Turkey's Path to Democratization

Turkey's Path to Democratization: Barriers, Actors, Outcomes

Muhammed Çetin

New York

Published by Blue Dome Press
535 Fifth Avenue, Ste. 601
New York, NY 10017-8019

www.bluedomepress.com

Library of Congress Cataloging-in-Publication Data
    Çetin, Muhammed.
    Turkey's path to democratization : barriers, actors, outcomes / Muhammed Çetin.
        pages cm
    ISBN 978-1-935295-51-8 (alk. paper)
        1. Democratization--Turkey. 2. Democracy--Turkey. 3. Turkey--Politics and govern-
    ment--1980- I. Title.
    JQ1809.A15C47 2014
    320.9561--dc23
    2014012779

ISBN: 978-1-935295-51-8

Printed by
Imak Ofset, Istanbul - Turkey

Contents

3. Obstacles to Democratization

4. Constitutional Reform and Barriers to Reform

5. Conflict and Its Resolution in Southeast Turkey

Preface

With the recent advance of globalization, commentators, researchers and journalists of all stripes and many nations have concerned themselves with Turkey's hard road to democratization. Is it still underway? What are the hindrances or blockages? What are the motivations and roles of civil society groupings in this evolving democracy? What is the current stance and role of the military, given Turkey's recent history of recurrent military coups d'états? Will Turkey ever succeed in gaining admittance to the European Union?

In addition, as a result of the frequency and extent of military action in the Middle East, much has been made in the media of Turkey's real or imagined role as an intermediary in the shifting world order. Turkey's role in NATO clearly interacts with Turkey's constantly changing relations with neighbors in the region. Is Turkey moving West or is it turning to the East? What are the implications for Turkey and the region of the relatively new "state" of Northern Iraq—now commonly known as "Kurdistan"?

Paradoxically, many foreign "experts", while insisting that Turkey is an "outsider" to the "European tradition" insist on measuring events in Turkey according to a variety of yardsticks crafted by that tradition. In fact, as with every country, there are vital areas in which Turkey's history and recent conditions are specific and cannot be evaluated according to measures commonly used when discussing most Western European societies. There are yet other respects, still largely unexamined by foreign commentators, in which Turkey's history is very similar to other European societies. In the twentieth century, for example, Turkey suffered under military regimes similar to those endured by Spain, Italy, Portugal, and Greece, and much of South America, and for similar reasons. This similarity is rarely acknowledged outside Turkey, let alone examined. Thus, Turkey is viewed through a number of distorting "orientalizing" lenses, and all its troubles attributed to "Islamism."

However, to understand contemporary social phenomena in Turkey, one needs to understand the changing circumstances in which the attempt was made to establish, and then hold on to, a nationalist, laicist, and Westernized republic after the end of the Ottoman Empire. With respect to the emergence, dynamics and outcomes of social and political movements in Turkey, the political system, its institutions and processes, and the larger social and cultural ethos, constitute highly significant material factors. Thus, it is necessary to trace the seeds of collective action in Turkey to the early Republican years, when a new state and society formed. To this end the book starts with a brief history of the early years of the Republic of Turkey.

A few months before this book went to press and just before local and metropolitan elections in March 2014, the police in Turkey laid charges against more than 40 people for bribery, rigging state tenders, violating the laws on construction in protected sites, forgery and smuggling gold to Iran (breaching the sanctions). This was not the first time rumors of corruption had touched the government, but this time the investigation involved government ministers and their families. Prime Minister Erdoğan immediately swung into action to stifle the investigation.

Without any disciplinary procedure, several thousand members of the police and bureaucracy and over a hundred judges and prosecutors were dismissed, and many more reassigned to other regions or cases. Simultaneously, as in the 2013 Gezi Park protests, the Prime Minister directed a highly pugilistic rhetoric at a selection of scapegoats to deflect public attention toward foreign "foes" (Turkey's allies and trading partners, such as the US and Israel) or a minority group as the "enemy within" (in this case, the Hizmet movement, at other times the Kurds, the Alevis, etc.).

While a number of public officials dared to brave the Prime Minister's ire and publicly contradict his claims, evidence of corruption continued to leak on the internet. In response to this defiance, the government issued an order to close Twitter and YouTube down in Turkey.

At the same time, although the Speaker of the House questioned the extent to which the executive was interfering with the judiciary, the ruling party managed to push through Parliament a bill extending the executive's power over the judiciary, undoing the constitutional reforms of 2010—reforms which had been endorsed by the Venice Commission, the European Union, and, indeed, by the public in a referendum.

In the course of the election campaign there were mass resignations from the AK Party among local councilors and 10 Members of Parliament have resigned from the AK Party so far. I was among them.

In spite of this political turbulence, the populace prioritized economic stability and growth over financial probity, and the AK Party won 43% of the vote in the local elections on a turnout of 80%. This was perhaps not so surprising. The opposition parties in Turkey were still demonstrating their lack of capacity to produce viable policy alternatives, even at the level of local services. Thus, the various civil society organizations which expressed their concern were reduced to asking the public to vote *against* something negative (corruption), rather than *for* something positive (a raft of alternative policies or principles).

Prime Minister Erdoğan claims the results of the local elections as a triumph for his government, but that does not seem to have calmed his fears. He has been widely criticized for his abusive and divisive speech. Yet, for all the threats of revenge and claims to unbridled power, the government remains impotent or indifferent where it really counts: in the chamber of Parliament. Hope is waning for the expansion of citizens' rights and freedoms and the dismantling of the authoritarian statist political culture of Turkey.

These events have thrown up new questions. The "heroes of the periphery" seem to have swallowed whole the political strategies of their former foes. Will the "new elite" be even more protectionist than the old? What will be the outcomes in the next few years?

The aim of this book is to provide some background, from an "insider" perspective for journalists, academics, researchers, and new undergraduate students of Turkey and its internal and external relations, as well as for the general reader.

The articles presented here were written weekly over a period of three years for publication in the English-language newspaper *Today's Zaman*. They have been grouped according to themes important for an understanding of the to-and-fro of public life in modern-day Turkey, and within each theme they are arranged chronologically, that is, in the order in which they were first published. They were written prior to the turbulence of 2014 but throw light on the underlying processes in Turkish politics and help to contextualize the latest events. They are supported by references, mainly to web addresses, to aid the reader who wishes to do further reading on the events being discussed. Wherever possible, I have referred to English-language resources. In only a few cases this has not been possible, or extra references in Turkish are desirable, and there are therefore references to Turkish-language articles or websites.

It is my humble wish that this book may be of some use to those who are interested in Turkey's development at this vital point in its history.

1
Historical Background

Introduction

This chapter recounts the socio-political developments of the Republican era. The narrative provides the background necessary for the articles that follow. I shall point in particular to the distinguishing characteristics of the socio-political context; the key events in the period up to 1994; and the ideas, attitudes and events of this period that have shaped and influenced the various kinds of mobilization in Turkey.

The Republican Era: One-party Rule

In July 1923, the Turkish people won sovereignty over eastern Thrace and all of Anatolia. In August, the delegates in the national Parliament fell to infighting over the political course and nature of the future regime. After lengthy disquisitions and eventual intimidation by Mustafa Kemal, Parliament abolished the sultanate and deposed the sultan but retained the caliphate with no political authority. However, many in Parliament did try to invest the caliphate with such authority, aiming thereby to retain influence with other Muslim lands and populations. Then Mustafa Kemal proposed an amendment and, on October 29, 1923, transformed the nation into 'the Republic of Turkey'.[1] In 1924, at his urging, Parliament abolished the caliphate, the Ministry of Religious Endowments and the office of Shaykhulislam (the highest religious authority) and assigned their responsibilities to two newly established directorates under the government. It abolished the Ministry of the General Staff, and shut down sharia courts

---

[1] Mustafa Kemal Atatürk said: 'Sovereignty has never been given to any nation by scholarly disputation. It is always taken by force and with violence [and] some heads may roll in the process.'

and madrasas. The Law on the Unification of Education placed religious secondary education under the Ministry of Education, reorganized the madrasa at the Süleymaniye Mosque (Istanbul) as a new Faculty of Divinity and enforced coeducation at all levels.

These changes put the military and religious cadres under government control and the potential for an Islamic state (the most likely challenge to the legitimacy of the Republican regime) was thereby quashed. In addition, Parliament accepted that Turkey was no longer a world power—its frontiers were to be bounded by the Turkish-speaking population of the Republic—and it would not entertain any vision of transnational leadership in any respect. The initial, occasional and individual, reactions to these changes were suppressed by the state apparatus. Later, when 32 parliamentarians, unhappy about the changes, broke with the party and formed the Progressive Republican Party, Mustafa Kemal's People's Party changed its name to the Republican People's Party (RPP). The partition of the state by the Treaty of Sèvres, the invasion by the Allied Forces, and the British influence on Kurdish nationalist aspirations, nurtured a peculiar Turkish nationalism and aggravated relations with the Kurds, who previously had for the most part supported the Turkish nationalists. A law was passed in 1924 which forbade publications in Kurdish, widening the chasm between the Turkish nationalists and the Kurds. When a Kurdish nationalist rebellion in religious garb, led by Sheikh Said, erupted in 1925, the Turkish government issued a law on Maintenance of Order, granting itself extraordinary powers to ban any group or publication deemed a threat to national security. That threat has been used repeatedly ever since by defenders of the system and vested interests. A good example was the establishment in 1925 of the Independence Tribunals (ITs). Enabling the execution of 1,054 people, the ITs played a significant role in suppressing rebellions—the Sheikh Said rebellion, for instance, was ended quite quickly with his arrest and execution.

ITs also snared many others, including Said Nursi, the most important Islamic thinker of the Republican era. Nursi was an Islamic modernist whose writings mapped out an accommodation between the ideas of constitutional democracy and individual liberty and religious faith. During the war years, he had fought against the foreign invasion and for independence, and spoken out against both modern Islamic authoritarianism and economic and political backwardness and separatism. His ideas for a modern Islamic consciousness emphasize the need for a significant role for religious belief in public life, while rejecting obscurantism and embracing scientific and technological development. Although he was not involved in any rebellions, the ITs sentenced him, along with many hundreds of others, to internal exile in western Anatolia.

In 1926, the government declared that it had uncovered a conspiracy to assassinate Mustafa Kemal and in the next two years turned the ITs on all its enemies. All national newspapers were closed and their staff arrested on the grounds that they were compromising 'national security'. The Progressive Republican Party was shut down, its leaders accused of collaborating in the conspiracy and arrested for treason. Under public pressure several prominent figures were released but others, though they had once worked closely with Mustafa Kemal, were executed.

Laicism

A strongly Kemalist Parliament—for all practical purposes a one-party state—enacted a series of measures between 1925 and 1928 to secularize public life. Mustafa Kemal believed that Turkey must renounce its past and follow the European model of progress. He accordingly set about eliminating all obstacles to a laicized and Westernized nation-state.

Dervish houses[2] were permanently closed, their ceremonies, liturgy and traditional dress outlawed. Kemal publicly denounced the fez[3] and the hijab (veil) as symbols of politicized Islam, as the headgear of a barbarous and backward religiosity, as a foreign innovation. Asserting that Turkish peasant women had traditionally worn only a scarf around their hair, he depicted the hijab as representing subordination of women by a reactionary political ideology. Parliament passed a law requiring men to wear brimmed hats and outlawed the fez. Women were given the right to vote and stand for election. The day after Christmas 1925, Parliament adopted the Gregorian calendar, in place of the Islamic one, as 'the standard accepted by the advanced nations of the world', and it changed the Muslim holy day of Friday into a week day, and instituted Sunday as a rest day.

---

[2] The lodges belonging to Muslim religious orders (Sufis).

[3] In fact, the fez had barely existed a hundred years in the Ottoman Empire and was associated with the state and its functionaries, not with the religion, whose dignitaries traditionally favored the turban.

The following year (1926), Parliament repealed Islamic Law and adopted a new Civil Code, Penal Code and Business Law, based on the Swiss, Italian, and German codes, respectively. In 1928, it deleted from the constitution the phrase 'the religion of the Turkish state is Islam'. The constitution did not yet state that Turkey was a secular state—that was to come in 1937—but the intent was clearly to secularize and to make Westernized forms of social order more visible in the public sphere.

In 1928, the new alphabet based on the Latin was accepted instead of the Arabic script. It was argued that the new alphabet would help raise literacy. If conceivably true, the low literacy rate could hardly be blamed on a script that had served written Turkish well for about a thousand years. The low levels of literacy were more particularly the result of the pro-longed wars, an ineffective system of public education and the belief that having an effective education system was an unnecessary luxury during wartime. Rather, reform of the script had historical, cultural, and political intent: use of the Arabic script had identified the Turks as belonging to Islamic civilization and history; use of the Latin characters would identify them with the direction of European civilization and modernity. At a stroke, the new regime totally renounced its past and embraced the revolutionary concept of history. In not learning the Arabic script, the children of the Turkish revolution would also not learn Islamic tradition and, indeed, would be unable to read its greatest literary monuments, or the documents produced only a few years before in the Ottoman Empire.

In the 1920s, the State looked to develop an indigenous, elite entre-preneurial class that would be loyal to and defend the new status quo—a nationalist bourgeoisie. In 1927, it provided to these privileged private citizens transfer of state land, tax exemptions, state subsidies, discounts on transport, and control of state monopolies. During the 1930s these citizens formed the core of the statist-elitist-laicists, whose actions will come up in the articles later in this book. They were also the first of the protectionist vested interests to exploit State-owned Economic Enter-prises (SEEs) and other state resources.

The shift to protectionism and statism hardened as the 1930s wore on and deepened the effect of the ensuing economic woes: agricultural prices collapsed causing peasants to fall into severe debt; industrial wages stagnated. The Republican revolution had reached a deadly pla-teau. Government economic policy drew fierce criticism and occasionally led to violent public reaction. The state centralized economic planning and organized several investment banks as joint stock companies to provide credit to agriculture, develop the mining and power industries, and finance industrial expansion. It also monopolized communications, railroads, and airlines.

Cultural Revolution

The Republican regime was both deliberate and selective in what it remembered and appropriated of the past. It linked the emerging national identity to Anatolian antiquity. The history and language reforms were part of a sustained campaign to erase the pre-existing culture and education. Mustafa Kemal personally directed the scientific and literary activity of the later 1920s and 1930s. In 1932, he founded the Turkish History Research Society and charged it with discovering the full antiquity of Turkish history. He theorized that Anatolia had been first settled by Sumerians and Hittites, whom he claimed as Turkic peoples that had migrated from the central Eurasian steppes carrying with them the underlying building blocks of 'Western civilization'. Also at his command, a Turkish Language Society was established in the same year. The 'Sun Language Theory' was developed, asserting that Turkish was the primordial human tongue from which all others derived. These theories made a deep, enduring impression on the generations that grew up on the textbooks teaching them. Education was designed to make pupils and citizens proud of their Turkish identity and suspicious of the Ottoman past, while also countering Western prejudices about Turks and Turkey. The explicit aim of the Turkish Language Society was 'to cleanse the Turkish language of the accumulated encrustations from the Arabic and Persian languages' and from the conceptual categories of the Islamic intellectual tradition. In the following decades the Society's officials made a concerted effort to introduce substitute or newly coined words. They were largely successful. The current generation of Turkish speakers find works from the early Republican era—including, ironically, the speeches of Mustafa Kemal himself—unintelligible unless translated into contemporary Turkish. Publication in languages other than Turkish was forbidden. In the 1920s, eighty percent of the words in the written language derived from words of Arabic and Persian origin; by the early 1980s the figure was just ten percent. By providing historical roots outside Ottoman history, the Republic's ideology combined the goals of Westernization and Turkish nationalism, claiming that Western civilization really originated in a Turkic Eurasian past, which the Ottoman Empire had obscured. As political scientist Binnaz Toprak sharply observed, these policies produced 'a nation of forgetters'.

In 1933, a law reorganized the Darulfunun (literally, 'home of the arts', an Ottoman university founded in the fifteenth century) into Istanbul University and purged its faculty in favor of those supportive of Mustafa Kemal's program for national education.

In 1934, the State required all citizens to adopt and register family names. Many potentially useful administrative advantages might well be imagined from a system of alphabetized family names, but the change expressly required that the names be authentically Turkish: names derived from Arabic or Persian roots, or from other ethnic origins (Jewish and Armenian, for example), were not permitted. The measure thus reinforced the national, ethnic identity of the citizens, as distinct from (in particular) their religious identity. The state effectively bound the personal destiny and identity of its citizens to that of the nation-state.[4]

In 1936, the government monopolized the authority to broadcast. At the same time, nationalists were advocating the use of Turkish in Islamic liturgy. Parliament established a fund to produce the Turkish version of the Qur'an; Atatürk encouraged the use of Turkish for mosque prayers, Friday sermons and for the call to prayer. After some public resistance (and violent reactions from the state to this resistance), the prayer liturgy remained in Arabic, but the call to prayer began to be given in Turkish, and this was made compulsory in 1941.

The Republican People's Party (RPP) established 'People's Houses' and 'Village Institutes'. By 1940, more than four thousand People's Houses had been founded to facilitate the development of popular loyalties and to communicate to citizens their mission and values as formulated by the regime. In 1935, Mustafa Kemal demanded a new strategy for education, which went nation-wide in 1940 through the Village Institutes.

---

[4] In 1935, Parliament gave Mustafa Kemal the family name Atatürk, 'Father of the Turks'.

The graduates were expected to teach and emphasize techniques of agriculture and home industry, and to inculcate the fundamental ideology of the Republic. These Institutes were widely resented. The people accused the mastermind behind the Institutes of being a communist and the Institutes of being agents of one-party rule and atheistic. They mistrusted the system also on account of its control rather than transformation of their affairs, as it consistently failed to realize land redistribution or relieve them of the power of landlords.

In 1931, Mustafa Kemal had outlined his party (RRP) ideology in six 'fundamental and unchanging principles', declaring it to be 'republican, nationalist, populist, statist, laicist, and revolutionary—concepts incorporated into the constitution in 1937 as definitive of the basic principles of the state.

While the political system and 'ideology' of Turkey remains *Kemalism* or *Atatürkism*, the last three of the six principles became contentious over time. 'Etatism' or 'statism', meaning the policy of state-directed economic investment adopted by the RPP in the 1930s, was not universally accepted as a basic element of Turkish nationhood and was eventually abandoned. 'Laicism' or 'secularism' has been variously interpreted by those at different points on the Turkish political spectrum. It refers in fact to the administrative control of religious affairs and institutions by the state—rather than to separation of state and religion—and to the removal of official religious expression from public life, but in principle it also implied freedom, 'within these bounds', of religious practice and conscience. 'Revolutionism'—in much later years replaced by the term 'reformism'—as one of the least articulated principles, suggests an ongoing openness and commitment to change in the interests of the nation. In reality, as Turkish history since the early days of the Republic has repeatedly shown, some things can hardly be discussed, let alone changed.

Sociologist Emre Kongar considers the Turkish social and cultural transformation unique—in the totality of its ambition and in its success in replacing, with a synthesis of Western and pre-Islamic Turkish cultures, the previously dominant Islamic culture of an Islamic society. However, the drastic reforms—from grand political structures to the everyday matters of eating, dressing and celebrations—pushed through in such a short period of time, would need a longer period for assimilation. They were not all welcomed but, on the contrary, provoked hostile reactions, which has had the effect of enduringly politicizing certain issues in Turkey.

İnönü, 'the National Chief' and 'Eternal Leader'

After the death of Mustafa Kemal Atatürk in 1938, his reforms were consolidated by his successor, İsmet İnönü. Parliament granted İnönü the titles of 'the National Chief' and 'the Eternal Leader', with enhanced powers in anticipation of possible challenges to the regime, powers much greater than those of the last two Ottoman sultans. The Second World War began a year later. Through imposition of martial law in much of the country, İnönü's forceful use of the crisis ensured the maintenance of the Kemalist structure and kept Turkey out of the war.

During the war years there were shortages of basic goods and cash, as well as inflation. In 1942, the government imposed an extraordinary 'capital-wealth tax' on property owners, farmers, and businessmen. The tax schedules were not prepared with formal income data but left to the personal estimates of local bureaucrats, who divided taxpayers according to profits, capacity, and religion—Muslim, non-Muslim, Foreigner, and Sabbataist (Jewish converts). Many were financially ruined by this tax, against which no appeals were admitted. Resisters were arrested and then deported or sentenced to hard labor. The Turkish financial world was severely shaken. In 1944, İnönü suppressed student protest movements against his policies. Prominent figures were arrested and charged with 'plotting to overthrow the government'[5] and to bring Turkey into the war on Germany's side.

Turkey was still underdeveloped: there were shortages of tractors and paved roads; a mere handful of villages had electricity; barely a fraction of the country's agricultural potential had been realized. Villagers resented the increased state control, the increased taxation, and the sym-

---

[5]   What was meant by 'the government' was the single-party establishment (including parliament and government) identifying with and defending the regime. Whoever questioned or opposed this establishment was perceived as and accused of 'overthrowing the state or regime', a recurring theme in the history of the Turkish Republic.

bols of state-imposed secularization. Wartime price controls destroyed their profits. In addition, while already poor and over-taxed, villagers were forced to build schools, roads, and facilities for masters who often turned out to be aloof mouthpieces of the hated regime. The military police violently suppressed dissent. In the towns, the appalling economic conditions, censorship of the press, and restrictions on personal freedom fed a growing exasperation. Even after signing the UN Charter, Turkey prolonged martial law for more than a year, press censorship remained heavy, and no labor union activity was tolerated. Anti-government sentiment grew accordingly: state civil servants who had suffered heavily from inflation, and businessmen, both Muslim and Christian, who had carried the burden of the capital tax, united in opposition to the single-party authoritarianism.

Four parliamentarians, Celal Bayar, Refik Koraltan, Fuad Köprülü, and Adnan Menderes, formally requested that the constitutional guarantees of democracy be implemented. Köprülü and Menderes published articles in the press critical of the RPP. They and Koraltan were expelled from the party; Bayar resigned his membership. Following domestic and external pressures, İnönü in 1946 allowed the four dissidents to form the Democrat Party (DP). The DP served as an umbrella under which all who mistrusted or opposed the RPP government sought refuge and voiced the resentments that had been building up over previous years. Then, before the DP was able to organize fully, the RPP called early elections in May 1946, which it won.

However, the victorious RPP all but split in a tussle between its single-party statists and its reform-minded members. The RPP leader was forced to resign, and the party adopted a new development plan. Turkey joined the IMF (International Monetary Fund) and then implemented some economic and political corrective measures. The hated founder and head of the Village Institutes was relieved of his duties. The Education Department decided that religion could be taught in schools, and a Faculty of Divinity opened in Ankara in 1949. Under international pressure since signing the UN Charter, the RPP also relaxed its attitude toward popular Islam. Even so, in the 1950 elections, it won only 69 seats as against the DP's absolute majority of 408.

Democrats, 1950–1960

In 1950 power passed from a single-party dictatorship to an elected democratic government. But then something happened that would recur in different guises to haunt Turkey right up to the present: top army officers offered to stage a coup d'état to suppress the elected government and restore İnönü to power. For fear of international intervention, İnönü declined. The Democrat victory was received with jubilation; Bayar became the President, Menderes the Prime Minister.

From 1948 to 1953, production, especially in the agricultural sector, GDP and economic growth all boomed. More than 30,000 tractors were imported, which farmers could finance through credits; dams were built; cultivated land increased by more than fifty percent and total yields swelled; major cities were linked to a national highway system for the first time; the miles of paved highways quadrupled and improved feeder roads made it easier for thousands of newly imported trucks to get farm produce and goods to market. In these years the DP presided over a period of lower cost of living, increasing production and employment, tax reform, customs reforms, and support of private capital and foreign investment.

Then, from 1954, overall economic growth slowed. The expansion had been financed with borrowed money and fuelled by splendid harvests. With low levels of hard currency, the country was left with large trade and balance of payments deficits. In 1955, import restrictions returned and foreign investors refused requests for new loans. The privatization program never got off the ground. The largest firms were still the SEEs. The government's building of cement plants, dams, and highways all at the same time was simply trying to do too much. In September, the attempt of Greek Cypriots to unite with Greece caused riots in Istanbul and Izmir. When thugs attacked Greek merchants, martial law was declared. Some of the media began to act the role of an opposition party. The government threatened to prosecute the publication of news that could 'curtail the supply of consumer goods or raise prices or cause loss of respect and confidence in the authorities'. Two daily newspapers were closed for doing just that.

The largest industrial conglomerates in today's Turkey had their origins in this period. Mechanization of agriculture forced surplus laborers to migrate to the cities in search of work. Urban traders and businessmen accumulated enormous wealth and clamored for political leverage proportionate to their economic standing. The Confederated Trade Unions of Turkey also expressed the desire for greater political participation. As the DP identified with free enterprise and free expression of religious sentiment, it attracted many of the successful entrepreneurs and the conservative peasants. However, in its enthusiasm for the boom, the government had failed to foresee the social consequences: the rapid economic growth in particular roused political envy among those who felt threatened. The later years of the period were characterized by thugs, students, and security forces fighting on the streets, with media galvanizing discontent on certain issues in favour of vested interests—recurrent motifs in the country's modern history.

Particularly ominous was the growing resentment of the established 'Republican' bureaucratic, military, and intellectual elites, whose laicist and statist assumptions about national life were being challenged by democratically oriented policies. The ostensible reason for the military officers' resentment was that their salaries did not keep up with inflation. In 1950 the DP government, wanting to purge the revolutionary core in the army general staff, discharged the top brass with ties to İnönü. Then in 1953, uncertain of the goodwill and potential neutrality of the university faculties, it prohibited university faculties from political activity by law. A 1954 law introduced an age limit which forced faculty members and some judiciary to retire—these were the Republican cadre, then over sixty, who had been in post for twenty-five years.

Democrats looked to thread a way between the pressures from constitutional secularism and their electoral base. In 1950, they ended the twenty-seven-year ban on religious broadcasting with twenty minutes per week of Qur'anic recitations on radio, and introduced religious teaching into the public school curriculum. More Imam-Hatip schools[6] were opened and the call to prayer (*adhan*) was once again made in Arabic. The unloved People's Houses and Village Institutes were closed. Defaming Atatürk was made a criminal offence after a few busts of him were smashed.

---

[6] These are, despite the name, secular state schools, entirely within the national secular educational system. The cost of their construction has never been met by the Turkish state but through donations by ordinary people, who then handed them over to the Ministry of Education. The schools follow the national curriculum with extra basic courses on Islam for the training of preachers and Qur'an teachers by state trained, assigned and paid teachers.

The courts found the recently organized Nation Party guilty of using religion for political purposes and dissolved it.

In spite of the DP's concessions to the secularists and statists, conditions became strained. The defenders of the status quo in Turkey (who will come up again in the later parts of this narrative) counter-mobilized against the elected government and civil society. Citing the economic downturn, displeased businessmen and academics withdrew their support for the DP. A dean at Ankara University delivered a 'political lecture' and was dismissed; students were mobilized for protests; some academics resigned. From 1955 onwards, officers in the armed forces began noticeably to conspire against the government.

Discontent in the military stemmed from complicated social roots. Since the end of World War II, the prestige of a military career in Turkey had slowly declined. Democratization had marginalized those accustomed to playing a central role in the country's affairs. A small number of officers within the army formed a kind of oppositional, reactionary movement against the elected government, incorporating revolutionary ideology into the training of cadets and junior officers. Menderes, wary of the influence of the officers and İnönü, made a military reformer his minister of defense, but opponents among the military top ranks managed to have him dismissed. After that, Menderes ingratiated himself with the generals, but he was ill-informed about the junior officers who were frustrated by the hierarchy of the officer corps and hungry for economic and political power. After Turkey joined NATO in 1952, those officers started to receive advanced training in Europe and the US, and to interact with the American and NATO officials based in Turkey after 1955. They complained about 'purchasing power' and 'standards of living' in Turkey. In the 1957 elections, the DP, despite taking almost 48 percent of the vote, lost its majority. The RPP meanwhile found new support among intellectuals and businessmen defecting from the DP. Two months later, nine junior army officers were arrested for plotting a coup.

Through 1958–59, the DP government implemented some economic measures, rescheduled its debt, and received further loans from the US, OEEC (Organization for European Economic Co-operation), and IMF. In 1959, it applied for membership in the European Economic Community (EEC). A partial recovery began. However, discontent among state servants and the elite persisted. The RPP went on the offensive. İnönü's tour of Anatolia became the occasion for outbreaks of violence along his route. Menderes ordered troops to interrupt the tour by İnönü in 1960, but İnönü called their bluff and embarrassed the troops into backing down. Student protests and riots started in April. On one occasion, police opened fire, killed five and injured more. Under their top officers' direction, cadets from the military academy staged a protest march against the government but in solidarity with the oppositional student movement. Some elements of the armed forces openly displayed their opposition to the elected civilian authorities. Martial law was declared. On May 14, crowds demonstrated in the streets. On May 25, Parliamentarians fought within Parliament leaving fifteen injured. On May 27, the armed forces took over the state.

Military Coup d' État

Some circles in Ankara and Istanbul welcomed the military coup; much of the general public accepted it with sullen resignation. Declarations of nonpartisan objectives notwithstanding, the military's actions confirmed the general perception that the coup was an intervention against the DP government on behalf of the RPP. The DP was denounced as an instrument of 'class interests' aligned with 'forces opposed to the secularist principles of Atatürk's revolution'. DP Parliamentarians were arrested and the party closed down.

Calling itself the National Unity Committee (NUC), a junta of 38 junior officers exercised sovereignty and declared a commitment to the writing of a new constitution under which Parliament would resume its role. General Cemal Gürsel, nominal leader and chairman of the NUC, became President, Prime Minister, and Commander-in-Chief. The NUC grouped into three factions, which from the outset disagreed about aims and principles. One faction comprised old school generals (pashas) who wanted to restore civil order and civilian rule. The second faction, more interested in social and economic development, wanted a planned economy led by SEEs and to hand power to İnönü and the RPP. The third faction, made up of younger officers and communitarian radicals, advocated indefinite military rule in order to effect fundamental political and social change from above, a sort of non-party nationalist populism on the pattern of Nasser's Egypt.

The power struggle among these factions continued until the pashas dissolved the NUC and formed a new NUC, exiling fourteen radical junior officers to Turkish embassies abroad. The pashas only later realized how far the radicals had disseminated revolutionary views among the junior officer corps. They purged some of those, but sub-groups reformed, conspiring to seize control and overhaul the whole political and social system. Aware of the continued danger and wanting to prevent their 'economic marginalization', senior officers formed OYAK and the AFU. OYAK was a pension fund for retired officers financed by obligatory salary contributions; it developed very quickly into a powerful conglomerate with vast holdings. The AFU (Armed Forces Union) was set up to provide a forum for discussing issues of concern under the supervision of the top ranks: the pashas intended to gain control over the junior officers and to ensure there would never be another military rebellion that they themselves did not lead and direct.

Meanwhile, those who favored a return to a single-party system deadlocked the Constitutional Commission. After a purge, the Commission eventually produced a document. However, a rival group of professors submitted another draft and convinced the NUC to appoint an assembly made up of the NUC and 'some' politicians. The compromise constitution, written by two professors, passed in a deeply divided referendum in 1961.

The constitution brought significant structural changes to society and government. It established a bicameral legislature. The upper chamber Senate was directly elected for six-year terms, but members of the NUC and former presidents of Turkey became lifetime senators and fifteen others were appointed by the president. The lower chamber was popularly elected by proportional representation. Legislation had to pass both chambers. The national budget was reviewed by a joint commission of the two chambers. A Constitutional Court (CC) was established, fifteen members of which were drawn from the judiciary, parliament, law faculties, and presidential appointments. The CC reviewed laws and orders of Parliament at the request of individuals or political parties.[7] The president of Turkey would be elected by Parliament, from among its own mem-

---

[7] The chief editor of the *Turkish Daily News* Ilnur Çevik maintains: 'For quite some time the Constitutional Court, the supreme judicial body of Turkey, was regarded as a tool of the conservative establishment, which rejected reforms and did its best to maintain the current order, where our country has been reduced to a semi-

bers, for a single term of seven years. His office maintained a certain independence from the legislature. The constitution guaranteed freedom of thought, expression, and association, which the 1924 constitution had not included. Freedom of the press was limited only by the need to 'safeguard national security'. The state had the power to plan economic and cultural development advised by the State Planning Organization. The National Security Council (NSC) was institutionalized by law, chaired by the President and made up of the chief of the general staff, heads of the service branches, the prime minister, and ministers of relevant cabinet ministries. The NSC would advise government on matters of domestic and foreign security. Through its general secretariat and various departments, the NSC was gradually to develop into a decisive political force, as ever greater portions of political, social, and economic life came under the rubric of 'matters of national security'.

The coup was a grave error, set a bad example to the rest of the military cadre about ignoring the military hierarchy, and also aroused their ambitions for the successive military interventions in Turkish domestic politics, especially in 1971 and in 1980, which halted the democratization process so that Turkey lost valuable time in its economic as well as democratic modernization.

After the Executions: 1961–1970

Hundreds of DP deputies were tried on charges of corruption and high treason. The trials and executions of DP leaders during the national elections of 1961 made obvious the junta's true political ambitions. Partly in response to public appeals for clemency, the sentences of eleven of the fifteen condemned to death were commuted to life imprisonment. The former president was spared on account of his advanced age and ill health. Prime Minister Adnan Menderes and the Foreign Minister Fatin Rüstü Zorlu, and Finance Minister Hasan Polatkan were hanged in September.

In the general elections held a month later, İnönü's RPP won 73 seats. The core of the DP reformed as the Justice Party (JP) was only three seats short of a majority in the lower chamber. Cemal Gürsel, the coup leader, became President. The election results could well be interpreted as a repu-

democracy with a rather dismal human rights record' (Çevik, 1999a in Çetin 2009).

diation of the new regime and its constitution. Political instability marked the next several years, as a series of short-lived coalition governments headed by İnönü, with the support of the army, tried to implement the constitution.

In late 1961, workers began demonstrating in the streets demanding their right to strike. Junior officers, determined to prevent a new Democrat take-over, plotted a coup in February 1962 under Colonel Talat Aydemir. Aydemir, a key conspirator in the 1950s, had been unable to participate in the coup due to his posting in Korea. This time he took part and was arrested. Circumstances forced the JP and RPP into a brief coalition until May. When it collapsed, İnönü formed another coalition that, thanks to concessions, managed to last more than a year. Meanwhile, a second coup attempt by Colonel Aydemir was thwarted, and he was executed in May 1963.

Local elections in 1963 made it clear that the governed no longer gave consent to the RPP. İnönü resigned. The winning JP, however, failed to form a new government. Once again, İnönü managed a coalition with the independents, which survived for fourteen months, thanks largely to the Cyprus crisis preoccupying everyone throughout 1964. In February 1965, the budget vote brought down the government, and the country limped to elections in October.

Social and economic goals of public policy were never achieved because vocal opponents to development planning were in the cabinet after the first coalition. For instance, the cabinet rejected proposed reforms for land, agriculture, tax, and SEEs. The State Planning Organization advisors were forced to resign. The government's lack of political commitment to its work, the increasing politicization of appointments and its partisan protection of vested interests, instead of those of the whole nation, weakened state institutions.

In 1965, Süleyman Demirel's JP won the elections with an outright majority. Demirel assured the generals that he would follow a program independent of the old Democrats. He reconciled with the military, granting them complete autonomy in military affairs and the defense budget. However, the irregular economic growth of the 1960s gradually alienated his lower middle class constituency. The JP began to fragment, some following Colonel Alparslan Türkeş into nationalism, others following Necmettin Erbakan into religious pietism. Türkeş, a key figure of the 1960 junta, had returned from exile abroad in 1963, retired and later took over the chairmanship of the Republican Peasants' National Party (RPNP). Under his direction the RPNP adopted a radically nationalist tone. Erbakan formed the National Order Party (NOP) in 1970, the first of a series of political Islamist parties in Turkey. He gained a reputation as a maverick for freely airing intemperate remarks and advocating a role for Islam in public and political life.

In the 1960s, the RPP argued with the same old rhetoric that Demirel's policies had forsaken the principles of Atatürk[8] and would ruin the peasant and worker. Bülent Ecevit, who had been the Minister of Labor in the three RPP-led coalitions till 1965, asked the RPP to shed its elitist image and trust the common people to know what was best for them. Some deputies did not like his suggestions and left the party. However, Ecevit had understood that the voters had supported Menderes and later Demirel because they felt alienated by the RPP's arrogance and because the other parties' programs were better.

By 1970, Turkey faced a mounting crisis whose origins lay generally in deteriorating economic conditions, the massive social changes since the 1950s, a loss of confidence in the State, and the circumstances of the Cold War. On the other hand, there were some successes in Turkish–foreign joint ventures: an oil-pipeline, a dam, two irrigation projects, and associate membership of the EEC. By the end of the decade, the state monopolies, the publicly owned banks, and the recently founded OYAK had become fairly successful and sizeable enterprises.

Mechanization pushed labor to western Europe: the migrants' cash remittances from Europe were Turkey's most important source of foreign exchange.

In 1967 leftists formed the Confederation of Revolutionary Workers' Unions (DISK). Its president was Kemal Türkler, a founding member of the (communist) Turkish Workers' Party (TWP). DISK was anti-capitalist and politically radical activist, encouraging street demonstrations and strikes to achieve its objectives. Proportional representation brought

---

[8]   This remains the gravest accusation in Turkish politics against any person or group considered a symbolic or direct political challenge to the protectionist vested interests in the establishment. It is highly significant that, at rather predictable junctures in events, this accusation has also been directed against the country's prime ministers and presidents.

such small parties into Parliament, with the result that public life became increasingly influenced by the activities of small extremist groups of the left and right. Throughout the late 1960s and 1970s, they exerted an influence on politics beyond their numbers. The milieu in universities enabled leftists to form on-campus 'idea clubs' with agendas anticipating the imminent radical transformation of society. Spreading outward from the universities, politicization and polarization increasingly infected public life. National dailies, language, music, art, and festivals came to be known as leftist or rightist; people could be identified on the political spectrum by the vocabulary they used in everyday speech.

One of the most notorious extremist groups that emerged in this period was Revolutionary Youth (*Dev-Genç*). It grew out of an effort to link the 'idea clubs' at universities nationally under Marxist leadership. It advocated the violent overthrow of the state. The left in general stressed opposition to imperialism, to the West, and to American bases. Americans and their interests represented, to the leftists, subservience to international capitalism and militarism in Turkey. The correspondence in 1964 between American President Johnson and then Prime Minister İnönü, published in 1966, in which Johnson threatened not to back Turkey in the event of a Soviet attack, turned public opinion dramatically against the US. For leftists, the letter confirmed that the US had no real interest in Turkey beyond a cold calculation of its place in the international power balance. They accused Demirel and the JP of being 'American stooges'. Demirel announced a government and police crackdown on 'communists.'

The leftists were also targeted by the right, which, in general, coalesced around a common anti-communism, in many (but not all) cases advocating conservative Islamic piety and values as normative for Turkish society. A large portion of the Turkish populace was indeed socially and religiously conservative—a fact not lost on Demirel, who was not above occasionally manipulating traditional Islamic social values or fears of the Soviets for political purposes. More virulent forms of nationalism and anti-communism became evident in the late 1960s. There was sporadic anti-American violence: in 1966, rioters attacked the US consulate, the office of the US Information Agency and the Red Cross; increasingly violent demonstrations accompanied the visit of the US Sixth Fleet; the US Information Agency in Ankara was bombed. Leftist and rightist groups both took part in demonstrations that turned increasingly violent in late 1967.

In 1968, leftist students seized the buildings at Ankara University demanding abolition of the examination system and fee structure. In May 1969, a rector and eleven deans protested against the government and resigned. In August, demonstrators belonging to the leftist unions occupied the Ereğli Iron-Steel plant. Riot police were unable to evict them. Airport employees went on strike in September. Fighting took place all over the country during the elections in October. The JP maintained a shaky Parliamentary majority. The RPP was still in its identity crisis. Six other parties entered Parliament, though none won even seven percent of the popular vote. Then, in 1970, because of economic problems, unpopular corrective measures and a three-month-late budget, JP dissidents forced Demirel to resign.

Military Coup II

Civil unrest and radicalization continued to grow in the 1970s. DISK organized a general strike in the spring. In August, ominous news of a shake-up leaked from the General Staff. In December, students clashed at Ankara University. The Labor Party headquarters and Demirel's car were bombed. In February 1971, more than 200 extreme-leftist students were arrested after a five-hour gun battle with the military police at Hacettepe University in Ankara. On March 4, leftist students kidnapped four American soldiers and held them for ransom. A battle ensued when police searched for the soldiers at a dormitory in Ankara University; two students died before the Americans were released. On 12 March 1971, the military seized control of the state, citing the crisis in Parliament, the incompetence of the government, and street and campus clashes between communists and ultra-nationalists, and between leftist trade unionists and the security forces. This was a sad repetition of their previous seizure of power (in 1961) and the same themes recurred in their discourse to justify their action.

The generals said they had acted to prevent another coup by junior officers rather than because they had a specific program to lead the country out of its difficulties. Publicly blaming the political parties for the crisis, they selected a government that would implement the 1961 constitutional reforms. Under martial law, the military arrested thousands—party and union leaders, academics and writers; also they closed down Erbakan's party, as well as several mainstream newspapers and journals.

The National Intelligence Organization used severe repression, including torture, to extract confessions from suspects. The cabinet made no progress and was forced to resign. Constitutional amendments scaled back civil liberties, freedom of the press, and the autonomy of the Constitutional Court. Universities and the broadcast media lost their autonomy to supervisory committees. The National Security Council 'advice' to Parliament became binding. A system of State Security Courts (SSCs) was introduced that, in the following years, would try hundreds of cases under the rubric of national security.

Bülent Ecevit succeeded İsmet İnönü as the RPP chair. Erbakan put together a new party with much the same leadership and called it the National Salvation Party (NSP). Elections were held in 1973. Though they had very little in common, the RPP and NSP formed a coalition, the first of several that would govern Turkey with diminishing levels of success till 1980.

In Cyprus in July 1974, Greek Cypriot guerrillas, fighting for union with Greece, overthrew the Cypriot President in a coup and replaced him with a guerrilla leader. Killings began. Turkish troops landed in northern Cyprus to protect the Turkish-Cypriots and secured one-third of the island. There the Turkish-Cypriots organized what later, in 1983, became the Turkish Republic of Northern Cyprus (TRNC). Turkey paid a high price for this move. the substantial cost of assistance to TRNC, a 50 percent increase in its defense budget; diplomatic isolation and damage to its standing in the EC. Further, the US cut off assistance and imposed an embargo, which contributed to Turkey's grave economic position in the late 1970s. In 1976, Turkey signed a new four-year defense agreement with the US, but the US Congress did not approve it due to Greek and Armenian lobbying.

Collapse of Public Order

Ecevit resigned in 1974 in order to call elections that he thought, after the Cyprus action, his RPP could win. However, leaders of the other parties did not allow an election to be called. Ecevit's move brought governmental impasse until late 1980. A series of unstable coalitions followed, none of which possessed the strength to manage the economic problems, or control the political violence.

Some enterprises that had taken advantage of foreign capital during the 1950s had grown tremendously in the 1960s. To maintain their position and leading role, and to lobby the government for support, in 1971, owners of the 114 largest firms formed the Association of Turkish Industrialists (TUSIAD). However, the quadrupling of oil prices in 1973 raised the cost of the imports Turkey depended on and consumed about two-thirds of Turkey's foreign currency income. Inflation and unemployment climbed steadily after 1977. By 1978–79, there were even shortages of basic commodities.

After the 1971 coup, the crackdown on radical leftists by the security forces started a spiral of attacks and retaliations to which there seemed to be no resolution. With Alparslan Türkeş's appointment as a minister of state from 1974 to 1977, the violent campaign of radical groups against all who disagreed with them escalated and contributed substantially to the collapse of public order by 1980. A 1977 May Day celebration by the leftist unions turned into a battle among themselves and with the police, leaving 39 dead and more than 200 wounded. Leftists retaliated with a wave of bombings, killing several people at the airport and railway stations. A state of virtual war prevailed between DISK[9], the Turkish Workers' Party and other leftist groups on the one hand, and the Istanbul police force on the other. Clashes between rightist groups and leftists killed 112 and wounded thousands in Sivas and Kahramanmaraş. Ecevit declared martial law.

Violence was at a peak on university campuses. In 1974–75, students disrupted classes, rioted and killed one another, forced the temporary closure of universities, waged battles, and carried out killings and bombings at off-campus venues frequented by students. Academics were beaten and murdered. At Ankara University in 1978, a leftist student, Abdullah Öcalan, formed the Kurdish Workers' Party (PKK) and began a separatist war in the south-eastern provinces. Americans and NATO personnel were targeted and murdered by the leftists. Although banned, May Day demonstrations organized by leftist labor continued. Clashes between rightists and leftists increased. Members of the security forces, journalists, party officials, labor union leaders, and ministers were murdered; strikes went on for weeks and months.

---

[9]   The Confederation of Revolutionary Workers' Unions

The divided government, meanwhile, did not take up an austerity plan suggested by Demirel's economic advisor Turgut Özal. In February, Fahri Korutürk's presidential term expired: for six months Parliament was unable to elect a successor. The economy was in tatters, with inflation running at 130 percent and unemployment 20 percent. Murderous confrontations between the radicals had taken 5,241 lives in two years. Erbakan's fundamentalist meetings in Konya stirred up the military. And again, for the third time in twenty years, on September 12, 1980, the military seized direct control of the state. Their discourse framed their action in exactly the same way as in the two previous coups.

The constitution after the 1961 coup had restructured Turkish government and institutions in such a way that it caused the political system to fail. Personal and political liberties were not implemented, nor reforms to land, tax and the SEEs. The system crashed in insurmountable difficulties. Due to inability, or unwillingness, to revise the prevailing political culture for the needs of an open society, together with the consequences of economic crisis, deep fissures opened in society between those who had benefited from the rapid and haphazard social and economic development since 1945 and those who found themselves victims of the inflation, unemployment, and urban migration it engendered. There were those who had benefited from multiparty democracy through their links of patronage with powerful officials, and those who still lived with the residue of the one-party era with its authoritarian model of leadership, the equation of dissent with disloyalty, and party control of state offices. Turkey's standing in the Cold War contributed to the polarization of society and was also exploited to mask the sources of its problems, and made it impossible to achieve the political consensus necessary to adopt reforms. A major source of the political and social degeneration of the 1960s and the chaos and anarchy of the 1970s was the radical tendencies of students, militants, academics, unions, and officers of the state security apparatuses. Finally, the armed forces, which Parliament had failed to subordinate to civilian rule, put an end to that rule, which the armed forces had themselves established a mere ten years earlier.

Military Coup III

In September 1980, the military arrested and placed the prime minister, party leaders and 100 parliamentarians in custody. It dissolved Parliament, suspended the constitution, banned all political activity, dissolved and permanently outlawed all political parties, forbade their leaders to speak about politics—past, present or future—and seized, and subsequently caused to disappear, the archives of the parties of the past thirty years. Martial law was extended to all Turkey. Several thousand were arrested in the first week. The junta wanted in this way to signal its determination to institute a new political order.

The coup leaders, the five commanders of the armed forces, formed the National Security Council (NSC) and gave themselves indefinite and unlimited power. General Kenan Evren became head of state and appointed a cabinet composed mostly of retired officers and state bureaucrats. Martial law commanders in all the provinces were given broad administrative authority over public affairs, including education, the press and economic activities. Return to civilian rule would follow fundamental revision of the political order. In the meantime, the 1961 constitution, where it did not contradict the provisions of martial law, would remain in effect until replaced.

Evren said the country had passed through a national crisis, and separatist forces and enemies, within and without, threatened its integrity; that Kemalism had been forgotten and the country left leaderless; and that the junta would correct this and enforce a new commitment to Kemalism, with Evren providing the necessary national leadership. Much of the country viewed the coup with relief, expecting that near civil war conditions would soon end. Indeed the rightist–leftist street clashes ended immediately. However, within months, the army opened a new front against Kurdish separatists, which gradually escalated by 1983, and it also suppressed Islamic political activism.

Turgut Özal was retained in the post-coup cabinet as Deputy Prime Minister and Minister for Economic Affairs. They decided to continue the economic policy he had planned under the former government. Özal negotiated with the IMF, World Bank, and EU. They released new credits and rescheduled former and more new debts. In this way, the state began a transition from an economy directed from above to an economy open to integration with world capitalism.

New 'Order'

The military regime forbade all strikes and union activities and disbanded the labor federations, imposed a strict curfew, and arrested more than 100,000 within eight months. Martial law authorities attempted to be even-handed, arresting the rightist and religious as well as leftist members. Several newspapers were closed for publishing articles critical of the regime. By 1983, about 2000 prisoners had faced the death penalty.[10] The trial of extreme rightist Mehmet Ali Ağca, who had tried to assassinate the Pope in 1981, revealed the extent of interactions between extremist groups and organized crime within Turkey and abroad.

Universities were placed under the supervision of a newly created Council of Higher Education (YÖK). The junta held the power directly to appoint university rectors and deans, and purged hundreds of university faculty. Over the 1980s, the number of universities rose from 19 to 29. The right of university admission was broadened, effectively diluting the power of the old university faculties and the traditional elite classes, whose children made up the student bodies. In 1981, the centenary of Atatürk's birth, the state arranged conferences, volumes of publications and the naming of numerous facilities and institutions—even a university—to commemorate 'The Centenary'. Evren's face next to Atatürk's on banners and in public ceremonies linked him and his military regime to Atatürk and Atatürk's regime.

In the autumn of 1981, the generals nominated the members of a consultative assembly, directly appointed by the NSC and martial law governors, to draft a new constitution. Its mandate was to purge the country of the effects of the 1960 coup, including the 1961 constitution, which was partly blamed for the fragmentation and polarization of Parliament, the judiciary, bureaucracy, and universities, for needlessly politicizing all public life, and for breeding the violence of the late 1970s. An annual holiday commemorating the 1960 coup was abolished.

The new constitution was approved by referendum in 1982. While recognizing most civil and political rights, it laid heavy emphasis on the protection of the indivisible integrity of the state and national security, extended a measure of impunity for the extensive use of force during riots, martial law or a state of emergency, strengthened the presidency, and formalized the role of the military leadership. The president was charged with ensuring 'the implementation of the constitution' and 'functioning of the state organs' and would become the guardian of the state, serving a single seven-year term with potentially wide powers. He would appoint

---

[10] Of these fifty were eventually executed and the rest, though spared the death penalty by later civilian governments, served life sentences.

the cabinet, the Constitutional Court, the military Court of Cassation, the Supreme Council of Judges and Prosecutors, and the High Court of Appeals. He would chair the National Security Council (NSC), now made a permanent body with the right to submit its views on state security to the Council of Ministers, who were required to give priority to the NSC's views. Parliament again became a unicameral legislature. Any party short of ten percent of the national vote would not receive parliamentary representation. A new discretionary fund was created and put at the personal disposal of the prime minister, outside of the parliamentary budgetary process. Restrictions were placed on the press and labor unions. The State Security Court would rule on strikes, lockouts, and collective bargaining disputes. The government lost its mandate to restrict private enterprise. By a 'temporary article' appended by the NSC, General Evren became President, without being elected.

The NSC forbade more than 700 former parliamentarians and party leaders to participate in politics for the next ten years. It shut down several newspapers for some time for failing to observe severe restrictions on political articles. Due to the brokerage firm and bank crisis in 1982, Özal left the cabinet. In 1983, the NSC permitted the formation of new political parties. Some new parties that looked like reincarnations of the old parties or were directed from behind the scenes by former leaders were barred from the elections and closed down. The NSC approved three parties: the Nationalist Democracy Party (NDP), led by a retired general, the Populist Party, headed by a former private secretary of İsmet İnönü, and the Motherland Party (MP), formed by Turgut Özal.

President Evren did not hide his dislike of Özal but this only made his party an early favorite with a public very tired of the military. Evren's stated preference for the NDP probably condemned it to a third-place finish. The MP won 45 percent of the vote and an absolute majority in Parliament.

The Özal Years

For the decade before his death in 1993, Özal dominated Turkish politics. He set his sights on a fundamental shift in the direction of economic policy, to encourage exports and force Turkish products into a competitive position in the world market. His policy instruments were: high interest rates to combat inflation, gradual privatization of inefficient SEEs, wage controls, and an end to state industrial subsidies. Through the mid-1980s, the economy grew steadily: whereas in 1979, 60 percent of exports were agricultural products, by 1988 80% percent were manufactures; the annual inflation rate was lower than it had been; and the government completed large-scale infrastructural development projects. Privatization proceeded very slowly, although the government was successful in breaking up state monopolies. The size of the bureaucracy was still considerable. Major cities grew as industry drew agricultural labor off the land. Economic liberalization rapidly benefited the largest industrial holding companies and some SEEs.

Having a clear-cut economic policy, and executing it with relative consistency, Özal skillfully managed the bureaucrats and the economy.

By mid-1985 Özal was determinedly pursuing political liberalization as well. Martial law had been lifted in fifty of sixty-seven provinces. Eight provinces in the southeast remained under a state of emergency, and anti-terrorism measures stayed in place throughout the country. Turkey's application for the full EEC membership that Özal championed was rejected in 1987. Economic liberalization did not automatically bring political liberalization with it. Özal succeeded in introducing new faces to political life in Turkey, but he was not allowed to normalize it completely or to exert civilian control over the military. By referendum, he let the former leaders of the former parties return to politics and called early elections for 1987. His Motherland Party won an absolute majority—292 of the 450 seats; İnönü's Social Democrat Party came in with 99 seats. Demirel's True Path Party took 59 seats. No other party, including Ecevit's or Erbakan's, reached the threshold.

An aspect of Özal's liberalization was his encouragement of a role for Islam in public life. Özal understood that Islam was the source of the belief system and values of most Turkish citizens, and that it was excluded from the public sphere only with increasing awkwardness and artificiality. He said in 1986, "Restrictions on freedom of conscience breed fanaticism, not the other way around."

In 1984, seeking to recruit religious sentiment against the influence of communism, the military regime required compulsory instruction in Islam in all schools. Picking up an initiative of the Menderes government, the regime sanctioned construction of 34 public Imam-Hatip training schools in one year. Özal's government permitted the graduates of these schools to go on to the universities. Also, members of parliament and the cabinet were visible in attendance at mosques on holy days and other religious observances. Parliament permitted university students to cover their heads in the classroom. Advocates of the headscarf presented it as an issue of civil liberty: in a democracy, they argued, the individual ought to be free to wear any clothing within the limits of public decency; since the constitution guaranteed freedom of religion, laws forbidding the wearing of headscarves violated the citizens' civil rights. For its opponents, the headscarf was a reference to the veil that Atatürk had famously made a symbol of the 'reactionary' Islamic order. They claimed that wearing it was a political gesture directed against the secular state guaranteed by the constitution. In 1989, President Evren himself petitioned the Constitutional Court for a repeal of the new law permitting headscarves. Thousands of university students demonstrated throughout 1989 as the issue went into litigation, first being banned, and then re-permitted by an Act of Parliament. The Council of Higher Education (YÖK), in defiance of Parliament, banned it on university campuses.

Polarization became especially evident in the 1980s, as a new generation of educated but religiously motivated local leaders emerged as a potential challenge to the dominance of the secularized political elite. Assertively proud of Turkey's Islamic heritage, they were generally skillful in adapting the prevalent idiom to articulate their dissatisfaction with various government policies. Certainly, through the example of piety, prayer, and political activism, they helped to restore respect for religious observance in Turkey. In reality, the controversy about the headscarf on campuses is the larger question of the role of Islam in Turkish public life. The visibility of a new consciousness in the public sphere was disturbing for some laicist-Marxists, like *Cumhuriyet* columnist Akbal (1987):

> If these young girls must cover their heads then they can quietly stay home and wait for a bigot husband like themselves! In that case no one would have anything to say against them. In her home she can cover her head, or any other part of her as tightly as she wants. What do we care, what does the society care! But those girls who say *'I want to have education, I want to become a doctor, a lawyer, an engineer, a chemist, a state official or a teacher'*, there is only one path we can show them and that is the path of modern civilization. [Emphasis in the original.]

Many of the new technocrats, diverse professionals, businessmen, and wealthy entrepreneurs started to emerge from outside the traditional classes of Republican elites. Personally religious or conservative, they were more willing than their predecessors to give open expression to that.

For the unyielding laicists, Islam must be confined to the private domain. Since for them 'modern civilization' is at stake, any form of public visibility for Islam is perceived as a direct threat to, and loss of, the constitutive public sphere and system, and as a rebellious attack on Atatürk's reforms and the secular regime he established. More objective commentators have argued, however, that it would be rash and senseless to assert that all women who adopt the headscarf or the new, urban Islamic dress in the city are supporters of the Islamist party or to associate it with politicized Islam in Turkey.

President Özal

Following allegations of corruption, then inflation after 1987, electoral losses in several large cities and coming third in the local elections of 1989, and the defection of several MP deputies to other parties, Özal left party politics and ran for the presidency. He was elected the eighth President of Turkey in 1989.

Iraq invaded Kuwait in 1990. Affirming Turkey's loyalty to the Atlantic alliance, Özal used his position to redefine Turkey's role in regional and world politics. He believed that the solutions to Turkey's economic problems lay in close co-operation with the US and full membership of the EU. He saw in this also the potential for a political solution to the Kurdish problem. Initially, his efforts paid off. The Gulf War, however, left Turkey in a complicated relationship with Iraq and the Kurds. The Kurdish autonomous zone in northern Iraq, seen from the Turkish military's perspective, constituted a potential incitement to the Kurds of Turkey. Since 1989, Özal had been seeking a non-military resolution of the conflict and advocating greater cultural liberty for Kurds. The end of the Gulf War in 1991 seemed a propitious time to carry that project forward. Özal directed the cabinet to repeal the 1983 law forbidding the use of languages other than Turkish. Two prominent Iraqi Kurdish leaders met with Turkish Foreign Ministry officials, twice with the Turkish military, and later with Özal. In October, Demirel came to power in a coalition government with İnönü of the SDP, which the Kurdish groups supported.

After the 1980 military coup, Turkey's civilian politicians had never succeeded in gaining control of the military's actions in the southeast. Through the mechanism of the NSC, the generals had repeatedly intimidated politicians, including Özal and Mesut Yılmaz. When, during demonstrations in 1992, more than 90 Kurds were killed by security forces, the Kurdish deputies in the SDP resigned in protest: the chance of a negotiated solution receded. Meanwhile, the number of 'unsolved' murders in the southeast climbed. These killings were carried out by clandestine paramilitary groups, some of whom probably operated independently, but evidence began to mount of their being funded by the state.

The conflict escalated in 1992 and 1993. Nearly 250,000 troops deployed to the region destroyed some 2,000 villages, displacing an estimated 2 million people, and themselves suffering more than 23,000 casualties. Local people fled to major cities all over Turkey. The Turkish army conducted a number of military operations across the border in northern Iraq to wipe out terrorist bases used against Turkey. In 1993, PKK leader Öcalan announced a unilateral ceasefire. Some were surprised, but Özal had been directly involved. The military, however, interpreted this as a sign of the terrorists' weakness and, assuming final victory was close, intensified operations. Negotiating with Özal through Jalal Talabani, Öcalan renewed the ceasefire. At this critical juncture, Özal died suddenly in April 1993, while still serving as president.

After Özal, Turkey struggled to reconcile the changes of the 1980s and 1990s—the legacy of the late president—with the traditions of the Republic and the requirements of modern democracy. A strong, stable government seemed elusive as Turkey was beset by economic difficulties, political scandals, corruption, the ongoing battle against terrorism, and Kurdish separatism. In fact, each of these issues was as old as the Republic.

Within a month, Süleyman Demirel became President and Tansu Çiller Prime Minister. In 1993, the Kurdish ceasefire broke down and military operations against the PKK resumed as before. The PKK ambushed a bus and murdered 33 off-duty military personnel. Heavy new fighting erupted, and hope of a political solution to the conflict seemed lost. Neither Demirel nor Çiller was capable of opposing the wishes of the generals or prepared to risk a civilian–military confrontation by challenging the military's assumption of a free hand in dealing with southeastern Turkey.

The ongoing struggle brought serious economic problems and estrange-ment from the EU. It also compromised the integrity of the state through the influence of organized crime.

The government was unable to control spending, and consequently there was high public debt and an accelerated 'dollarization' of the econ-omy in 1994. International agencies therefore downgraded Turkey's cred-it status. That prompted a devaluation of the Turkish Lira that cost Tur-key an estimated $1.2 billion. An austerity package caused the Lira to lose half its value.

Political Islam?

After Tansu Çiller's government lost a vote of confidence, the country went to the polls in 1995. Erbakan's Welfare Party (WP) won the largest vote, 21.4 percent, followed by Çiller's True Path Party (TPP) and Yılmaz's Motherland Party (MP). Ecevit's Democratic Left Party (DLP) and Baykal's RPP also won seats. Among the parties failing to reach the threshold were the Nationalist Movement Party (NMP) of Türkeş and the (leftist-Kurd-ish) People's Democracy Party, which showed strongly in the Kurdish regions but less among Kurdish populations in the major cities. Erbakan was unable to attract coalition partners to form the government. In 1996, Çiller and Yılmaz formed a coalition government that lasted only eleven weeks. Later, Çiller's coalition with Erbakan brought the WP to power and made Erbakan the prime minister in 1996. Erbakan once again put political Islam on the Turkish agenda.

An extended public debate about the role of religion and the mean-ing of political Islam ensued. Erbakan's former campaign speeches were dug out in order to heat up controversy—for instance, his 'either with or without blood' outburst during the 1994 municipal elections; his praise of Iran for resisting the West; his pledges to take Turkey out of NATO; to set up an Islamic NATO, an Islamic UN, an Islamic version of the EU, and an Islamic currency. These speeches carried more force as political ges-tures than policies and were incapable of attracting broad-based support in the country. Nevertheless, similar or even more inflammatory postur-ing by other WP deputies and mayors dominated national headlines. Perceptions of the WP government were ambivalent: was it a thing to be feared, a threat to secularism and the regime; or was it a sign of a healthy Turkish democracy, that they had a right to hold, express and persuade others to share their position? The reason the WP had done as well as it had in the elections was that it articulated a vision of the just society in Turkey through the use of a commonly understood religious idiom, the traditional values—widely interpreted as meaning Islamic morals and behavior. It also benefited from an 'anti-Ankara' sentiment, as voters reacted against a government and state apparatus riddled with corruption scandals and out of touch with common people. Nevertheless, a sizeable portion of the voting public did not like the WP's rhetoric and mistrusted their motives. Laicists opposed the WP's recruits in a variety of lower level government positions.

Erbakan made a series of visits to Muslim countries, which drew criticism from the laicists. In 1997 his government was brought down—not by its failure to lower the budget deficit or curb inflation, nor by various scandals, but by a rally in Sincan, a suburb of Ankara. Electoral success gave the Welfare Party (WP) access to the privileges (and responsibilities) of power as never before, but they failed to use them in the service of the nation.

'Post-modern' Military Coup

At a rally in honor of 'Jerusalem Day' hosted by the (WP) mayor of Sincan, the speech of the Iranian ambassador, anti-Zionist slogans chanted by the crowds and the posters displayed by Palestinian visitors were enough for the army tanks to rumble into Sincan.

A top-level military commission calling itself the 'Western Working Group' launched an investigation into the WP. On February 28, 1997, the National Security Council (NSC), projecting themselves as guardians of the Kemalist reforms, and in particular of secularism, released a public statement that: "destructive and separatist groups are seeking to weaken our democracy and legal system by blurring the distinction between the secular and the anti-secular. [...] In Turkey, secularism is not only a form of government but a way of life and the guarantee of democracy and social peace [...] the structural core of the state." The military's 'supervision' of Erbakan's government eventually forced its resignation in June 1997. Following this, the pressure on the Muslim communities increased, with some secularist leaders openly expecting a 'settling of accounts' with political Islam.

In what the commander of the navy admitted was 'a post-modern coup', the politicians were forced by the military commanders either to implement the measures they proposed or put together an alternative government that would do so. Erbakan agreed to an eighteen-point plan to reduce the influence of Islam in Turkey, that is, to curb Islamic-minded political, social, cultural, and economic groups. The ban on certain faith communities, their SMOs and other religious institutions would be enforced, the 'reactionary' personnel in governmental positions and state posts would be purged, the spread of state Imam-Hatip schools would be stopped, and tighter restrictions would be maintained on 'politically symbolic garments like women's headscarves'. Many companies were denounced as 'backward', and state institutions and people were warned not to buy anything from those companies. In addition, TUSIAD, the business federation, issued a report in line with the military's agenda, urging that the power of political party leaders be curbed. Erbakan was asked and agreed to sign an order purging 160 military officers for so-called 'Islamic' activities and sympathies.

Since the military coup of 1980, nothing has been as divisive in Turkish political life as the NSC decisions of February 28, because those decisions affirmed the army's supremacy over political life.

The reason the military did not take over the state administration was that they had proved to themselves and to others that they could engineer far-reaching change in the political system and govern everything from their barracks. Through the NSC, the military possessed a constitutionally defined executive authority that it had used since the 1980s to exert its power on a range of issues. This 'post-modern' coup caused the Turkish political scene to become even more confused and unpredictable. Erbakan resigned in 1997.

The generals behind the coup 'asked' Mesut Yılmaz, the leader of the Motherland Party, to form a new government, and he did so. In 1998, the Constitutional Court closed the WP "because of actions against the principles of the secular republic." Six WP leaders, including Erbakan, were banned from political leadership for five years, and individual members also faced criminal charges of subverting the constitution. The mayors of

Sincan, Kayseri and Istanbul[11] received prison sentences[12] for 'inciting religious hatred'. Within a few weeks, most WP deputies had joined a successor party, the Virtue Party, which subsequently became the largest in Parliament.[13] In the end, for all its accomplishments at the municipal level, the WP had fared no better than the other parties at finding solutions to the basic economic and political problems of Turkey. It had instead aggravated them.

Prime Minister Yılmaz pressed ahead with what came to be known as the 'February 28 Process'—the efforts to limit Islamic influence in public life. Parliament required pupils to complete eight years of primary education—a measure designed to eliminate students' admission to state Imam-Hatip schools and other faith-inspired communities' secular and state-inspected schools. During the military rule in the 1980s, the graduates of the state Imam-Hatip schools had been allowed to continue higher education in social sciences and other post-secondary institutions. The schools enrolled one-tenth of the eligible 'secondary education students'.

The February 28 Process also enforced regulations banning headscarves from schools, universities and the entire public sphere. Asked about civil servants beginning to turn up for work wearing headscarves, one of the highest ranking military officers had called it "the end of the world." Public protests and hunger strikes broke out all over Turkey, but to no avail. The secularist circles and media, especially the radical secularist and leftist newspaper *Cumhuriyet*, tried hard to frame the public debate and spared no effort to reinforce the authority and power of laicism to define the terms of public discourse, including the meaning, style and judgment on head-covering, sometimes with pejorative top headlines or stories. The administration also moved against Islamic influence in other areas. The police detained twenty leading Muslim businessmen on charges that they had provided funding for Islamic activities, and in 1998 the chief prosecutor in Ankara's State Security Court asked for the closure of MUSIAD, the Independent Industrialists' and Businessmen's Association,

---

[11] The Mayor of Istanbul was then Tayyip Erdoğan, the Prime Minister of Turkey since March 14, 2003.

[12] Four years, 7 months; 10 months; 10 months, respectively

[13] This is another recurrent theme in Turkish politics. After all coups, the people has always voted for and restored into government positions the parties and leaders that the military overthrew or expressed strong dislike for.

and filed charges against its president for inciting hostility based on religion. All the people charged were eventually acquitted.

When Yılmaz attacked Çiller on the grounds of corruption, Çiller's coalition partners, the WP, shielded her from prosecution. But before long, Yılmaz himself was implicated in revelations of corruption on such a massive scale that the foundations of Turkish democracy were threatened. It all came out as a result of a car accident.

Crash and Corruption

In a traffic accident that occurred in Susurluk in 1996, three occupants of a car lost their lives and one was injured. Since the identity of the victims and the story of how they happened to be riding together in the car came out, the case has gone on unfolding and remains an open file.

The three dead included Abdullah Çatlı, a criminal right-wing hitman wanted in connection with the attacks and murders of leftist students in Ankara in 1978–79. He was also involved in the jailbreak of Ağca, the Pope's assailant. At the time of his death, Çatlı held a gun permit and, among his thirteen passports in various names, one Turkish diplomatic passport. The second passenger was Çatlı's girlfriend, a former beauty queen. The third was a senior security officer and deputy police chief of Istanbul, who had commanded police units in missions against Kurdish terrorists. The survivor in the car, Sedat Bucak, was a True Path Party Member of Parliament with close connections to Çiller, and led a Kurdish clan receiving government funding to fight Kurdish separatists. Also found in the car were guns and silencers.

At first, President Demirel denied government involvement in criminal activity. The Minister of the Interior resigned when it became clear that his initial statements about the crash were not only false, but that in fact he had had a long relationship with Çatlı. Newspapers published reports, based on police and intelligence documents, showing that state organizations had been hiring death squads to murder Kurdish rebels and 'other enemies of the state' since the mid-1980s, and that these death squads had evidently received a strengthened mandate in 1991. Türkeş, the former junta colonel and the leader of the Nationalist Movement Party, publicly acknowledged that Çatlı had been employed by the government to carry out clandestine missions on behalf of the police and the army.

Another former Interior Minister Sağlam admitted that the National Security Council had approved the use of 'illegal' means to dispose of 'enemies'. The weapons used were in some cases traced back to the security forces. Funding for the death squads was raised through bank presidents, who in return received kickbacks from the drug trade that the squads were allowed to run, the profits being laundered through casinos licensed by the Ministry of Tourism.

The published versions of official reports directed by Prime Minister Yılmaz were incomplete and misleading with respect to the period of Çiller's premiership. In fact, missing persons and mysterious murders dated back earlier than that, to 1991, Yılmaz's first term as premier. Yılmaz's statements, that outside the military police, the armed forces were unaware of, and uninvolved in, the activities of the death squads, remained unbelievable. New information became available almost daily, revealing the depth and complexity of interrelationships between the police, military officers, banks, the government privatization process, cabinet ministries and parliamentarians, business tycoons, organized crime and far-right gangs. It pointed to two ultimate sources of the problem. The first was the fanatical pursuit of the war against Kurdish armed insurgents in southeastern Turkey and other enemies of the state, and the second was the corruption of the ongoing strategy to privatize SEEs. Both the True Path Party and Motherland Party were implicated in the escalating spiral of scandals. But the issue went even deeper. Bülent Ecevit and the chief of general staff had known all about it since 1973. Far-right nationalist and marginal fundamentalist groups had apparently been secretly armed and used as paramilitary death squads with the knowledge of the highest officials of the state. Investigations of Çiller's abuse of the prime minister's fund suggested that the account had been used to pay such hit men and squads.

Three TPP associates were convicted while Çiller's associates defended themselves throughout 1998 against charges involving their personal finances. Yılmaz's government collapsed in 1998 as Parliament investigated his connections to organized crime.

The scandals of the 1990s were not evidence of anything wholly new in Turkish politics. This was how the Turkish political system had worked for decades, as an elaboration of systems of patronage. This is the result of political patrons' access to dramatic sources of wealth in the form of control of the formerly state-owned industrial ventures and businesses (the SEEs). Beginning in the early 1980s, a very large portion of Turkey's industrial capacity was put up for sale. The stakes were enormous, and it is hardly surprising that, in the struggle for control of this huge financial potential, some of the darkest forces in Turkish society came out in ways similar to what has been seen all over East Central Europe since the break-up of the USSR and the fall of the old Stalinist regimes. The ugliest aspect of it all is that retired generals or military personnel took the highest administrative or consultative positions in such ventures, and that murderous gangs were able to operate with the acquiescence of the Turkish military and bureaucrats, who found them useful against the separatists and other political dissidents. These gangs included not only neo-fascist groups but also marginal fundamentalists. A police shoot-out with an illegal Kurdish fundamentalist group called Hizbullah (unrelated to the group of the same name in Lebanon) in eastern Anatolia in early 2000 led to the discovery of huge caches of weapons and the remains of dozens of persons murdered by this group, which had received state support for its opposition to the PKK, the separatist (leftist) Kurdish armed group.

The Return of Ecevit

After Yılmaz's resignation, Ecevit, head of the Democratic Left Party (DLP), became prime minister. He was virtually the only prominent political leader untouched by scandal, and he took the nation to early elections in April 1999. His victory in those elections was helped by the capture of Öcalan, the PKK leader. Ecevit formed a coalition with Devlet Bahçeli's[14] NMP and Yılmaz's MP. As prime minister, Ecevit confronted issues, some as old as the Republic, and others unexpected by earlier generations.

In 1997, EU member states did not offer Turkey a pre-accession partnership. This stunned Turkey, which had held associate member status since 1964. Some EU member states feared that Turkey's large population, cheap labor, and agricultural and industrial products might outbid the comparatively high-priced European labor and products. They also raised political objections to Turkey's membership, such as the relationship

---

[14] Türkeş's successor in the Nationalist Movement Party

with Greece, abuses of the civil rights of political dissidents and minorities, the use of torture, the military's influence over elected government, and its very rigid attitude towards religion. Dutch parliamentarian Arie Oostlander reported (on Turkey's accession to the EU):

> The underlying philosophy of the Turkish state implies an exaggerated fear of the undermining of its integrity and an emphasis on the homogeneity of Turkish culture (nationalism), an important role for the army, and a very rigid attitude towards religion, which means that this underlying philosophy is incompatible with the founding principles of the European Union.

In 1999, Öcalan was captured, tried, and sentenced to death for treason for his role in leading the Kurdish separatist struggle against the Turkish state. Öcalan made some statements of reconciliation, calling for an end to the separatist war and pleading that the Turkish and Kurdish people were in the end indivisible. The Turkish military interpreted these remarks as evidence of PKK weakness.

Also in 1999, an earthquake struck the most heavily industrialized Istanbul–Izmit corridor. The aftermath of the quake showed both the weaknesses and the strengths of Turkey. The state was completely inadequate and ineffective and came to people's assistance too late and too slowly after the disaster. One dimension of corruption emerged with the death of more than 17,000 people: contracting procedures had allowed construction companies to put up shoddy structures that ignored building codes.

By 2000, the generation of men who had led the country since 1961 was passing from the scene. The coalition government failed to amend the constitution to enable Demirel to serve a second term as President; rebellious deputies urged Demirel to retire in spite of the potential for political and economic destabilization; the Supreme Electoral Board barred Erbakan from participation in politics; Türkeş died; after Demirel, Supreme Court Judge Necdet Sezer became President. A younger generation was calling for a more democratic, open, liberal, and humane public regime, for their leaders to translate the nation's enduring values, potentialities, and aspirations into a form that could be meaningfully articulated in present conditions and carried forward to the future.

President Sezer did not merely disappoint the younger generations; he proved to be the staunchest protector of the status quo and, through his continual vetoes and unilateral actions against the government and parliament, a most vigorous opponent of the efforts for modernization and accession to the European Union.

Implications of the Historical Background

Like all the Ottoman intellectuals of his generation, Mustafa Kemal was brought up on the revolutionary, democratic, and nationalist ideas of the Young Turks, the Committee of Union and Progress and, through them, the French Revolution. The War of Independence primed Mustafa Kemal to come to power, to eliminate the sultanate-caliphate, and enable his socio-cultural and political ambitions to radically Westernize Turkish society. He was convinced that the only way to save his country was a radical change in the political system along the lines of the Western European nation-states. He worked his strategy through the representative bodies authorized by local communities, the Republican People's Party, the government, parliament, the institutions which these bodies set up and, later, through the statist-elitists. He controlled and guided the political power and cadre of a new laicist nation-state that would necessarily establish the conditions for the revolutions he had planned.

However, with and after Atatürk, the emergence of a protectionist bureaucracy, then of an intelligentsia, and the subsequent transformation of both through a broadening of the bases of their recruitment, education, and politicization, have deeply scarred Turkish history and society ever since. Domestic and international developments have not influenced the role and leadership of the protectionist elitists, namely the military, civilian bureaucracy, and academics. There is little recognition on their part that there might be a variety of models of social organization that could serve as a platform for Turkish society and interests in particular, and for global society and humanity in general. They do not see or appreciate that internal motivations and desires lead people, not political and external pressures. Inevitably, the road that the protectionist elitists paved in collaboration with vested interest groups only polarized society, increasing societal tension and unrest.

In any case, the radical reforms of the one-party era touched only some segments of society. Some segments did not take part in those top-down directly induced changes; also, some lived far away from the urban centers, or had little exposure to the reforms, or rejected and remained outside them. In short, the reforms were not as complete or extensive as some celebrated statist-elitist-secularists claim or wish to believe. Of course, some writers (notably, Daniel Lerner and Bernard Lewis) have lauded the resounding success of modernization in Turkey. On the other hand, its critics argue that 'Turkish modernization, when examined from alternative vantage points, contained little that was worth celebrating." So influential was their demur that by the end of the seventies 'modernization' had become a dirty word, and authors such as Lerner and Lewis were cited only as examples of the 'wrong' way of studying the late Ottoman Empire and republican Turkey. Divisions between those who unreservedly admire (even revere) the radical modernization and those who question it are mirrored in divisions between the urban and the rural, and between the east and the west of the country, which influence political views and trends in today's Turkey:

> Before anything else, the new republic would use all the power and energy at its disposal towards the substitution of Western culture for the Islamic. The insistence on changing Islamic institutions and structures prevented the modernizing elite of the Kemalist era from turning their attention to broader definitions of systemic change.[15]

The governing ideology in the one-party period also necessitated its favoring an authoritarian, tutelary attitude towards the public, and its interventionist economic policy. There was little accumulation of wealth except in the hands of the state, no wealth-owning class that would protect and support the revolution and lead progress. That is why, in the 1930s, state-owned conglomerates were formed to carry out the state-planned industrialization and economic development.

The State-owned Economic Enterprises (SEEs) came, over time, to dominate business, economy, and politics. Through political patronage, government officials and former military officers staffed the bureaucracy of the new republic, saw the opportunities to create and build state-sponsored personal fiefdoms, and seized control of the SEEs. Further, taking advantage of tax exemptions, state subsidies, low-interest capital, priority access to scarce resources, foreign exchange and trained personnel,

---

[15] Toprak, B. (1981) *Islam and Political Development in Turkey*. Leiden, E.J. Brill.

state officials and officers increasingly turned the SEEs against private sector competition. They became a real elite, a protectionist, republican class, with a strong grip on economic and political power.

When some politicians and parties sought to make reforms in the system, they could not do so without disturbing a protectionist elite unwilling to accelerate the democratization and economic liberalization that would harm their interests. Authoritarian rule and its suppressive measures, and scarcity of basic necessities, alienated people from the elitists' ideas and attitudes. The role played by faith (Islam) in the identity and lives of the majority of Turks was undeniable. When the elitists tried to revolutionize and Westernize (as well as the material aspects of the state's relations with its citizens) the inner dimensions of individual, family, societal, and religious identities, aversion and resistance were inevitable —as was the oppressive authoritarianism of the RPP in response to resistance, and its kindling, in turn, an even stronger desire for a free society and a liberal economy.

The invested sinecures—in theory for the people but in reality against them—facilitated and engineered the conditions for the protectionist elite's interventions and military coups. Through the coups they sought both to re-establish state authority according to their own understanding and to restructure the political and economic system. Everything in society came to be institutionalized around a set of static norms imposed from above. Military power, constitutionalized and thus embedded in the state structure, defined the boundaries of civilian power. The arrangements of key political actors, prior to or during transformations, established new rules, roles, and behavioral patterns, which became the institutions upon which the new regimes consolidated. Accords between the political elite and the armed forces drew the parameters of civilian and military spheres that would later become persistent barriers to change and, thus, democratization. Before the transition to civilian rule the rules of the game were set by the military. New constitutions were drawn up by consultative assemblies largely appointed by the military. Thus began the period of 'guided democracy' with its 'licensed' or 'accredited' political bodies and parties, under the direct supervision of the National Security Council.

Political liberalism, which would gradually expand civil society, promote democratization, protect human rights and prevent destabilizing political responses, has never been fully achieved. In practice, elitist or mil-

itary interventionist counter-mobilizations have allowed very little movement towards full democracy in Turkey—a fact acknowledged by European countries and authorities and, unfortunately, condoned by them 'at all
costs'—even the cost of disenfranchising those elements of the Turkish
population, 'however moderate', who support other political approaches.

The primary justification for the three coups in 1960, 1971, and 1980
was that rampant corruption and civil discord paralyzed the operation
of parliamentary democracy. No coincidence then that the February 28
Process occurred at a time when bribery and corruption were endemic
features of the economy. International records clearly put Turkey high
in the list of most corrupt countries (57th out of 91 countries, according
to *The Corruption Perceptions Index 2001*). The loss to the nation, as publicly declared by the Corruption Investigative Committee of the Turkish
parliament, was 150 billion US$ through bank graft and plunder by their
owners. It is noteworthy that some CEOs and top advisors of the banks
concerned, and of the holdings that owned those banks, are retired senior
generals. The office of the president, the inter-parliamentary committees
and other institutions clearly had, and through the Constitutional Court
exercised, the power they needed to prevent the incumbent government
or parliament from carrying out the reforms the nation needed. Since the
leadership could not overcome opposition from other institutions and had
to abide by the rule of the Constitutional Court, it could not carry out policies like economic and political liberalization, and so progress to democratic and political efficacy was stifled.

After the collapse of the USSR and the Eastern bloc, and the end of
the Cold War, Turkey's statesmen and civil societies worked to establish
close commercial and political relations with the Balkan, Caucasian, and
Central Asian states. A thin sort of culturally Islamic revivalism came into
view. However, there was little prospect of any movement for an Islamic
state gaining wide popularity in Turkey in the 1980s. Islamist fundamentalists occasionally staged dramatic acts of violence, but numerous polls
of the general population have found that no more than between two
and seven percent of Turks favored the establishment of a political order
based on Islamic law. Throughout the 1980s, electoral returns gave Erbakan's Welfare Party no more than ten percent of the popular vote nationally. Sometimes the specter of an Iranian-style Islamic revolution was
raised, but Turkey was not Iran. No one in any way resembled Khomei-

ni. The majority of Muslims in Turkey are consciously resistant to any sort of radical or fundamentalist Islamist movement. Even those who may be considered or consider themselves to be conservatively religious have grown up as citizens in a secular order and accepted its basic premises. Accordingly, Turkey's Islamic or faith-inspired movements accept the fundamental premises of democracy.

Since the 1950s, there has been strong public demand for transformations in different sectors of the state apparatus. Societal changes and the demands for organizational autonomy have brought to light widespread issues and crises in the functioning of the country's bureaucratic institutions. The normal functioning of those institutions has been instrumentally subordinated to the dominant interests. Political scientists Dorronsoro and Massicard observed: "Organizations controlling—directly or indirectly—the Parliament have increased in the last decades." Another political scientist, William Hale (1999), summed up the political system in Turkey as 'amoral partyism' or a 'system of neo-patrimonialism' in which a party's 'clients' ignore any fiscal irregularities and political inconsistencies as long as they are benefiting—party leaders can therefore change alignments without any justification in terms of the party's supposed ideology. So, democracy in Turkey is "characterized by state dominance over civil society, political patronage and corruption, and political parties that operate as spheres of intraelite competition." The traditional protectionist leadership in Turkey has been based on a strict nationalist, secularist and bureaucratic-authoritarian understanding.

Several social and political scientists have detailed the particular features of the control and management flowing from this bureaucratic-authoritarian understanding over the last thirty years as: special interventions under pressure of particularist demands; clientelistic management of power; compromise with the traditional (protectionist) elites and with speculative and exploitative interests; unabashed spending of public funds for political purposes; the apportioning, by political entities, of publicly owned industry, SEEs, state agencies, and the banking system; and partisan control of information and the media.

As this chapter has also shown, given the logic of the dominant elitist–statist–secularist attitudes, questions have rarely been asked about certain issues, such as the heterogeneous bloc of interests mobilized around certain parties, the rationale of Turkey's model of development, the imbalances between the east and west of the country, and between ethno-religious communities, the separation and exclusion between the protectionist and modernizing groups, the people's need for faith and for a role for it, the place and significance of civic initiatives, the place, weight and status of Turkey in Europe and the world, and so on. Sociologist Ali Bulaç comments on the resulting waste of energy and resources:

> The governing elite in Turkey, as a hard core, is resistant to any development, reform, or legitimate democratic demands [...] Democratic developments and increases in civil initiatives carry the accumulated energy from the periphery towards the centre, but resistance at the core continues to cause a waste of social energy.

In terms of the capacity to govern, the response by the Turkish political elite has consisted of the introduction of restricted reforms along with a resort to repression and counter-mobilization against its own people. In terms of capacity to represent, the reaction has taken the form of hyper-politicization and under-representation. This system of relationships has resulted in distorted modernization and the breakdown and transformation of collective actions, the hyper-politicization of all issues, short-term interest, patronage, and nepotism, societal conflicts and tensions, sectarianism and terrorism, and embezzlement, massive graft and corruption. Political analyst Heinz Kramer sums it up well:

> Turkish society, therefore, needs to be directed to and transformed by institutionalization; the selection and renewal of modernizing personnel in organizations; democratization; globalization; the disengagement of old antagonistic elites and demands; and the acknowledgement of Islam as a guide to the spiritual well being of people.

Conclusion

Societies differ in the amount of social movement activity they have, in how such activity is structured, sponsored, and controlled. In Turkey, it is largely either the state apparatus or civil society that sponsors movements or counter-movements. By contrast, in western Europe or North America, states often act or arbitrate neutrally, even though some state apparatus and democratic processes might look quite similar on other grounds. Accordingly, imputed or constructed meanings, especially within the sociology of social movements, are not fixed or static but subject to change and variation with the social context. Meanings, concepts, societal conditions and resulting action are indeed different, albeit overlapping.

Mobilizing and counter-mobilizing actors do not have equal access to the same cultural stock. Even if they do or claim that they do, the reality constituted by the skills, orientations, styles, interests and supporters or collaborators of the groups is sure to be somewhat different from what it appears or they claim it to be. How the socio-political elite, media, and interest groups conceptualize the nature, identity and outcome of mobilizations and counter-mobilizations is highly dependent on local conditions and context.

We have seen in the foregoing that the protectionist group within the Turkish establishment collaborates with other ideological, media and interest groups to their reciprocal advantage and (nearly always) to the disadvantage of ordinary citizens. The templates of organization and repertoires of contention in Turkey and the Turkish societal context are very different from those that obtain in Western Europe and North America. Cultural stock and repertoires of contention are not static; they grow and change—something that has been demonstrated also in the accounts of state-sponsored organized crime, that is, the unfolding entail of the Susurluk incident and the February 28 Process.

2
Fostering Civic Society and Democratization

Civil Society and Civic Organizations

September 11, 2008

Almost two weeks ago, as the new commander of land forces, General Işık Koşaner, gave a speech about the enemies he despises. These included separatists, faith-inspired groups, networks that consist of a postmodern clique of some academics, media and finance circles and NGOs. These were labeled as "postmodern" traitors "manipulated by global powers" and a "global enemy"[16]. Rather than dealing with comments and criticism of his remarks, it is useful for us to ask what exactly civil society is and what functions civil society organizations, such as faith-inspired groups and NGOs, fulfill in contemporary societies.[17]

In fact civil society is an arena of friendships, clubs, churches or other faith groups, business associations, unions, human rights groups and other voluntary associations beyond the household but separate from the state. Civil society organizations are essentially outside the institutional structures of government. They give us as citizens opportunities to learn the democratic habits of free assembly, non-coercive dialogue and socioeconomic initiative. They are self-governing, and we join or support them voluntarily. Despite their diversity, they are not part of the government

---

[16] For a view sympathetic to militarism and military coups in Turkey and which omits to mention the ultra-nationalist, anti-civil society, anti-democratic component of this speech, see Robert Tait's article for the Guardian www.guardian.co.uk/world/2008/aug/29/turkey.islam.

[17] This speech available in Turkish at arsiv.ntvmsnbc.com/news/457549.asp#story Continues. Accessed 30 June 2013.

apparatus. Unlike other private institutions, they are set up to serve the public, not to generate profit for those involved in them. So, civil society organizations embody a commitment to freedom and personal initiative. They enable us to make full use of our legal rights of citizenship to act on our own authority so as to improve the quality of our own lives and the lives of others.

These organizations embody the ideal that we have responsibilities not only to ourselves but also to our communities. So civil society organizations provide society with private institutions that are serving essentially public purposes. They have connections to a great number of citizens. The fact that we citizens may belong to any number of civic organizations and professionalized networks in the civil sector adds to the flexibility of these organizations and increases their capacity to channel private initiatives in support of public, cultural, educational and humanitarian purposes and philanthropic services.

Civil society organizations contribute to our potential as citizens to discover and implement new solutions following our own development agendas. They boost voluntary participation; they build networks of committed citizens in mutually trusting relationships; in them we pursue, through respectful dialogue and collaborative effort, the shared goal of improving community services. It is obvious that virtuous individuals working largely on their own cannot build a society rich in mutual trust and good relations. True richness, that is, reciprocity, trustworthiness and civic virtue, can only arise from a dense network of social relations.

Faith and faith-inspired organizations are a substantial part of civic society. They contribute significantly to the preservation and development of relations and bridges with other communities of the same faith and also with other faiths outside their own fold.

The opportunity for us as citizens to associate with such organizations is an important dimension of participatory and democratic culture because each of us, as an individual, can freely join the associations and services of our choice, and we are also free to leave such a group if and when we please. Individuals are motivated to participate in such civic organizations or networks for many different reasons, ranging from self-fulfillment and self-expression to self-development or anything else.

The fact that a civic, autonomous initiative is situated outside the conventional channels of political representation—party, government, state, etc.—does not mean that it stands in some way against the political, governmental or democratic system. This would be a grave misreading of the reality of diffused civic networks, especially of collective action. Because they are not oriented for profit, faith-inspired or civil society organizations are very different from political actors and formal state institutions and agencies. They do not aim to compete with the government or state institutions and agencies. They deal with human beings individually through independent, lawful, civic organizations, although the natural consequences of their actions extend to the civil-public sphere. However, this is not the "top-down" approach characteristic of the state or government. The action or projects of civil society take place in many different ways at various levels of society, wherever citizens perceive a need that they feel capable of fulfilling by organizing together. Without them our society and our day-to-day lives would be much poorer in every way.

In short, the civil society sector demonstrates a shift in orientation from macro-politics to micro-practices. While their origin and services may arise from civil-society or faith-inspired initiatives, their discourse and practice also affirm the idea that religion and the state are and can be separate and that this does not endanger, undermine and damage our "national unity, national values and security parameters."

Economic and Social Crises and Disintegration

April 30, 2009

Modern societies need to find solutions to the growing economic and social crises before they lead to further disintegration and unforeseen and undesirable consequences. The international press and media are full of reports that the rates of burglary, crime, murder, suicide and racially motivated violence are on the increase in this or that country. Layoffs from work, rapid changes in people's financial status, the thwarting of people's individual goals and the sudden occurrence of a global depression are leading to breakdowns in collective values and collective order as well as raising questions about the limits on the attainment of wealth, pleasure and power.

This does not indicate an absence of clear societal norms and values. Yet it shows that individuals lack a sense of social regulation. Traditional values which have always been believed to keep families and society intact have been ignored, disrupted or undermined. As a result of this, people remain unguided in the choices they make in their personal and community life in many situations.

Looking at the current crises, traditional social contacts and cultural values no longer give a sense of authoritative normative regulation or consensus over social regulation in the larger society. Individuals now want to achieve beyond their means. They are so committed to achieving their goals and desires that when they encounter obstacles, they seem unable to adopt alternative goals and may readily turn to deviant means such as crime to achieve them. Extreme value is attached to the personal attainment of wealth and success at the expense of everything—friends, family and moral values. This leads to individuals' alienation from one another, and dehumanizing strategies are used by individuals and organizations for gain. This kind of understanding has profoundly changed not only the way people live but the way society is organized. It has brought the destruction of the old family and community values promising a better world. This is the reality of individualistic, materialist and capitalist understandings.

The understanding of a traditional society was criticized on the grounds that goals are limited by social order and morality. In contrast, the understanding of modern society was presented with its promise of unchecked desires, deregulation and disengagement. Normative social values became less present in individual life. This has led to unlimited desires, unachievable goals and unhappiness. Having more leads to wanting more. Pursuing unattainable or unlimited goals condemns individuals to chronic dissatisfaction and unhappiness.

Against all these elements, social, political and religious leaders emerge and speak. However, this has failed to have the desired effect on people because, while preaching about frugality, moderation, limiting our passions and desires, and on our values, these leaders were staying in the best hotels, flying in their private jets and helicopters, and producing a new social elite, not to mention the scandalous "treatments" they receive in massage parlors. So faith and society started to lose their moderating role.

Now, in the face of the latest economic and social crises, we should all question ourselves about over-consumption, social disintegration and the social disorders of our affluent societies. Do we have more than we truly need? Food, clothing, home appliances, cars and excessive luxury in our houses vary in size, color, form and price. Is the life or society we live in ideal or is it plagued by social disorder? Is our affluent lifestyle really perfect for us and those around us? Social disintegration and the individual or social problems we go through arise from indulging in too much material accumulation, over-consumption and our detachment from traditional (moral) values. We talk about environmental degradation and pollution. What about moral pollution? Erosion of good old small-town values, for instance?

In the face of social, economic and individual crises (see, for example, the murder of 57 people in the US this month alone), families and communities need to spend more time and effort on strengthening the bonds within the family. A good, strong family relationship does not just mean money spent on family members. Family members, especially children, need more time, care, understanding and compassion.

As for administrators, they need to focus more on the sources of tension and unhappiness in society. The relations between production, cost-benefit, social welfare systems and social norms need to be carefully revised. While doing this, indeed, we must not sacrifice our individuality and our freedom of choice. However, free will without moral choice and values may reduce humanity to machines without purpose, and in that there is scant chance of bettering ourselves. Without moral guidance, people in complex societies cease to exist as true human beings.

Concerned citizens, civil society organizations and governments across the world rally to offer concepts and approaches to the current crises. There is obviously hope for a better and sustainable society and future. We need to first recognize the problems confronting the stability of our societies, then turn to valid remedies to recover from them. Social disintegration is not inevitable. People have already been given what is needed.

Turkey and the Transition to Democracy

October 8, 2009

I n the last 40 years, many nations have had to deal with various obstacles as they have built or restored democracy. Along with the government's latest initiative, Turkey now needs to develop a set of criteria in order to shape its development of a civic, democratic society based on the rule and supremacy of law.

Democratization is now under way in more than half of the states that were authoritarian 25 years ago. Numerous examples can be given, from countries in Latin America to the Far East. Interdisciplinary studies are full of examples of democratic expansion efforts in many countries, such as Taiwan, Scotland, Croatia, the Czech Republic and so on.

There are many particular conditions that affect the development of civic-democratic societies, including historical conditions, the alignment of the elite, the protectionist status quo, corruption, economic development or stagnation, the role of the media, business community, judiciary and military. Consequently, studies reveal that, as in Northern Ireland, for example, the democratic road is not always rosy. It is often bumpy but well worth following.

Nearly half of the 100 countries that have started down the path of transformation to a democratic society since the 1970s have experienced some kind of relapse or other. One common obstacle to democratization is the trade-off or incompatibility between democratization and economic development. In some countries, as frequently seen in Latin America and Africa, living conditions have actually declined over the last 15 years as a result of some measures carried out in the name of democratization.

Moreover, the emphasis and issues are not the same in societies where the attempt to establish democratic governance follows ethnic conflict. In such societies that aim to move away from ethnic conflict to democracy, transitional problems concern minority rights, forced displacement, refugee return and reconstruction, and the prosecution of extrajudicial killings and war crimes. In a country transitioning to democracy following a conflict, democratization starts with political elites; other civic organizations and citizens increase their involvement gradually with each positive step that the incumbent government takes toward restoring legitimacy and the rule of law.

An excessive role for or weight of the military quashes democratic rule, hinders modernization and results in the breakdown of the state, as seen in the cases of Sierra Leone and Liberia. Failure in democratic development encourages the growth of authoritarianism and militarism, which further impedes modernization and democratization. As in Turkey, issues of "state security" or "threats to the regime" become the highest goals. This notion nurtures nationalist identities and ethnic loyalties, which hamper the development of a multicultural civil society, the rule of law and participatory democracy.

Understanding the multiple challenges facing democratic transitions is vital. If a transitioning state cannot sustain peaceful political and economic development, the strains of transition and reform prove so great that the government and any democratization process it has initiated will collapse. Then, not only do the historic democratic gains made so far come to seem illusory to the masses, but that misperception has far-reaching implications for the surrounding countries that were ready to follow the example of democratization. Consider, for example, how Iraq, Syria and Iran might be affected by the success or failure of democratization in Turkey.

Studies of countries in different parts of the world have discussed essential obstacles that influence the process of democratic transition, its length, success or failure. Pre-existing obstacles are sometimes overlooked or underestimated at the beginning of the democratic transformation. They therefore can cause not only the failure of the democratic process but also actually increase tension in society.

In the case of Turkey, democratization is a thorough-going process concerning every sector of society rather than a one-off initiative of some pro-Kurdish activists and Democratic Society Party (DTP) members. Any process of democratization is necessarily influenced by pre-existing socio-economic and political realities. As Turkey continues with the democratic initiative it should be handled carefully, so that it should not be seen as a project which is imposed by one side and rejected by most. The sensitivity and importance of the issue require that the demands raised by all sides go through a meticulous process of mutually beneficial analysis.

Democratization requires compromises for the common and greater good in order to reach a socio-politically and culturally acceptable and practicable model.

Many communities in the world have gone through such democratization processes in recent years. These experiences should be reviewed and shared by academia and the media with the larger society and the government of Turkey in order to achieve an effective separation of powers and so that a civil society is encouraged. Building an institutional infrastructure for liberal democracy in which ethnic, cultural and religious freedoms thrive will be a driving force for development in and around Turkey. Such democratization and development does not call into question the legitimacy or sovereignty of the state, but is a call for human dignity and a diverse and prosperous society.

Role of Civil Society in Turkey's Judicial Reform

June 10, 2010

Records from the court-ordered wiretap of former Justice Minister Seyfi Oktay have revealed cronyism in the higher judiciary, with many judges and prosecutors asking the minister directly for higher positions in the judiciary. It seems the former minister and his cronies had exerted inappropriate influence on cases, the courts and the appointment of judges and prosecutors for almost 15 years.[18]

In 1946, for the needs of post-war Europe, Sir David Maxwell-Fyfe, a British politician and attorney general, said, "The law is a living thing. It is not rigid and unalterable. Its purpose is to serve mankind, and it must change and grow to meet the changing needs of society." Today's Turkey also needs reform in law, and the rule of law must be strengthened and evolve to serve all its citizens.

Civil society needs to involve itself with this living law creatively, rather than seeing it as fixed, unalterable and as a means to be used in power struggles between mighty groups. Also, in a modern democracy, civil society should engage with the law and "humanize" the state and its institutions, bringing it into line with "public conscience." That is, citizens urge governments to comply with and implement the law and to develop it for the benefit of all rather than for the narrow interests of particular groups.

In addition, the law in any particular society is formed with respect to its ethical foundations, arising from its common conscience. Therefore, in contemporary societies citizens are encouraged to be continually involved in refining their consciences in the light of current affairs, and also to monitor the rulings and actions of the judiciary. Thus, the law is not static but evolving, and cannot be abandoned to the dictates of partisan politicians and legal professionals of a certain period. Civil society

---

[18] For a newspaper report of the content of the wire-taps, see www.todayszaman.com/news-212642-jurists-object-to-court-verdicts-influenced-by-oktay-his-team.html.

must therefore play a big part in reflecting the public conscience and international law.

However, this view encounters official and public cynicism in Turkey today. People are perplexed as to whether the law has real force and applies equally in all circumstances. Although some articles of the Constitution are well articulated, when they are applied to cases affecting certain interest groups, the protests start. Some of the judiciary condemns ordinary citizens for meddling in the law, saying that individuals are "unqualified" to uphold the law or to "take the law into their own hands." It seems only the select few can be involved, those chosen from among certain associations of prosecutors and judges; it is apparently not up to the government or Parliament to deal with legislation and the execution of the law or the Constitution.

But these are all false arguments that hold our society back. They have prevented the courts from acting as a necessary balance to the power of the executive and ensured that they do not do their job of judging whether, for instance, gangs and putsch-minded people within the judiciary and the armed forces are acting within the law. This lack of judicial oversight has allowed our state to cover up illegal acts.

Nonetheless, one simple route for civil society to bring governments to comply with and develop international law is campaigning for the implementation of EU regulations and requiring our institutions to comply with existing international law. Through education and lobbying, civil society organizations encourage debate and urge governments to uphold international law by suggesting various policy changes.

Individuals and groups have also requested a judicial review of government decisions and the indictment of government and military leaders who have been complicit in plots, extrajudicial killings, coups and crimes against peace and humanity as well as those involved in the preparation of such crimes.

This is all part of the process of bringing our society into line with international human rights law. Civil society is often well ahead of institutional changes, so legal challenges may not work out at a particular time. Nevertheless, they often succeed at a later date, when attitudes have changed and institutions have caught up. Thus courts must continually be presented with the opportunity and challenge of implementing international law on human rights and of acting independently of the executive.

The strength and wisdom of a society lies in its people. We need the government and legal system that we deserve as contemporary citizens of a civilized international community. We believe we are not completely powerless but are responsible individuals. Thus we cannot stay silent when we see gross crimes being committed in our name. We have seen the active deployment of weapons and plots that could destroy the fundamental principles of law, the Constitution and international law. Taking the law seriously, we call our institutions to account. We become part of the force behind the evolution of our society, taking a part in shaping the law and ensuring its implementation.

Civil Society, Education and 'Masters' in Turkey

July 8, 2010

A pervasive feature of Turkish socio-political life is the talk of the self-appointed "masters" of the nation, who pronounce judgment on every issue, whether well-informed on it or not. These masters assume ultimate authority.

They are the true owners of Turkey. To them, the current government, president and those who voted for them are ignorant, backward and deserve reproach. The masters rule on judicial and constitutional issues while blatantly ignoring the law, the Constitution and ethics. They monopolize tender bids and investments and milk the national budget and public resources.

They assume the right to use state resources, positions and ranks against the public to make putsches under the pretext that the regime is threatened. They claim a vote by one of them is worth thousands of votes from the commoners. They alone can know, discuss, own and decide everything in Turkey, but they are never accountable. Whatever their title—professor, general, judge, prosecutor or entrepreneur—they reveal a lack in their character: the results of a sound education.

All the plots, murders, negligence, corruption and lack of professional ethics among the bureaucracy require an open call to all civil society organizations: How can we link education on a national level to participation in policymaking to facilitate political equality, representation, accountability and legitimacy? How can civil society regulate the conflicting interests of the unelected elite and the public and limit the exercise of arbitrary power? How can it reform the morality and ethics of such "masters"? Civil society must help to establish the balance between the private and public, between individual interests and rights and the common good.

Civil society organizations have a great role in the functioning of democracy and the exercise of citizenship. They can build spaces that allow the constitution of common good and the transcendence of particular interests. In addition to providing schools, health and relief services, they form a sphere of morality as an element of the public space and a basis for the civic community. So the question for Turkey is, "How can we ground mass education in the civil society tradition?" In other words, how can public education supplement the public system with alternative expertise and advocacy to replace that of the self-proclaimed masters and guardians of Turkey?

Substantive uncertainty always ensues when the hegemony of certain powers in a system is challenged. However, this dominant culture, which is organized around a core of shared interests rather than universal values, must give way to a pluralism that accepts different values, beliefs and worldviews as normal and important in individuals' self-understanding. Civil society organizations should develop reform programs across the political spectrum, in policymaking, implementation and service delivery through contractual relationships, strengthening democracy, citizenship and social capital and advocacy on behalf of disadvantaged or marginalized groups. The proper relationship between civil society organizations and the state helps the integration and accommodation of diverse viewpoints instead of the current polarization and isolation.

Turkey needs civil platforms for debate and policy-making that cut across obsolete dichotomies. Civil society organizations can engage the diverse agents of education, government, voluntary organizations, public-private partnerships and faith communities to produce an education that unites the citizenry without coercive uniformity. This will affirm pluralistic commitments without dangerous fragmentation. A democratic civil society can sustain a democratic state.

Considering the conduct of the exclusivist, protectionist, elitist bureaucracy in Turkey, we need to make room for diversity in ethnicity, religion, culture and mental outlook in education. Otherwise, the uniformity advocated by the main opposition parties in Parliament could easily result in a new kind of despotism.

This cultural, ethnic and religious pluralism needs to be accommodated in conceptual and political frameworks with sufficient flexibility to combine choice with equity. There must be a commitment to shared civil and political culture with openness to exploring and reaffirming the distinct backgrounds or cultures of different groups.

In order to curb social ills and incivilities observed in society, education should not be stripped of its moral dimension nor increase indifference to moral issues and universal ethics. Its moral dimension should contribute to the moral fabric of our society without denying the rights of citizens. Finding feasible arrangements may be challenging. It requires examining cases where this tradition has already been institutionalized and where civil society organizations play a constructive role as advocates of education and universal rights for all.

Civil society efforts should not be a partisan project or a cause of exclusive interest groups of this or that stripe or persuasion. They must be democratic and pluralist projects. The power to shape and formulate the main tenets of education, governance and justice ought to rest with the people, not with their former masters.

New Turkish Generals and the Greatest Good

August 5, 2010

As Turkey's Supreme Military Council (YAŞ) gathers to consider candidates for promotion to the rank of general,[19] it is a good time to discuss what makes a "good officer." What deficiency in the military curriculum leads to the incessant planning of coups and putsches in the military?

I believe significant time should be allocated for the education of our military officers in philosophy, axiology, ethics and religion. These lessons will help them learn, for example, *summum bonum*—the greatest good, the ultimate importance or the ultimate end that human beings ought to pursue. This concept can be an end in itself, containing all other goods.

Philosophy, axiology and ethics could teach our officers that all desires cannot be satisfied, that they may be conflicting. This would enable them to weigh the relative value of goods and ascertain which of them must be secured at the loss of others. They should learn to differentiate conscientiously between their physical comfort and personal happiness and the moral, the virtuous and the collective good. In fact these are not entirely mutually exclusive. The difference lies only on the surface. Studying axiology and ethics could make our officers understand how, why and to what degree humans should value things—person, idea, object or anything else. They need this study of good and evil more than the courses they take on economics, based upon the material cost-benefit dichotomy. Then they would be able to value the conduct of persons rather than objects.

Axiology or ethics could teach them how human beings develop, believe and act or fail to act on certain values. They might clarify the values that orient or reorient them in their individual and social life, lest

---

[19]   The August reshuffle period is when military officers are promoted or retirement decisions are taken. Before and during this time likely-to-be-retired generals make headlines out of real and imagined "national security threats", including civil society movements and faith-inspired movements or communities.

their personal choice, judgment and behavior fail to guide them at different stages of their professional and human development. Military officers need to learn the values rightly held by the majority and community, and why and how different groups of people may hold or prioritize different kinds of values influencing social behavior.

Such an education could form a basis for officers' ethical actions consistent with universal values and measures. This foundation would provide support for their integrity, service to humanity and altruism. These values constitute the integral parts of true human culture and generate sound behavior. With them, officers would not indulge illegal expectations, or lose their personal identity and sense of worth, but remain good, helpful and important. They might help people solve common human problems rather than initiating plots and coups to the detriment of society. They could come to understand people of other cultures or origins and the values, beliefs and assumptions that motivate their behavior and aspirations because every life, including the future generations of a nation, is priceless.

The clarification of values could help them learn what is worth working for and what their lives are for. They might cease imposing their own egoistical, marginal, partisan, ideological, undemocratic passions on the majority. Their cognitive, moral and professional education must be based on values such as democracy, justice and service to all without discrimination. Their perspective should be based more on global norms and the value of life and saving lives as opposed to taking them, rather than on abstract claims, exclusivist ideology and the interests served by a killing junta.

Our officers should learn to take part in our culture even if their personal values do not entirely agree with some of the normative values sanctioned in the culture. They must learn to synthesize and extract aspects valuable to them from the multiple subcultures they live among. If any officer or group of officers expresses a value in serious conflict with the norms of Turkish society, society with its authority ought to use various means of encouraging conformity or stigmatizing the non-conforming behavior of such marginal officers. Fair legal probes, prosecution and imprisonment can justly result from conflict with social norms that have been established as law.

Human life cannot be traded for professional promotion and marginal benefits. Some officers' great ambitions for their future promotions are not commensurate with the low value they assign to soldiers' lives. People will judge officers' actions by their conformity with rules, morality, ethics and the service mentality, not by the good consequences arising from actions for the officers themselves. Turkish society does not take pleasure in watching its beloved children maimed and killed.

Fostering Democratic Character:
Cooperation or Forced Compliance?

September 16, 2010

In the period surrounding the September 12 referendum[20] in Turkey, the discourse and attitudes of many of the parties to the public debate raised doubts as to whether some interest groups have any real understanding of the nature and requirements of democratic citizenship.

And if indeed they have an understanding of what democracy requires from them, it seems they may have no genuine intention of fulfilling those demands. So the question becomes how, as a society, we can foster in citizens the personal virtues that are essential for democracy to take root and flourish. For the realization of democratic education and democratic life, we need to reflect on the relationship between democracy, public virtue, responsibility, liberty and education.

Democracy cannot function without a public, and a public requires citizens who are responsible to and for themselves and the whole society. Society then needs to exert every reasonable effort to provide and protect the individual freedom that democracy entails. Society is also supposed to educate its citizens into free and democratic citizenship, a substantive idea of the common good and the virtues of democratic polity.

As a system of government, liberal democracy is able to define norms, virtues or virtue in the citizenry. Through its procedures and institutions, it mediates between the individual good and shared concerns for the common good. Democratic citizenship entails our active involvement in the making of laws and in keeping elected officials informed of our wishes. It requires citizens to choose and support leaders, projects and poli-

---

[20]   The September 12 referendum was called by the ruling party when the opposition in parliament used various means to block all attempts to amend the 1980 Constitution, which had been written by the military following a coup. The government submitted the amendments to the public vote.

cies that are wise, just and for the common good, that are good for members of the public generally.

However, remarks made by opposition party leaders and the higher judiciary on the results of the referendum show that they understand democracy in a different way. They see it as an arena for the clash of competing interests in which particular people work to use the power of the government for their own gain. This understanding will not sustain but destroy democracy. It implies that they use their own positions to impinge on other citizens' liberty and rights.

Over decades studded with coups, governance in Turkey decayed into an oligarchy of the military and judiciary as power concentrated in those powerful groups. They acquired more and more power over citizens' public and private lives. The public voted in the referendum because democratic power has never been evenly distributed and because of this continuing "clumping" of power.

With the referendum, the public showed that it has the disposition to identify the problem and the will to search for a common solution. If democracy is a project of individual liberty then we, civil society, can now assume fully our constitutional role as citizens in fostering democratic virtues in young people. Democratic education will instill in them visions of the proper forms of social life, in which they will enjoy and enjoin rights, justice, equity and societal cohesion, in which competing visions will be freely, respectfully and peacefully discussed and settled.

However, the negative reaction to the referendum from certain groups indicates continued intent to prevent citizens from forming projects that will increase their civic power and bring prosperity to society as a whole. The establishment of cultural and human rights, liberties and hope for an industrialized democratic country depends on peacefully replacing the obsolete oligarchic way of the state bureaucracy in accord with the will of the majority. Otherwise, the bureaucratic tutelary minority will harden into a caste at the expense of the majority.

So the understanding of democracy is a shared responsibility. We want for all children what all the best people want for their own children. Democratic citizenship necessitates democratic education in which all social, cultural and spiritual needs, values and meanings are considered. Liberal democracy is a cooperative way of life. So we need to prepare our youth to be citizens of that sort of society, to fashion good lives for themselves.

Education is one important means by which democratic understanding and participation, liberties and rights are fostered in the interest of the common good. The next thing to consider is the transition from this personal discipline and virtue to democratic social life, personal achievement and collective happiness. Further, education must foster those virtues necessary for the polity to be democratic, again without undue impact on others' rights, liberties and intellectual and moral development. For neither chaos nor forced compliance, the only two options that the current opposition in Turkey has ever offered or produced so far, counts as democratic.

3

Obstacles to Democratization

Hegemony or Democratic Participation?

July 24, 2008

J udicial moves against the democratically elected ruling party, former high-ranking military officers' leadership of gangs and organized crime, and talk of yet more coups; in the claims and counterclaims, outside observers of the Turkish political scene must be wondering what the outcome of these events will be—the continued hegemony of the protectionist elite or the triumph of democratic participation?

The Turkish political system has long been subjected to various degrees of internal manipulation through a structure of dominance in social relationships. This imposes constraints within the system and leads the protectionist interests to enact draconian measures without clear public support.

Those representing protectionist interests assume control over the rules and mechanisms of decision making itself as if this is their exclusive privilege. In the views reflected in the "Action Plan"[21] leaked from the military we see how they are reluctant to give up their tutelage of the masses, even though they have had hardly any relations with them, in truth. For the protectionist elite, any initiative that does not originate from amongst them and any attempt to shift power relationships within the political system or to acquire influence over decisions is either a threat, a matter of crisis for the regime or a national security issue.

The problem, then, is how to give a precise definition to the parameters of pluralist participatory democracy. Undoubtedly, social relations influence such participation in both directions. From the perspective of

---

[21] www.todayszaman.com/news-247681-action-plan-put-into-action-in-propaganda-websites.html

the protectionist ruling groups, political participation serves to confirm the priority of their own interests and to secure the subordinated consensus of other social groups; participation takes place within the confines and rules determined by their dominating system, thus—to a greater or lesser extent—promoting their interests. To them, the subordinated groups participate politically so as to increase their influence in the decision-making processes or to alter institutional power relationships. They therefore are always more or less excluded from involvement in decision making, and their efforts are seen as non-institutional. The protectionists assume that social, cultural and political representation in Turkey, as well as the identification of any societal problems and their solution, is their sole and exclusive prerogative. This is, again, best seen in the February 28 process and the Şemdinli[22] and Ergenekon[23] (Turkish Gladio) cases and in arbitrary impositions on faith-inspired projects and civil society; it was also observed in the constant vetoes exercised by former President Ahmet Necdet Sezer,[24] in the baseless insistence on the quorum of 367 during the presidential elections[25] and in the Justice and Development Party (AK Party) closure case.[26]

These counter-mobilizations against participatory democratic acts and institutions were not based on democratic procedures or political consensus but were and are realized through ideological interpretation. The protectionist system propagates itself and permeates daily life and existential choices. It filters and represses some demands by presenting them as an absolute, existential threat to the very structure of society. When it cannot compete with any alternative in argument, action and services,

---

[22] www.hurriyetdailynews.com/default.aspx?pageid=438&n=court-says-senior-officers-involved-in-semdinli-bombing-2006-07-19

[23] Report from Young Civilians, "Ergenekon is our Reality" available from ergenekonisourreality.wordpress.com. Accessed on16 August 2013.

[24] "Gül's Kemalist predecessor Sezer was a strict legal expert who used his veto to block many of the AK Party government's initiatives." Niels Kadritzke, Headscarves, generals and Turkish democracy, *Eurozine*, at www.eurozine.com/articles/2008-02-01-kadritzke-en.html. Accessed on 14 August 2013.

[25] www.todayszaman.com/news-114470-367-the-number-that-blocked-turkeys-political-system-by-assoc-prof-adnan-kucuk-.html

[26] www.todayszaman.com/news-136603-the-state-versus-the-people-by-joost-lagendijk-.html

it simply assimilates any alternative under the familiar rhetoric of threats to the regime, or some variation thereof.

Despite the fact that their interpretation and counter-mobilization is anti-democratic and anti-egalitarian, they attempt to legitimize their acts by reference to events and to exploit division, radicalization and tension in society. Their true self-interest resurfaces at different conjunctures as improprieties, corruption or concealment of other vested interests. One way for protectionist actors to seek a reduction in the risks involved in a decision is to secure a preventive consensus through the use of ideological manipulation. This preventive consensus usually appropriates the name of "Kemalism."

Protectionists implement decisions according to the practical effect of the particular forces and interests intervening in the implementation process. They exert direct pressure on administrative and governmental bodies to secure an advantageous application of any new ruling. They do not represent their interests through transparent replication. Instead, they set boundaries and determine both the potential and limits of action within the system. Their coercive character and decisions are not a functional necessity founded on consensus.

This produces a closed political system in which the principles of law, democracy and social justice can be abandoned, but the most sensitive principles—those of the republic, secularism and national security—are bound up tight and exploited. This understanding or notion of democracy runs into problems because, as Fethullah Gülen has stated, "The world is a culturally diverse place and no single group, nation or culture has the monopoly on democratic ideas and practice.... Democracy, though it still needs to be further improved, is now the only viable political form, and people should seek to modernize and consolidate democratic institutions in order to build a society where individual rights and freedom are respected and protected.... If we are to proceed to an even more perfect democracy, that can again be achieved through democratic processes." Certainly not through protectionist organizations and their clandestine efforts, such as Ergenekon.

Greek Protests and Turkish Provocateurs

December 18, 2008

Violence, looting and vandalism overwhelmed Greece last week after an adolescent was accidentally shot by police during a protest. Certain Turkish "columnists" have jumped on the occasion and demanded to know why Turkish youth or citizens do not react in the same way as those in Greece, and why, when there is any mistreatment in Turkey by the security forces, whether police or military, all hell does not break loose against them so that they dare not repeat that mistreatment in the future.

I will not go into the details of the events in Greece. Herkul Millas' op-ed "A crisis of values in Greece" in Today's Zaman on Dec. 14 explained clearly enough what is occurring and why.[27] My concern is the columnists and journalists in Turkey who are using this opportunity to target the police regardless of what this might cost the people, the nation and the state.

In the work of such writers we see a clear example of how transmitting information can easily turn into transforming it. It is not sensible or sensitive professionalism, but adversarial journalism. Rather than educating people and broadening their minds about nonviolent and peaceful protest, this type of journalism serves to prevent Turkey from achieving stability and consolidating true democracy and human rights.

This is not the first time that some press and media organs and their "wise" columnists have done so. We have seen this ideological blindness before: during the Susurluk case,[28] the February 28, 1997 coup, the irrational insistence on the quorum in the last presidential election, the military's e-memorandum, the Justice and Development Party (AK Party)

---

[27] www.todayszaman.com/news-161172-a-crisis-of-values-in-greece-by-herkul-millas-.html

[28] See Historical Background, page 34.

closure case and recent commentary on the case of the Turkish Gladio, the Ergenekon terror organization.

No one can condone violence, coercion, torture or killings at the hands of security forces. We openly and explicitly condemn it. However, neither can we condone violence, looting, vandalism and anarchy by anyone, anywhere or in any way. Just ends cannot be achieved through unjust means. The means we use must be as pure and lawful as the ends we pursue.

In contemporary societies, people are entitled to protest in order to express dissatisfaction publicly or to influence public opinion or policies. People can protest peacefully, without the use of violence, without loss of life and without any negative effect on the public or country.

In modern democratic societies, peaceful and non-humiliating protest is, in any case, more effective than violent protest. Violence should not be an "alternative," as suggested by "wise" Turkish columnists. It is not an efficient way to raise awareness of a cause or a struggle. It is counterproductive. This does not have to mean passivity or accepting authoritarianism and oppression. Political history gives us examples of peaceful heroes, such as Rumi, Gandhi, Abdul Ghaffar Khan, Martin Luther King and many others.

Violent protest invariably leads to injuries and even fatalities. It threatens overall public safety and affects bystanders and the innocent. The general public cannot feel secure. What is the meaning of destructive acts, such as setting fire to cars, smashing glass, demolishing public facilities, throwing stones everywhere and at everyone and ripping up plants, trees and flowers? Why are some protesters armed with knives, pipes, batons and even firearms? We will not forget the photos of a "revolutionary" anarchist ripping up the tulips in Istanbul. Not only the protesters, but innocent bystanders and even journalists themselves, get caught and hurt in riots and skirmishes.

In dealing with protesters, police usually employ a range of tactics that are officially designated as non-lethal. Yet, we know that people can indeed die or be injured as the result of their use. None of this would happen if people preferred peaceful protest to violence. There are many methods of peaceful protest: collective marches, picketing, theatrical performance and protest songs, for example. There are other forms of education, persuasion and targeted communication via the mass media.

These methods are more effective and nobody gets injured by them. Those who use them can easily win the sympathy of others.

Where is the morality and proper mental framework in suggesting violent protests, causing damage and meaningless destruction? If you are civilized, violence is not the way to solve problems. In a violent protest, how can one identify the right cause? It only harms the ordinary citizens' health, wealth, property and life.

If cooperation and consensus between all parties and compliance with legal means and ends are the fundamentals of contemporary democratic societies or civilized people, what kind of culture and country do these columnists who advocate violence belong to? We may prevent outer physical violence through proper ways and means, but how are we to prevent the inner violence of spirit of such columnists? On the eve of the municipal elections, when the understanding between the Sunni and Alevi citizens of Turkey is improving, when the leaders of the terror organization Ergenekon are failing to respond to cross-examination, is there something those "wise" journalists of Turkey know but we do not? It is revolting and irrational to suggest the use of violence to achieve a more peaceful society.

How to Be an Americanist

January 29, 2009

I n one of the latest developments in the Ergenekon investigation, remarks made by the former head of the Higher Education Board (YÖK), Dr. Kemal Gürüz,[29] reveal the extent to which the position he and other Ergenekon suspects hold is inconsistent, contradictory and unreliable.

We believe in the basic legal premise that people are innocent unless proven otherwise, so rather than accusing Gürüz of complicity in the murders carried out by Ergenekon or other unlawful dealings and activities, here I will evaluate his deeds against his own claim: "I am an Americanist to the core."[30]

Now, Ergenekon is known for its enmity toward Americanism and American political interests and values. Supporters, defenders and those accused of being members of Ergenekon express this position on a daily basis in their press releases, media appearances and in the trial itself. Can we forget the media coverage of protests against the investigation into Ergenekon in which the protesters displayed banners saying, "No to the USA, the EU and NATO"? Are we now to ignore their argument that they have no interest other than saving Turkey from American hegemony, that they are striving to prevent Turkey from becoming a mere satellite state of America, and that Turkey needs new political alignments other than those with America and Europe? Indeed, Gürüz took part in such demonstrations and encouraged his colleagues to take part too.

So, what does "Americanism" mean? Americanism is normally regarded as a loyalty, strong affection or support for the nation or culture of the United States. It involves attachment to very basic concepts underlying the experience of being American. The list of concepts may vary accord-

---

[29] www.todayszaman.com/news-278193-who-is-who-key-figures-in-the-february-28-postmodern-coup.html

[30] www.cnnturk.com/2009/turkiye/01/18/ne.ergenekonu.ben.amerikanciyim/509452.0/index.html

ing to different people but it usually involves principles or values such
as freedom, equality, individualism, respect for faith and the rule of law.
A broader list of definitions includes "faith in a greater power, a rooted
concept of morality, the rule of truth, mutual freedom, equal access to representation, respect for private property, equality of opportunity, personal responsibility, presumption of innocence, the due process of law, local
governance and a national focus."

Yet, if the "Americanism" Gürüz claims for himself involves the principles and values above, then Gürüz is not an "Americanist" at all. What
Gürüz did during his chairmanship of YÖK, what he achieved through
the people he assigned to universities and committees, and the ways he
and his associates ideologically interpreted and interfered with the democratic process and parliamentary and government affairs can by no means
be reconciled with any of the values expressed in any adequate definition of Americanism.[31]

As an example, remember the almost 40,000 female students who
were not admitted to lectures, lecture halls, campuses and universities, and
for that reason lost their places at university—never mind their impaired
psychological, financial and social status because of such fascist discrimination. There was the academic sacked because his headscarved mother came in a car to pick him up from the campus after working hours. In
the same way, headscarved students are not awarded their diplomas, or
are denied the positions in their department or university that they have
truly earned.[32] Young women's headscarves have been pulled off by
Gürüz's colleagues in abusive and aggressive scuffles. People have been
blacklisted or not promoted because of their likely political or religious
inclinations or even because of the type of music that their spouses listen to at home. State grants and student or research admission quotas
are allocated unjustly and ideologically. I will not go into further details

[31] For an interview in Turkish where Gürüz speaks freely of removing a rector from
his post for ideological reasons ("for reactionary activities"), see gundem.milli-
yet.com.tr/atalay--font-color-darkblue-irticaci-mi---font-/guncel/gundemdetay/
21.01.2009/1049747/default.htm.

[32] www.todayszaman.com/news-124951-veiled-tales-3-you-cant-lecture-here-if-
your-mother-wears-a-headscarf.html. For Guruz's own ideological refusal to allow
students to wear headscarfs, see www.milliyet.com.tr/universitede-turban-ko-
nusu-tartisilamaz/guncel/haberdetayarsiv/26.11.2002/247988/default.htm
[8/20/2013 2:40:13 PM]

of why Turkish universities are failing in terms of accredited academic research and publications in the scientific field. There is not space enough in this column to list the reasons for such failures, nor the financial misdemeanors and corruption at the administrative level. Nonetheless, the academics involved in all these misdeeds and failures are never too busy to show off in meetings and protest marches claiming that the regime is threatened.

America is a nation of freedom and laws, founded upon a written constitution. This produces the rights and opportunities and provides the moral backbone by which all else is supported. People from various cultures, faiths, religions and races live and work in the US. There are headscarved students, lecturers and administrators in American universities. They are not seen as a threat to education or society and its values. Americans benefit from such people and lead the world in education, science and politics.

When it comes to the self-proclaimed Americanism of Gürüz or people like him, we cannot but ask whether it is self-deception, delusion or a simple political game to protect their own interests or plots, now that their schemes and unlawful dealings have started to emerge. One day they enjoy their meetings under the banners of "No to the USA, EU or NATO" and "Ordu Göreve" ("Turkish Military to Your Mission," meaning that the military should come out of their barracks for a new military coup).[33] The next day, when their schemes are revealed, wishing to be unquestionable, untouchable and protected, they are "Americanist to the core."

Or are they, as Bernard Chazelle of Princeton University describes them, in "a pathological condition of old lineage which feeds on a witch's brew of hypocrisy, resentment, illiberalism and a deep-rooted aversion to change"?

---

[33] www.cnnturk.com/2012/turkiye/10/11/hoca.pankarti.gorememis.cunku/ 680223.0/index.html[8/20/2013 4:49:34 PM]

Censorship or Freedom of the Press in Turkey

March 12, 2009

T he freedom of the press has been at the center of some controversy recently in the Turkish media. Dailies belonging to businessman Aydın Doğan, whose companies have been accused of tax evasion, have alleged that the government is censoring the press and the media.[34] Turkey has a lively press. However, it remains a difficult environment for independent journalism due to dealings between governments and media owners, military-media relationships and ethno-religious issues. Perhaps the most obvious example of censorship in Turkey is the blocking of particular Web sites in order to prevent access to certain views and information.[35]

There is a wide variety of media outlets: more than 40 national dailies (nearly 20 of them mainstream), several national weeklies, almost three dozen local papers and two English-language national dailies. There are also about 25 national radio stations, hundreds of local radio stations and nearly 30 national—and a great number of local TV—channels. Radio and TV journalism has entered a new phase because of the preconditions for Turkey's accession to the European Union, particularly since the Justice and Development Party (AK Party) government's new initiative, the TRT 6 Kurdish-language television station.

Today the stakes are higher than in the past. Due to competition among media tycoons, issues are often exaggerated to serve their interests. The latest example is the claim about suppression of freedom of the press in Turkey.

---

[34] www.todayszaman.com/news-168474-finance-ministry-lambasts-dogan-media-over-fine.html

[35] www.todayszaman.com/news-122630-turkey-bans-youtube-yet-again.html; www.todayszaman.com/news-136375-turkey-blocks-access-to-youtube-again.html; www.todayszaman.com/news-213469-turkish-court-blocks-access-to-44-proxy-sites-enabling-to-visit-youtube.html

Censorship is a policy of controlling, restricting or suppressing the public expression of ideas, opinions and information within a society. The censor considers itself bound to protect the governing authority and interests or the social and moral order. It suppresses information before or after something has been published. Not all censorship is equal, nor is it always directed by the same force.

Moral censorship aims to remove what is morally questionable, obscene, pornographic or graphically violent. Military censorship keeps military intelligence and tactics from the enemy and attempts to suppress what is politically inconvenient in terms of national security issues. Political censorship holds back information from the populace to exert control over it. Religious censorship aims to remove any content objectionable to a certain faith. In corporate censorship, editors in corporate media outlets intervene to halt the publication of information that portrays their business or business partners in a negative light or that may cause a potential loss of advertising revenue, shareholder value or tender bids.

Censorship is a typical feature of dictatorships and other authoritarian political systems. Democratic nations are usually believed to have less censorship, instead promoting freedom of speech. With regard to the current controversy, if accusing the government of censorship, the media organs concerned need to provide some evidence for their claims: How does the government maintain the extensive program of state-imposed censorship they accuse it of? What is the main mechanism of official censorship in Turkey? Are there government censorship personnel in every large publishing house or newspaper? How many censors are employed to review information before it is disseminated by publishing houses, editorial offices and broadcasting studios? Is it possible to escape government control, if there is any? Do all press agencies and radio and television stations have government representatives on their editorial staff? What was overtly or covertly imposed on their media organs or editors? Why have they previously turned a blind eye to military censorship of the media, such as that imposed on the weekly magazine Nokta, for example?[36]

Why have national security and defense suddenly become an issue for them when in the past they complained about the use of this rationale to suppress information? When basic religious rights were restricted in

---

[36] uk.reuters.com/article/2007/04/13/uk-turkey-military-magazine-idUKL 1316903020070413

public and governmental spaces, when attempts were made to remove the freely elected government, where were they then?

In today's tele-wired society it is almost impossible for any government to censor all media. In this protest against "censorship" we are hearing yet another threat to request illegitimate action against lawfully elected representatives. We are seeing media bias in this accusation of political and economic censorship. The media organs concerned would like to reduce the effects of any of their competitors or new actors in the field. They represent a class of oligarchs threatened by the emergence of real economic opportunity for other firms. The economy and politics are no longer monopolistic arrangements but offer genuine competition and innovation, and this does not please them.

Those media organs and their staff are attempting to mold the national interest to suit their individual interest. We watched the same schemes in the party closure cases and military interventions of 1960 and 1997. However, at present the Internet and online radio and journalism operate over national borders. Information on political and economic dealings can no longer be concealed from the public. Most Turks, like people in most parts of the world, are committed to the ideals of liberty, freedom, human rights, equity, justice and peace. They do not want religious, intellectual or political censorship. Also, Turkey now has many more reliable media organs that can investigate and inform the public about the bias and cheap and ultimately trivial schemes of some.

Polemical Journalism and Its Consequences

May 21, 2009

Since the 1990s, polemical journalism has become very common in Turkey and has totally ignored any libel laws. Since the polemic writers are backed by ideological and interest networks, they do not worry about the potential cost of libel. While disputing a matter, position or belief, they do not intend an argument or dialogue between two people who hold different ideas or wish to persuade each other. They act to controvert, shame, disgrace and thus negate any rights or freedoms to anybody or anything they oppose, even though that person or institution has not done anything wrong or worthy of reproach. This week we have also witnessed a clear example of this in an ill-reasoned article replete with factual inaccuracies from Soner Çağaptay in *Newsweek*.[37] The errors in the article have been dealt with elsewhere so here I shall look at the principles lying behind the issue.

Although different forms of dialectical reason have existed throughout history and various lands, it has a simple prerequisite that the participants, though they do not agree, share at least some meanings and principles of inference. So their aim or intention is to resolve the disagreement through rational discussion, and ultimately the search for truth, not to foment hatred, disorder and conflict. Since Socratic times, one way to proceed is to exercise the discretion to withdraw your hypothesis as a candidate for truth, if the hypothesis is seen to lead to a contradiction. You may not be able to prove your thesis, and you may not accept the antithesis, but you are at least willing to concede a third thesis or synthesis (combination of the opposing assertions). Since ancient times, this form of reasoning has been based on the exchange of arguments and counter-arguments. That exchange of relevant points of views leads to a dialogue, a synthesis and a qualitative transformation in the direction of positive

---

[37] www.thedailybeast.com/newsweek/2009/05/15/behind-turkey-s-witch-hunt.html

thinking and positive action. It improves the minds, hearts and souls of interlocutors by freeing them from undetected, unperceived errors and by being persuasive—convincing through dialogue.

It is clear as day, however, that some groups and their spokespersons do not reason, argue or examine their interlocutor's claims and premises in order to draw out a contradiction or inconsistency among them or to improve them. Recent developments in and about Turkey manifest this aspect of our public life: the blind opposition in the Parliament to a new constitution and to the EU accession process, an unconstitutional court ruling ordering President Abdullah Gül to stand trial,[38] militant secularist opposition to and sabotage of the president's and government's efforts to resolve the gangrenous Kurdish issue, the eccentric arguments from the leader of the Kurdistan Workers' Party (PKK) terrorist organization about defending the regime and acknowledging ties with the Democratic Society Party (DTP) while the DTP closure case is hot,[39] together with misinformation provided by Turkish "bloggers," as well as "research" commissioned with the aim of preventing Turkey from becoming an open and civic society.

We have seen that these groups, the alienating "white Turks," the elitist-statist protectionists, the militant secularist bureaucracy and the exclusivist coup lovers, supporters and makers, have no intention of resolving the tension between a thesis and its antithesis by means of a synthesis. They do not attempt to "overcome the negative," that is, at least preserving the useful portion of an idea, thing or society, while moving beyond its limitations. Their antithesis, if they offer one other than killing journalists, scholars and even Christian missionaries to foment chaos and prepare the necessary conditions for their consecutive putsch schemes, staging military coups and staying in power for at least 25 years without any elections, is always selected to suit their own subjective purpose. So their arguments are not defensible against a multitude of other possible syntheses, but rhetorical, contradictory and not logical. This type of think-

---

[38] www.todayszaman.com/news-175719-court-demands-guls-prosecution.html; www.todayszaman.com/news-176377-sincan-judge-readies-for-criminal-complaint-after-gul-ruling.html

[39] www.todayszaman.com/news-174801-pkk-is-guardian-of-the-regime-claims-karayilan.html; www.todayszaman.com/news-174447-pkk-leader-we-want-bloodshed-to-end.html

ing, of course, leads to systemic blockages, dysfunctions, alienation and crises rather than progress, unification and realization of the rational, constitutional state of free and equal citizens.

Polemical journalism and its effects on dialectical thinking in Turkey, as everywhere, is dogmatic, and, if it persists in this way, it may have many serious consequences: it only provides advantages to its cronies; it provides justification for rejecting alternative initiatives, projects and policies; it obfuscates the integral relationship between opposite perspectives that can be normally held and accommodated within Turkey; it ignores the fact that the understanding of differences and multiplicity requires understanding their relationship with the whole of Turkish culture, civilization and contemporary democratic systems. It therefore does not make any marked contribution to our intellectual, spiritual and democratic culture. It stifles liberal thinking and the development of liberal democracy. Its identification and utilization of might rather than right encourages totalitarian modes of thought and action. It only justifies irrationalism and facilitates fascist ambition. It lowers the universally acknowledged standards of intellectual responsibility and honesty. In the end, the damage done inevitably has an impact on the environment and the lives and well-being of the perpetrators, too. *Newsweek*'s editors may feel that controversy may help sales of their new Turkish edition. But they and Çağaptay should remember that they also exist in society and ponder this week how unwise they may have been.

Infotainted Infotainment

July 9, 2009

Human beings are social creatures. This sociability immerses us in an emotional and mental environment of other people's thoughts, emotions and experiences. We become preoccupied with issues and individuals that we have never met and never will meet. We read and discuss things from our environment and the media, including inaccuracies, distractions and trivia. All too often, as consumers of this infotainment we vacillate between mental pollution and an intellectual vacuum; we talk about nonsensical things that don't matter at all.

Advertising and political propaganda in the mass media are major factors in this mental pollution and intellectual vacuum. They produce social pressures that more positive influences from our family, peers and education can scarcely withstand. Certain centers use the media for misrepresentation, manipulation and psychological warfare for the sake of political status and domination, provoking psychological problems, deviations and polarization in society.

The mix of infotainment and misinformation has produced profound cynicism in society. There are many now who show no interest in social or political issues. They suspect they are being pressured into believing things that may not be accurate. They do not want to think about anything that may bother them, just so they feel good all the time. They hold that they live in a free society so they do not want any pressure from their peers or other groups. They ignore politicians and political issues in the media because they see both media and politicians as unable or unwilling to set rational and coherent policies. They see all political debates as devoid of intellectual honesty and ethics. In other words, part of the public responds to this environment with ignorance, apathy and lack of direction.

Fortunately, another part of the public sees this apathy as an escape from civic responsibility and refuses to accept it. To them this vacuum is far more harmful than any predicted environmental pollution. They see it as an escape from the age-old question of what it means to be a good person. These people are active in the public space and refuse to be deflected by trivia and misinformation.

And, of course, there are some people in between these two poles who remain very confused because the issues are often distorted by the manner in which they are conveyed, the debates are shaped by various influences and interests, and there are sharp divisions between policies and reality.

Simple examples can be given. Currently, media and public attention are very much engaged with Michael Jackson's death. This event has pushed aside almost all other issues and left them in its shadow. Large parts of the media have taken a break from covering the elections and protests in Iran. The Honduran coup and president's flight and plight have not come to an end but are scarcely discussed at all. While providing extensive coverage of the Jackson memorial ceremony, some CNN programs only gave President Obama's visit to Russia a passing mention, and even then it was to ask how Obama's daughters have been experiencing the visit.

I wonder how Jackson's death and funeral engage the Somali families fleeing conflict-ridden Mogadishu for the relatively safe city of Dusamareb? For Turks, which is more important, Jackson's funeral or President Gül's potential endorsement or veto of legislation to allow military personnel who have participated in coups d'état to be tried in civilian courts? What about the 2 million children of American military personnel in dire need of psychological therapy because of their parents' deployment in war-ridden regions of the world? Who will provide psychological therapy to the families of British military personnel documented to have tortured, killed and mutilated Iraqi combatants? What do we know of the Turkish scientist who found that a tank full of chicken feathers provides a very economical alternative to millions of dollars worth of carbon nanotubes in hydrogen-driven cars? What can be done about the ongoing discord and violence between the Chinese authorities and ethnic groups in the region of Xinjiang?

We are human beings, we are social, and we cannot pursue a life in an intellectual, emotional and spiritual void. Whatever happens in one corner of the world can affect us and have an impact on our individual and collective lives. Yet, we cannot be omnipresent and we cannot be all-knowing and all-embracing. The providers of information and the public, too, need to recognize that our environment and conditions require us to be selective and to focus on limited issues. Then individual, local, regional issues and affinities can be successfully dealt with.

As to political matters, they are all multidimensional and require serious reflection and depth of knowledge about local and global issues. Short-term viewpoints and cynical and provocative journalistic approaches are not adequate or effective. Columnists can make real contributions to policy debates. However, policy matters and engagement with public affairs require balanced and thoroughgoing exploration of issues and a refusal to "dumb down" the debate. Otherwise, the contribution of journalists will simply reinforce the trivialization of public debate.

Kurds and Journalists, Real and Symbolic

October 1, 2009

There may seem at first glance to be little in common between the recent court cases against journalists Şamil Tayyar and Mehmet Baransu[40] and the dispute over whether Democratic Society Party (DTP) members of Parliament have parliamentary immunity[41] and whether they can be questioned by the police.

The underlying problem is, however, the same and goes to the root of the very definition of the state in Turkey and its relation with democratic rights, civic and free society and constitutionalism.

The journalists wrote about the deep-state organization Ergenekon, for which they were imprisoned and subsequently released. The original Ergenekon is a story, a myth, a symbol, a heroic epic about the history of the Turks as an ethnic group, not as a modern, democratic, multiethnic nation. Currently, some Turkish citizens value the myth of Ergenekon without necessarily approving of the actions of those who have apparently assumed its name or rejecting modern lifestyles including democracy. Some dispute the very existence of Ergenekon, while acknowledging that a number of individuals may have done wrong. Few people deny that something is afoot or that there is a "deep state." Coup after coup in Turkey has shown this to be more than likely. So the action of the judiciary, its jailing of two journalists for daring to discuss an organization which, according to some, may or may not be real and then freeing them on condition that they do not commit the same or similar offense within five years, is like suspending Damocles' sword over their heads with an extra frisson: If the Ergenekon terror organization is real, then surely it must be dealt with in some way. If not, why jail people for talking about it?

---

[40] www.todayszaman.com/news-187703-tayyar-sentence-proves-press-freedom-still-under-threat.html

[41] www.todayszaman.com/news-155669-turkey-faces-a-new-impasse-over-political-immunity.html

The dispute here is clearly about the meaning of symbols and whose myth of the nation will prevail. Some will use all means at their disposal: the media, the military and the judiciary. Some, it seems, may not use words in the media without fearing a symbolic sword and a very concrete prison cell.

DTP members of Parliament too are in trouble over their relation to the national myth of Turkey. As they know, in some people's view, Kurdish people, their language and culture present a symbolic challenge to that part of the Turkish myth that insists on the homogeneity of the nation, that myth that denies multi-ethnicity and indeed, many kinds of diversity. All other considerations concerning the current issue are minor. The irony is that this time it is the right not to speak that is being denied, but the existence of DTP members of Parliament, like their refusal to speak to the police, is both symbolic and very real.

For onlookers without much previous knowledge of Turkey, it is difficult to distinguish the various groupings in these disputes. Organizations, whether armies, governments, political parties or media groups, are not monolithic entities but often loose groupings of participants with different priorities. Stances shift and turn. It is easy to look on and convict the whole nation. But the prime minister of Turkey himself was once in prison for reciting a poem, the symbolism of which could be read in many ways, so it seems unlikely that he is fundamentally opposed to freedom of speech. But the symbolism of his imprisonment is also read in different ways by different groups: a persecuted hero or a villain.

Other public figures have also fallen foul of those who claim to protect the nation and its myths and symbols and indeed of the whole process of making and interpreting them. Fethullah Gülen had a similar verdict imposed on him: "Not guilty, but don't do it again."[42]

We clearly see now in Turkey that an exclusive group in the state bureaucracy has managed to impose their interpretation of information and events on the public for many years and is seeking to continue this imposition. Their understanding of politics and power was established by the constitutions of the many military coups we have suffered. Many anti-democratic organizations have their origins in those coups. In society,

---

[42]   Çetin, *The Gülen Movement: Civic Service without Borders*, 111; Harrington, *Wrestling With Free Speech, Religious Freedom and Democracy in Turkey*, 110.

different groups will attempt to promulgate values and explanations for activity that preserve their narrow interests. These explanations become the dominant patterns of shared meanings or collective frames of reference, setting the limits of what others may do, shaping the criteria by which they decide and assigning authority within those constraints. The acts of these journalists and members of Parliament are a symbolic threat to the interests that have dominated Turkish society for decades, challenge their legitimacy and so are met with real force.

But as evidenced by Prime Minister Recep Tayyip Erdogan's current premiership and the elections of the Justice and Development Party (AK Party) and President Abdullah Gül, the triumph of the deep state is not inevitable. People brought them to power against all opposition presented by the deep state. The control of national symbols has already slipped from the grasp of the vested interests in the deep state, but this may only make them more irrational and dangerous. Symbolic challenge has real results.

Harassing the Press in Turkey

December 31, 2009

C an investigative reporters, columnists and editors be criminally prosecuted for publishing unclassified information that does not have a high security value and that results in no harm to the security of Turkey?

Legal actions like those taken against two journalists last week for covering groundbreaking stories, such as Ergenekon, a clandestine crime network that has alleged links within the state, and a military action plan that included shady plots to kill non-Muslims in the country, are worrisome and an obstacle to freedom of the press in Turkey.

It is universally accepted that a free and independent press is critical to good governance and the constitutional order in modern democracies. The press should be free to publish news reports without fear that the state will criminalize those publications. Publicizing the wrongdoings of some officers and criminals is not the same as stealing state secrets or spying for the enemy. There is a distinction between discussing publicly available information and leaking sensitive national security information. Plotting against the people and publishing or discussing leaks about those plots are not equivalent. It is one thing to question the wisdom or propriety of publishing sensitive information on national security or to allege media bias and compromise in efforts against separatism or terrorism; it is quite another to call for the criminal prosecution of journalists for reporting on matters of public concern, even when those matters do not involve national security. Not every disclosure or discussion is a criminal act. Indeed, sensitive information should be treated sensitively, not only by journalists but by all. However, people are growing wary because of recent applications of vaguely worded statutes, particularly in the face of clear breaches of the law and Constitution by state and military authorities. If the courts and judiciary continue to prosecute journalists for reporting on already publicly available information, it will further hamper freedom of speech and expression and set a dangerous precedent.

The defenders of Ergenekon have already initiated more than 3,000 criminal investigations against journalists.[43] Who is breaking the law—the assassins, plotters and putschists or those who leak and publish such schemes and plots? Honest judges and courts are already busy with hundreds of leaks and breaches. Even legal scholars who are pro-democracy and constitutionalism say the legal questions are not straightforward. Deep-state supporters are making threats that they may be able to carry out legally to prevent further exposure of their countless violations of the law. They use the vagueness and ambiguity of the existing laws in theory.

Prosecutors demanded a sentence of between 18 months and six years for Star columnist Şamil Tayyar for violation of the confidentiality of the Ergenekon investigation in his published articles. In the event, he received a 20-month suspended prison sentence. But what Tayyar discussed was already in the Ergenekon indictment and available to the public in print and electronic versions. There are already 30,000 entries on the web about the information over which he was charged. On the same day Tayyar received his sentence, Mehmet Baransu, a reporter from the Taraf daily, was charged with violating the principle of confidentiality of an ongoing judicial process. Baransu exposed the military plot known as the "Cage Operation Action Plan." This was a plot to assassinate prominent non-Muslim figures and to massacre children in order to put domestic and international pressure on the Justice and Development Party (AK Party), which would in turn lead to diminishing public support for the party. Fortunately, Baransu was released by the court.

Tayyar and Baransu are not the only journalists facing charges. The trials of journalists are intended to give an explicit message to all journalists to be more cautious about what they write and to engage in self-censorship or face arrest or assassination. With these punishments and bans, the oligarchic minority within the system aims to block Turkey's democratization and consolidation of the rule and supremacy of law.

---

[43] www.todayszaman.com/news-190423-journalists-concerned-about-mounting-pressure-on-journalism.html; www.todayszaman.com/news-189525-journalists-weary-of-facing-charges-for-ergenekon-coverage.html; www.todayszaman.com/news-190337-yet-another-journalist-targeted-over-ergenekon-articles.html

But what if those journalists and their newspapers aren't exposing criminal wrongdoings? What are we doing to keep these journalists out of prison? What would happen in Turkey if the chaotic plans of the Cage plot and Ergenekon had been put into practice? The right to have access to information destroys the myth of state and military officials' untouchability and privileges. The incumbent government should act to eliminate nearly 15 laws in the Turkish Penal Code (TCK) that limit freedom of expression, some of which the European Union has been requesting Turkey abolish for almost two decades. Otherwise, Turkey will continue as a country under the rule of oligarchic judges and the military rather than under the rule of law and democracy.

Coups in Turkey: None So Blind

January 28, 2010

The Sledgehammer Security Operation Plan, drafted only a couple of months after the Justice and Development Party (AK Party) government came to power, detailed plans to trigger unprecedented chaos in Turkey, assassinations, clashes with Greece, the usurpation of Turkish and international resources and business interests, and the elimination and replacement of civilian authorities with subversive junta members from the Turkish Armed Forces (TSK). The ultimate goal of the military takeover would be a Baathist-type authoritarian and repressive regime in Turkey.

The plan's mastermind, retired General Çetin Doğan, at first denied the nature of the meeting he chaired or that there were any recordings of him; however, after further revelations by the Taraf newspaper, Doğan acknowledged that it was his own voice on the recordings of the Sledgehammer coup planning meeting.[44]

Doğan was not alone in denying the existence of such meetings or the presence of such people within the TSK. After close to a week, four media groups and their journalists were still resisting seeing or writing about the planned coup d'état.[45] Considering the attitude and political stance of those media barons and of their journalist employees toward the AK Party government, this could be "understandable" in Turkey. However, the strangest and most irrational reaction came from Deniz Baykal, the leader of the opposition Republican People's Party (CHP).

Faced with 5,000 pages of documents, audio cassettes and CDs, Doğan's partial admission and a case already initiated by prosecutors, Baykal calls the allegations "scenarios fabricated" by a certain group and compares

---

[44] Original report by *Taraf* at www.taraf.com.tr/haber/darbenin-adi-balyoz.htm and by *Today's Zaman* at www.todayszaman.com/news-199685-dogan-admits-to-coup-plan-in-voice-recording.html

[45] Some later changed their tune: www.todayszaman.com/news-191281-skeptical-journalists-papers-reconsider-views-on-army-plot.html

them belittlingly to a soap opera.[46] He claims that "Turkey has developed in the past 30 years and has left the possibility of a coup behind. There has been no coup, but rather continuous discourse using the words 'coup d'état'."

This is not the first time that Baykal's mentality and discourse have run against the norms of social democracy. Throughout the Ergenekon case and investigations of other coup schemes and plots, which are just variations on the aborted Sledgehammer, Baykal has declared that he does not believe such plots or people exist and that he is the advocate for the accused.[47] It is not a "normal" social democrat who advocates for those that attempt military coups with the aim of making Turkey an undemocratic society, in which political and cultural rights are curtailed and ethnic and religious groups are wronged and unrecognized.

After all, along with glorious and honorable events, Turkish history is replete with the unruly military staff burning with lust for power and wealth against the common good. Thousands of people—sultans, their family members, viziers, other state officials and military officers, scholars and intellectuals—were the objects of schemes, plots, killings and elimination at the hands of military officers or ordinary soldiers. No need to go back so far in our history. What about the improvised "Action Army" (Hareket Ordusu), which caused instability and chaos in the Ottoman state in the 19th and 20th centuries? What about the officers within the Committee of Union and Progress, which brought about the demise of the Ottoman state and millions of its citizens? What about military officers' intrigues during the tenure of İsmet İnönü? Since İnönü was the leader of the CHP, Baykal must know about his predecessor's interference with the military during the Republican era.

In 1950, after the elections, did top army officers not offer to stage a coup to suppress the elected Democrat Party (DP) government and restore İnönü to power? From 1955 onwards, did not officers in the armed forces begin to noticeably conspire against the government? Since the end of

---

[46] On the accusations of fabrication of evidence, see www.todayszaman.com/news-275822-abundant-evidence-refutes-forgery-claims-in-sledgehammer-case.html; www.todayszaman.com/news-255093-kosaners-confessions-a-blow-to-sledge-hammer-skepticism.html. Accessed on 22 August 2013.

[47] www.todayszaman.com/news-197698-baykal-criticizes-cosmic-search-while-continuing-to-support-ergenekon.html

World War II, democratization has marginalized those accustomed to playing a central role in the country's affairs. Some officers in the military have formed a kind of opposition movement against the elected government, incorporating revolutionary ideology into the training of cadets. And since 1960 has Turkey not suffered several coups at the hands of such military personnel? Doğan himself admits that he is one of them. Just look at the dates since the 1990s. They have been fouled by aborted coups such as Moonlight, Sea Sparkle and Glove, and no doubt several as-yet-unknown coups, as well as plots devised within the army with the intention of fomenting chaos and conflict, such as the "plan to finish off the AK Party" and other civic and faith-based initiatives in the guise of "actions to fight reactionaryism."

So how can Baykal and his cohorts give us any assurance that there have been no attempts at coups under way within the last 30 years? Or are he and his like-minded colleagues so blinded or deluded by their own personal and ideological interests at the expense of the whole nation that they do not realize that it is high time for pseudo-social democrats to retire and take a much-needed break from the strain of pretence.

CHP: Institutionalization vs. Personality Politics

May 27, 2010

The election of Kemal Kılıçdaroğlu as party leader,[48] along with a wholesale change of the leadership team in the Republican People's Party (CHP), has implications for the party system, institutionalization, linkages between voters and candidates and, in short, democratization in Turkey.

Unquestionably, there are significant differences between the party systems of the advanced industrial democracies and of less-developed countries. Although there is no precise cut-off point between the two types of countries, most democracies in less-developed countries have much higher electoral volatility than the advanced industrial democracies. The second major difference lies in the party system and how the parties are rooted and institutionalized in society. The third is the stability of programmatic or ideological linkages between voters and parties. In the semi-democratic context of less-developed countries, programmatic or ideological linkages between voters and parties are weaker. The linkages between voters and candidates are more personality-based, rather than institutionalized, and therefore less satisfactory, stable or uniform.

This is why many commentators focus on Kılıçdaroğlu's personal weaknesses, the dodgy dealings of his children, his shallow approach to international and financial issues and the populist rhetoric of his inaugural speech.

The sudden election of Kılıçdaroğlu by ideological factions in the party indicates fragile programmatic and ideological links between its voters and the leadership. The portrayal of Kılıçdaroğlu as "Gandhi" by some media illustrates that many voters choose candidates on the basis of personal characteristics. This personalization indicates the weak institutionalization of political parties.

---

[48] www.todayszaman.com/news-262599-kilicdaroglu-ascends-to-chp-leadership-after-baykal.html

Weak institutionalization has adverse effects on democracy. It hampers electoral accountability, which is a key underpinning of democracy. Institutionalized party systems structure the political process to a high degree, yielding party competition, regularity and stability, with less skepticism (which should not be confused with constructive criticism). Institutionalization accords legitimacy to political actors and dealings. It results in fewer floating voters, hence, less likelihood of massive electoral shifts such as those in the last elections in Turkey.

In more institutionalized systems, party organizations are not subordinated to the interests of a few ambitious leaders; they acquire an independent status and value of their own. But institutionalization is limited as long as a party is the personal instrument of a leader or a small coterie. The removal of all but a few members of the leadership team of former CHP Chairman Deniz Baykal and their replacement with deputy Onder Sav's list of 80 requires no further explanation. Parties dominated by personalistic leaders have frequent supply-side changes, as political elites shift from one party to another; we see this in the shifting allegiances of Rahşan Ecevit and Kamer Genç.[49]

The new leadership of the CHP will not be central in the struggle to expand citizenship. It does not seem to be able to make any serious contribution to societal cohesion. Nor is it fostering its own identity as a democratizing force. This will not lead to a higher level of development or a more stable party system.

In his inaugural speech, without even touching on ethnic, religious and other cultural issues of modern Turkey, Kılıçdaroğlu promised business as usual: political competition without institutionalization for the foreseeable future. This will not only lead to a general atmosphere of authoritarianism in the CHP, but potentially to the erosion of democratic gains over time.

For electoral accountability to function well, the political environment must provide citizens with adequate information and choice. Lack of information and choice undercuts electoral accountability. Where electoral accountability suffers, the promise that representative democracy holds, that elected politicians will serve as agents of the voters to advance some

---

[49] www.todayszaman.com/news-211010-winds-of-change-in-chp-no-more-than-a-light-breeze.html

common good or to advance the interests of specific constituencies, will be broken.

Voters identify their interests on the basis of their position in society—class, religion, ethnicity or nationality and urban or rural residence. Implicitly or explicitly, parties advance the interests of different sectors of society, and individuals vote for a party on the basis of these programmatic or ideological interests. So, a voter might cast a ballot because of a politician's or party's program even though a competitor is ideologically closer to his or her preferred position. Voting can also be personality-based, without a strong link to the ideology or program of the party. Voters are therefore more likely to drift from one party to the next; this is the problem lying in wait for the CHP now.

Totalitarianism, Complicity and Turkey's Future

July 29, 2010

Since the beginning of the 20th century, totalitarian rule has brought about enormous political and economic failures and human loss and suffering. The atrocities of the Holocaust, the Soviet gulags, the killing fields of the Khmer Rouge, events in Abu Ghraib, and Diyarbakır Prison (after the 1980 coup in Turkey[50]) prove that totalitarian rule remains an ever-present danger in the contemporary world.

Totalitarianism is the key feature of the plots and putsches of some bureaucrats in Turkey's military and judiciary. All their schemes, and botched attempts at coups, which constitute charges in current court cases, exemplify totalitarianism as described in many academic analyses of it.

Totalitarian rule imposes an absolute control over all aspects of individual and public life. Expression of political, economic, social and spiritual understanding is subordinated to the guiding ideology of the government. The government functions under the control of a single political person, faction or hierarchy, closely interwoven with the state bureaucracy.

Totalitarianism values authoritarian leadership, whether a dictator or a collective. A monopolistic control of the armed forces and mass surveillance consolidates a system of terror and physical force. This leads to the loss of pluralism and the rule of law. A monopoly on mass communication and the media brainwashes citizens. Technology and informants are exploited to identify dissidents and coordinate action against them, especially through collaborators in journalism. Central control and direction of the entire economy and industrialization through state planning crushes all autonomous investments.

Ordinary citizens have no share in state decision-making. Tolerance and respect for minority and individual rights are replaced with fixed goals, regulation and restriction of speech. Minorities are scapegoated. The state monopolizes political power and penetrates deep into the societal struc-

---

[50] www.todayszaman.com/news-241518-diyarbakir-prison-was-a-house-of-torture-in-coup-era.html; www.todayszaman.com/news-216915-diyarbakir-prison-to-turn-into-human-rights-museum.html

ture, seeking to completely control the thoughts and actions of citizens. If need be, it politicizes everything spiritual and human, and dismisses any objective truths.

Totalitarianism portrays democratic values and their advocates as decadent parasites that must be sacrificed for a higher cause. Its tyranny leads to massive terror, allegedly aimed at stability but risking stagnation. It seeks not only to punish and kill its enemies but to dehumanize them and erase any trace of their existence from memory. It changes its list of enemies. The innocent abruptly become enemies of the state, regime or public. Once arrested, they are non-persons. Killings and mass murders are normalized as necessary bureaucratic operations.

Totalitarian rule does not recognize talent, intelligence or wisdom in case they threaten its leaders' self-importance. For totalitarian ideals, a false reality is easily produced through conspiracies. Objective enemies are created—people who have not committed crimes but who might commit them in the future because of their "mentality" and "tendencies." People are left in a paranoid state wondering why freedoms cease to exist and why people start disappearing. Suspicion and uncertainty drive wedges between atomized individuals and society. Thus the concepts of justice, morality and eventually individuality and human dignity are completely eliminated through torture. Opposing the authoritarian system assures not only the demise of one's self but one's family, friends and more

Once in power, totalitarian rule wills to prevail forever. Some governmental or organizational units are left in place, as a facade to conceal the complete control or coordination by the doctrinaire elites. Vague orders from the leadership are interpreted by elite factions to suit their own interests. Totalitarianism defies law but claims legitimacy at the same time. And its leaders never admit to error.

However, contrary to the common assumption, totalitarian rule mostly rests on the consent of the governed. For totalitarianism to occur, there must also exist a combination of a lack of civilian political power, an absence of the sense of duty and human dignity, indulgence in short-term partisan interests, passion for higher position, and waste and blindness caused by hospitality and grandeur at the state's expense. When these merge with propaganda reinforced by an unscrupulous intellectual community, complicit political parties and hungry interest groups that have already estranged themselves from mass culture, the stage is set in any country, as it was in Turkey.

Our brutal reality must be faced honestly by intellectuals, the ruling party, the government and all civil democratic leaders of Turkey. The history of these events in Turkey is a warning to all those who advocate and comply with change that does not take into account mistakes committed thus far by authoritarian murderers.

Bags of Ill Will from the Turkish Naval Base

December 16, 2010

This week the trial of the participants in Balyoz (Sledgehammer) begins. Balyoz was a "coup simulation" run in 2003 by the former commander of the land forces, along with other gendarmerie and navy personnel.

The 1,000-page indictment accuses almost 200 high-ranking officers of "attempting to prevent by force the government of the Republic of Turkey from carrying out its duties." Some of the officers accused are still in the service, while others have retired. The indictment is based upon actual recordings made during the so-called "coup simulation." In the course of the "simulation" the real names of elected civil servants, authorities and politicians were used. Due to the shrewd, some would say, officious and unwarranted, intervention by the former Chief of General Staff General İlker Başbuğ, none of the high-ranking officers will be held in custody while standing trial.[51]

There are the usual civilian accomplices, of course, like the Support for Modern Life Association[52] and the Contemporary Education Foundation.[53] At odds with their claims to be educational is the fact that these organizations always turn up in the midst of plans to incite chaos and lay the groundwork for a coup d'état.[54] Their names and the names of their personnel repeatedly crop up in indictments that they maintain links with various outlawed terrorist groups in order to prime and support coup attempts. Their dirty linen has been aired in public over and over; some

---

[51]   www.todayszaman.com/news-208956-basbug-pressured-judiciary-to-remove-ergenekon-prosecutors.html

[52]   Çağdaş Yaşamı Destekleme Derneği

[53]   Çağdaş Eğitim Vakfı

[54]   www.todayszaman.com/news-229809-ultranationalist-group-hoped-for-chaos-ahead-of-2009-local-polls.html

of their leaders have already fled Turkey and are being sought under Interpol red notices.[55]

The outcome of this trial ought to have serious consequences and implications for the military and civilian coup lovers and makers in Turkey. However, experts and specialists working on the reform of the Turkish Armed Forces (TSK) do not predict any dramatic changes in the command structure of the TSK because it already has a surplus of active duty generals. Thankfully we are not at war, so if the prosecutors succeed in having a few generals sent down for working against a democratic, parliamentary government, for conspiring with separatist and terrorist groups and for sharing vital data and state secrets with "unfriendly" nations and organizations, the armed forces won't miss them much.

While many fear that this trial might not be successfully concluded, new developments are taking place. An active duty officer at the Gölcük Naval Command in the Bay of İzmit near Istanbul recently alerted civilian judges that a dozen large sacks of confidential materials were about to be destroyed. Under the supervision of civilian and military authorities, the documents were seized from concealed compartments in the command room of the base. The public has already been informed that the recovered materials are related to the many coups d'état and ongoing trials of officers involved in subversive and undemocratic activity, such as the Cage Plan and the Action Plan against Reactionaryism—a plot against the elected Parliament and faith-inspired communities. Documents contain vital information and substantial evidence related to "unfavorable" commanders and state dignitaries who would be confined, deported or "incapacitated" in the event of military action against an acting government. There is also information about a network of sex, drugs, extortion and blackmail within the TSK, and about the liaison between military commanders and some university rectors and directors in anti-government actions. Undoubtedly, the sacks will be a treasure trove of evidence for prosecutors.[56]

While it is always disheartening to hear of yet another discovery of bags of ill will concealed on a military base in Turkey, there may be hope for us yet. Those who still dream of a Turkey under their military and judicial tutelage reinforcing an authoritarian, elitist and ultra-laicist hegemo-

---

[55] www.aksam.com.tr/guncel/interpolden-kirmizi-kurs/haber-183479

[56] www.todayszaman.com/news-229294-coup-plans-and-blacklists-among-docs-seized-at-golcuk-command.html

ny, those who siphoned money from international charities under the pretext of educating the younger generation must be increasingly aware that the world is no longer revolving as they envisage in their crooked ideologies and self-interested schemes. Law-abiding individuals, legal institutions and the uncompromising awareness of the public are now demanding freedom, human rights, equality, participatory democracy, societal cohesion and peaceful progress. And last but not least, they want a fair trial for all coup lovers and supporters who have cost this nation and country so much.

Unsolved Killings Block Peace and Democracy in Turkey

January 27, 2011

This last week Turkish society has been commemorating slain journalists, academics and civilians. The commemorations have made it abundantly clear that Turkish society is still deeply disturbed and struggling to come to conclusions about the profusion of unsolved political and ideological crimes and killings the nation has endured.[57]

A number of the alleged assassins in these cases were apprehended, but several were detained for years without their cases being pursued through the courts, and the detainees have now been released by the Supreme Court of Appeals on the grounds that the cases had not come to conclusion after 10 years of investigation.[58] And yet the establishment of democracy, the rule and supremacy of law and the Constitution, and legal accountability demand that the state and governmental institutions and organizations, individuals and families of the slain should diligently and consistently cooperate to bring the murderers and those behind them to justice.

How is it that in 20 years we have not made any progress in a series of unsolved political assassinations? Intellectuals, journalists, academics, chiefs of police and intelligence officers have been murdered, including Uğur Mumcu,[59] Çetin Emeç,[60] Bahriye Üçok,[61] Muam-

---

[57] www.todayszaman.com/news-241525-call-made-to-include-armenian-journalists-killed-in-1915-in-slain-journalists-list.html

[58] www.todayszaman.com/news-304954-ugur-mumcu-case-risks-becoming-an-issue-of-history.html

[59] www.nytimes.com/1993/01/27/world/critic-of-islamic-right-slain-turkey-arrests-11-suspects.html. Accessed on 13 October 2013.

[60] For a report (in Turkish) of Emeç's widow's growing doubts about the official account of his assassination, see haber.gazetevatan.com/cetin-emec-suikastini-21-yildir-aydinlatamamis-zihniyetin-gazetecilere-bakisi-degisir-mi-hic/363543/4/yazarlar

[61] Report on demands to reinvestigate Üçok's murder: www.radikal.com.tr/turkiye/bahriye_ucok_suikasti_yeniden_sorusturulsun-946502

mer Aksoy,[62] Onat Kutlar, Turan Dursun, Ahmet Taner Kışlalı,[63] Necip Hablemitoğlu,[64] Hrant Dink[65] and Gaffar Okan. And there are many others whose deaths are less well sung and whose names this column is not sufficient to list.[66]

There are many reasons the killings remain unsolved. At times, deliberately, consciously, overtly or covertly the investigative units' efforts were not given the required priority. A Chief Public Prosecutor's Office proved negligent in its investigations.[67] Many now conclude that some cases have deliberately not been solved.[68] This is not a wild accusation: Turkish parliamentary investigation commissions have reported that all aspects of many cases were not sufficiently probed and have for this reason filed criminal complaints against the Supreme Board of Judges and Prosecutors (HSYK). Furthermore, the commissions maintain that cases were manipulated in particular directions.

As a nation we appear to lack the political will to solve the cases because so many big people, state institutions or authorities stand, as perpetrators, behind the long-standing failure to bring the murderers to justice. Nevertheless, the dark games behind all these political killings are undeniable now.

These are not "ordinary" murders we are discussing. Behind them are particular interest groups—militant secularists sponsoring false-flag terrorism, ideologically motivated fundamentalist and terrorist organizations, and organized crime. However, they have all become shrouded in a fog of legal uncertainties, so the masterminds, the ones who pulled the puppet strings, have not been exposed. In some cases, dispensable indi-

---

[62] On Aksoy's still unsolved murder (in Turkish): gundem.bugun.com.tr/devlet-bu-cinayetleri-cozemedi-haberi/220987

[63] www.turkiyegazetesi.com.tr/Genel/a48854.aspx

[64] arsiv.ntvmsnbc.com/news/454303.asp

[65] www.todayszaman.com/news-220451-lawyers-challenge-hanefi-avci-on-hrant-dink-murder.html; www.todayszaman.com/news-207583-hrant-dink-murder-could-have-been-prevented.html

[66] www.todayszaman.com/news-213566-families-of-murder-victims-demand-justice-ahead-of-fathers-day.html

[67] www.haberler.com/mumcu-cinayetinde-meclis-arastirma-komisyonu-4121540-haberi

[68] www.bianet.org/bianet/ifade-ozgurlugu/143803-meclis-oldurulen-gazeteciler-in-faillerini-arastirsin

viduals have been sacrificed and put behind bars for the assassinations, but most people believe that all the perpetrators involved have not been and cannot be revealed or brought to justice due to the negligence, manipulation or protection of certain state institutions and authorities. The public knows very well that the state, or the deep state, has in some way or another played a role in or facilitated many of the killings; this behavior is typical, as shown in the many recently unearthed coup plots. This is well illustrated in the details of the case of the slain journalist Dink. It is now known that some military, security and state intelligence personnel or organizations guided and manipulated the individuals involved in the killing, targeting some people and protecting those responsible for his death.[69]

The politically motivated killings and unjust and inhuman treatment of people will end only once political will is shown. The need for will and determination is not limited to the legislative and executive branches in order to expose and bring to justice the perpetrators behind the murders. To our amazement, while some families cooperate with the investigations, others do not insist on revealing the people and organizations at the root of these crimes, whether out of fear or more base motives such as their retaining certain ranks in state and governmental institutions for their silence.

From the Susurluk case to Ergenekon there are professional and organized formations behind all the killings, organized crime and false-flag terrorism. The killings will remain unsolved, a terrible stain on Turkey's conscience, as long as we do not properly investigate and expose illegitimate links amongst the police, military, judiciary, mafia and politicians. All the illicit organized groups behind the murderous acts also target the democratic regime, civil society, freedoms, rule of law and dignity of the human mind and life. We hope the mourners' grief for the assassins' victims will not continue to be muffled by injustice. It is high time to bring the murders, perpetrators and their culprits to justice.

---

[69] www.todayszaman.com/news-232952-hrants-friends-meet-in-front-of-agos-protest-lack-of-justice.html; www.todayszaman.com/news-259044-turkey-should-find-real-culprits-behind-hrant-dink-murder.html; www.todayszaman.com/news-232835-strong-political-will-still-sought-to-solve-dink-murder-after-four-years.html

Where Have You Been All These Years?

February 17, 2011

I t is extremely revealing to follow discussions about subversive plots and groups like Sledgehammer and Ergenekon in terms of understanding their defenders' crooked mentality and attitudes.

Retired General Çetin Doğan is a prime suspect in the Sledgehammer case and is alleged to be the mastermind behind the coup plan. Upon his arrest,[70] his wife, Nilgün Doğan, told the Hürriyet daily, on February 14, that the health of her husband and other suspects in the case is very bad: "They are at the age at which they need to take good care of their health. They are past their prime, so they can't stay in damp prison cells and eat pasta frequently."[71]

She gives the impression that she is a caring, loving, compassionate and rational wife and mother. She implores the public to do something to save her husband and his fellow culprits from any judicial consequences. Listening to her and other such defenders of miscreants, it is impossible not to ask, "Where have you all been all these years?"

If you, and others like you, are so caring, compassionate, rational and human, then as wives, mothers and women, where were you when the 1960 coup happened? Why did you not say a single word against the coup d'état that overthrew the first elected government and that degraded and tortured thousands and hanged the three best ministers Turkey had ever raised? When cadets and lieutenants debased all human values, extinguishing cigarette butts on the body of Prime Minister Adnan Menderes and sexually assaulted him by pinching his body and buttocks in the cold, damp rooms of Imralı, did your conscience ever prick you to

---

[70] www.todayszaman.com/news-202827-retired-generals-dogan-and-alan-arrested-under-sledgehammer-plot-probe.html

[71] English-language report including some of Mrs. Dogan's comments at www.hurriyetdailynews.com/top-suspect-in-turkish-coup-trial-turns-himself-in.aspx?pageID=438&n=top-suspect-of-turkish-coup-trial-turns-himself-in-2011-02-14

say anything against such inhumane treatment? Before and after 1970 and 1980, when consecutive coups were planned and staged, Turkey lost almost 50,000 people. They were maimed, tortured and killed to pave the road for ambitious generals to become the unchallenged masters of a nation. Mrs. Doğan, have you ever sympathized with the wives, mothers and children of those killed in the dirty plots to keep those shameless generals in command? Just remember the words of former prime minister and President Süleyman Demirel, "All that blood was shed just to sail some generals into Çankaya[72]; it is interesting how it all stopped the day after the coup!"

General Doğan and many of the accused in the Sledgehammer and Ergenekon cases were on duty and instrumental in such coups and their cruel aftermath. So, did your compassion and conscience ever stir then?[73]

What about the extrajudicial killings and disappearances of 17,500 people, most of which took place within the military area under your husband's command or under others accused in the Ergenekon case? All those victims' children, brothers, sisters, wives and parents would gladly eat pasta and live in damp rooms if it would only bring their loved ones back to them. Have you ever imagined what it is like not to lock the door for more than 30 years in case your beloved might come back one night?

While your husband and his alleged accomplices were busy playing golf, enjoying summer camps and entertainment and planning coups d'état, did you pause to watch the surveillance videos in which terrorists attacked the military outposts that your husband and his colleagues commanded? With the rest of Turkey, did you watch in horror as young men's lives were needlessly lost and their families' futures darkened? Have you ever stopped to ask if those events arose from the decades of incompetence, negligence and nefarious plotting of your husband and his associates? Does your motherly compassion ever say, "Enough is enough," when you see videos of fallen soldiers and of their stricken parents at funerals?

Sledgehammer was not a war game as your husband has claimed. It was a deliberate plan to bring down Turkish and Greek jets to create a political crisis between Turkey and the EU. Sledgehammer planned to bomb mosques and museums during busy hours to provoke people on the street

---

[72] The Presidential palace
[73] For the outrage of suspects' wives, see hurarsiv.hurriyet.com.tr/goster/ShowNew.aspx?id=17065614

through agents provocateurs in the guise of religious fanatics, to kill the leaders of ethno-religious minorities, to undermine faith-inspired communities and in particular the Gülen Movement and the Justice and Development Party (AK Party),[74] and thus to produce an atmosphere of insecurity, chaos and mistrust. This would pave the way for overthrowing the democratically elected government and installing a fascist military junta that would prevail for decades in Turkey. Mrs. Doğan, you and your friends should realize that the 195 suspects, all of whom are retired or active duty members of the armed forces, are not just toy soldiers you give to your children!

Seeing all this, can your wifely, womanly consciences ask, "What is this silly complaint about pasta and humidity, compared to the tears, blood and pain of tens of thousands of people and millions of others in Turkey? Did all this suffering occur because of our husbands' degenerate ambitions and the unfailing support for them from people like us?"

Game over!

---

[74] www.taraf.com.tr/haber/akp-ve-guleni-bitirme-plani.htm

4

Constitutional Reform and Barriers to Reform

New Draft Constitution, Third National Program and Opposition

September 18, 2008

The Third National Program for EU harmonization[75] was welcomed by all parties in the Turkish Parliament except the Republican People's Party (CHP). The CHP, predictably, has taken an adversarial stance. Not only did the party refuse to schedule a meeting with chief EU negotiator and Foreign Minister Ali Babacan, but it returned the draft program by post. Seeing the importance of the program, all other parties have stated that they will make contributions to the draft following their meetings with Mr. Babacan. In a parliamentary, participatory or deliberative democracy, the CHP's reaction is flawed and inappropriate. As the main opposition, the CHP can no longer call the government to account if it fails to proceed with democratic reforms.[76]

The reforms in the program concern Turkey's future and support its EU bid. While the government is seeking social consensus for the adop-

---

[75] www.todayszaman.com/news-152599-eu-harmonization-package-to-expand-la-bor-freedoms.html; www.todayszaman.com/news-153280-government-to-intro-duce-structural-changes-to-ministries.html; www.todayszaman.com/news-150825-turkish-military-to-toe-eu-line.html; www.todayszaman.com/news-156952-turkey-to-conduct-its-counterterrorism-as-per-its-third-national-program.html; www.todayszaman.com/news-197383-government-to-expand-freedom-of-the-press-in-2010.html

[76] www.todayszaman.com/news-153072-eu-skeptic-chp-mhp-losing-their-right-to-criticize.html

tion of the necessary laws in Parliament in the coming legislative term—with Turkey already lagging behind in its EU-reforms—the CHP is wasting time in unconstructive skirmishes and political crises. In contrast to its party program, the CHP has acquired an ultranationalist and protectionist discourse. It consistently fails to offer any alternatives to the government's plans. It opposes any constitutional amendments proposed by the government but does nothing constructive toward raising living standards or consolidating rights and freedoms.

The Third National Program contains 131 legal amendments and 342 secondary revisions for the next three to four years made up of changes to the current Constitution, parliamentary bylaws, EU harmonization legislation, the Law on Political Parties, the Elections Law, Funding of Political Activities Law and the Political Ethics Law. These all require both critical review and grand consensus. The program has priorities, including judicial reform and improvements to social policies and fundamental rights and freedoms. It is expected to raise living standards, to contribute a great deal to the resolution of systemic blockages through institutionalization, to fully democratize Turkey, and thus to harmonize the legislature and executive branch in accordance with EU or modern standards.

Opposition centers on our unresolved concerns about the inalienable integrity of the Turkish people and state, and the indivisibility of the nation, state and territory, and national security against internal and external enemies.

Some anticipate that the CHP will block the work of the multi-party committees. The CHP has announced that Turkey does not need a new constitution and that the current 1982 Constitution—often criticized for being anti-democratic as the heritage of the 1980 military coup—is now fine due to past amendments. Their single suggestion is to remove the parliamentary immunity of those in office.[77] The prevailing opinion says the CHP will take the new constitution to court in order to annul its adoption in Parliament by another Constitutional Court ruling, and this is why they are not participating in the committee drafting the constitution.

After the coups of 1960 and 1980, public policy goals were not achieved because the Cabinet and Parliament contained vocal opponents

---

[77] www.todayszaman.com/news-153150-parties-to-draft-constitution-without-chp.html; www.todayszaman.com/news-182938-chp-removes-democratization-report-from-web-site-agenda.html

to development planning. Governments rejected or presidents vetoed proposed reforms concerning land, agriculture, taxes and State Economic Enterprises (KİTs). Many State Planning Organization (DPT) advisors were forced to resign or were reassigned to new, unrelated posts. Throughout those periods, governments' lack of political commitment to their work, increasing politicization of appointments and partisan protection of vested interests, instead of those of the whole nation, weakened reform initiatives and state institutions. In 1995 the committee formed to devise a new constitution stopped its work halfway through, and committee members did their utmost to prevent changes from being made to the Constitution. Since February 28 and in the latest Ergenekon developments, we have seen enough of those who benefited from "non-democracy" through their links of patronage with powerful officials and those who still live with the residue of the one-party era, with its authoritarian leadership model and party control of state offices. Many a time the CHP has gone to the Constitutional Court rather than to Parliament and caused the abolition of regulations passed by Parliament. Another excellent example is the last president, Ahmet Necdet Sezer, who proved to be the staunchest protector of the status quo through his continual vetoes and unilateral actions against the government and Parliament. He became a vigorous opponent of efforts for modernization and EU accession.

When socio-political reforms in the system are sought, this disturbs the protectionist elite, which is unwilling to accelerate the democratization and economic liberalization that might harm its interests. But arbitrary and authoritarian rule, its suppressive measures and lack of freedoms and rights have already alienated people from protectionist ideas and bureaucratic elitists' attitudes. The CHP's and bureaucratic elitists' undemocratic resistance to reform is kindling in citizens an even stronger desire for a free society and liberal economy. We no longer live in a closed society. When the CHP or other bodies do not adopt a positive stance toward democratization processes, the public and the democratic world can see how the CHP acts against the social-democrat values it claims to hold.[78] The recent effort for a new constitution or Third National Program is a great opportunity, and Turkey cannot afford to miss it.

---

[78] See also www.todayszaman.com/news-167231-chp-to-block-new-constitution-efforts.html

Burn the Flag + Respect the Flag = 'False Flag' Anyway

February 12, 2009

Recently certain Turkish "Atatürkist" associations in the US issued a "most urgent call," which reads: "At the invitation of the Atatürk Society of America,[79] the leaders of the below listed organizations met to discuss the alarming developments in Turkey.

"In this meeting, it was agreed that we are all deeply concerned that the traditions of democracy and secularism embodied in the Republic of Turkey are in jeopardy. As a result we decided to organize a peaceful demonstration to raise public awareness ... in front of the White House.... Join us against creeping authoritarian rule, intimidation of the free press, the erosion of secularism, [and] the threat of theocracy.... Join us, support the rule of law, freedom of speech, individual rights, [and] a free, democratic, and modern Turkey as envisioned by Atatürk.... Please bring Turkish Flags with you."

During the Nevruz celebrations in 2005, a provocative Turkish flag-burning incident took place in Mersin.[80] This led to mass demonstrations all over Turkey and sparked anti-Kurdish sentiment among the public.[81] Following these developments, the deep-state structure, Ergenekon-related organizations, the Republican People's Party (CHP) and other statist, secularist and elitist protectionists organized several demonstrations on behalf of the Republic and the flag.

However, in the Ergenekon case currently before the courts, evidence from surveillance records has made it clear that all the street theater, from the initial flag burning to the counter-demonstrations, was orchestrated by groups, most of which are also implicated in the Ergenekon case.

---

[79] ataturksociety.org

[80] arsiv.ntvmsnbc.com/news/315307.asp; webarsiv.hurriyet.com.tr/2005/03/25/618850.asp

[81] news.bbc.co.uk/2/hi/europe/4379675.stm; webarsiv.hurriyet.com.tr/2005/03/24/618315.asp; webarsiv.hurriyet.com.tr/2005/03/26/619328.asp

Amongst other things, the Ergenekon indictment, because of the revelations of Witness Number 17 and pictures taken by the police as well as others published in the media, claims that the person who gave the children a Turkish flag to burn was Ali Kutlu. Kutlu is a suspect in the Ergenekon investigation and a member of the Association for the Union of Patriotic Forces (VKGB). Kutlu told the witness that flags were burned by the VKGB in order to provoke the public and foment chaos in Turkey.[82] The VKGB selected Mersin as the pilot site, and their sister organization, the Kuvayi Milliye (National Forces), an ultranationalist organization with links to Ergenekon, organized the widely publicized oath-taking ceremony in which members agreed to kill and die, which took place at the Mersin branch of the National Forces. The VKGB urged local villagers in Mersin to engage in war, with the claim that Mersin was "under the control of the [outlawed Kurdistan Workers' Party] PKK" and that this is a "war of independence, and everyone with Turkish blood must participate in this war." Within this context, they tried to organize mass demonstrations and protests titled "Respect the Flag." The real intention, it has emerged, was to lay the groundwork for a military coup. This construction of a fake attack and unreal threats leading to military action by the state is the very definition of false flag terrorism.

A day after the flag-burning incident on Nevruz, the Office of the Chief of General Staff released a statement that the Turkish Armed Forces (TSK) will protect the Turkish flag until the last drop of the TSK's blood is shed.[83] A year later, Ergenekon organized almost 80,000 people for a "Respect the Flag" demonstration, raising tensions in Mersin and other cities, too. Yet, the Ergenekon indictment contains evidence from a telephone conversation in which one VKGB member noted, "There were 4,000 soldiers in the Mersin demonstration. No one was aware of it." To which another VKGB member replied, "First we made the soldiers march. Then civilians participated, and we withdrew the soldiers."

Within the last week, a similar flag-waving demonstration was organized in Izmir. The number of people gathered, including toddlers and

[82] www.todayszaman.com/news-148778-witness-points-finger-at-ergenekon-in-flag-burning.html
[83] Amongst other comments the press release said, "Such treatment of a nation's flag ... in its own land by its own so-called citizens is inexplicable and unacceptable. This is treason."

infants in strollers, hardly added up to 500. Rather than flags, most of the crowd held placards opposing the Ergenekon trial. Since most people now recognize the ill intentions and dishonesty behind such demonstrations, the outcome was a total failure and embarrassing for those would-be Atatürkist associations.

What exactly are they hiding under the flag? The Washington-based "Atatürkist" group should know that as it organizes its "pro-democracy" demonstration, the Turkish people await an explanation of why such groups did not accept the popular or parliamentary votes that brought to power conservative or practicing Muslims. We would like to hear the justification for the full-page ads these groups put in American and European dailies claiming that Turkey would soon become a theocratic state where women cannot go out on the streets, beaches and universities, work or even drive, that massive clashes would ensue and innocent blood would be shed. We want to know on exactly what grounds "patriotic" groups use scare tactics that cause so much damage to Turkey, Turkish people and Muslims.

The Turkish people, far from rallying behind these false flag groups, intend, through legal means, to finish off the Ergenekon beast, which has tortured, assassinated, burned alive and exterminated people in acid wells and which assumed exclusive, direct control over power, positions and resources within the system despite the will of the people, the rule of law, democracy and respect for freedom and the flag.[84]

At the very least, we expect those so-called Atatürkist groups to give up the money they take from the Turkish government and state for representing them abroad.

---

[84] A civilian response in Izmir to the army's threats is reported at news.bbc.co.uk/2/hi/europe/4388023.stm

Deceit, Betrayal and Nihilism of Coup Makers and Helpers

March 26, 2009

Every day that passes now is a test, not only for the Turkish media, the civic, military and judicial authorities and academics, but also for non-Turkish experts and journalists writing about Turkey. The world is now jaded about news of Turkish generals and military staff aspiring to military coups. It is accustomed to the sight of media owners and businessmen offering support to nihilist generals. Yes, onlookers are all too thoroughly acquainted with the ideological and sectarian groups within the opposition party; however, to hear of plotting by high-ranking judges, former (prime) ministers and former presidents to eliminate aspects of Turkey's hard-won democratic processes is surely enough to shake any "objective" observer from complacency.

In the fifth revealed voice recording (March 23) of retired General İsmail Karadayı, a former chief of general staff, he elaborates on the prospective military coup, adding that democracy in Turkey must remain under the tutelage and guardianship of the military junta for 25 to 30 years. Again we hear recited the anti-democracy mantras of the deep state: "The people, the constituency, cannot be trusted with electing the president. Selecting the president by the people's common vote is extraordinarily dangerous. People are ignorant ... ."[85]

Karadayı explains who must be the president, as well as who should be the prime minister and the minister of education. He reveals how he has contrived with Republican People's Party (CHP) Vice Chairman Onur Öymen and former CHP and present Democratic Left Party (DSP) member İsmail Tanla to pen a statement to appeal to the Constitutional Court against the election of the president by public vote and a press release to invite the military to assume its duty to save the system from the ordinary people.

---

[85] www.todayszaman.com/news-170496-karadayi-opposes-popular-election-of-president-in-new-recording.html

The conspirators among the chiefs of general staff are now known to have formed exclusivist salons and secret society organizations, such as the Council of Consultation (Encümen-i Daniş) and the Friends Association (Dostlar Grubu), from which they sent guidelines, indeed ultimatums, to presidents, prime ministers, governments and bureaucrats on how to carry out their state and public duties and projects; they issued instructions about uniting parties before elections, as in the case of the Motherland Party (ANAVATAN) and True Path Party (DYP) before the presidential election, and about whether those parties should attend the election session in Parliament during presidential voting and certain constitutional amendments.[86]

Other generals who retired after their roles in such schemes were revealed and who are furious at their thwarted ambitions and the likely effects on future financial gains also do not cease to conspire against participatory, parliamentary democracy. Through new brotherhoods, associations and platforms, they take part in many activities against the elected government and against other civic and faith-based initiatives that do not sympathize with such schemes.

But this is not a mere soap opera of salons, clubs and diaries. Behind the uniformed façade erected by these "tutors and guardians," the self-proclaimed "security valve for the tenets of the republic," the would-be "indispensable elements of stability in Turkey and the region" that assumes the right "to intervene in public and politics when conditions necessitate it," there lie more sinister vistas. There are acid wells, hidden weapons and ammunition caches, detailed plans for assassinations, death squads, an inexplicable accumulation of funds, text and phone messages containing schemes and boasts of plots. There lie false flag terrorism and the deaths of 17,000 people in southeastern Turkey.

"Objective" observers inside and outside Turkey who are not losing their loved ones, homes, property, land, honor, blood, future and hope at the hands of such "guardians" may claim to be bemused at the fate of their "democratic, secular, progressive" friends who are apparently being entrapped by backward zealots. All the facts and figures remain a faintly unreal item of news for them, mere data for their academic pursuits about

---

[86] www.todayszaman.com/news-232871-controversial-body-failed-to-design-right-admits-member.html; www.todayszaman.com/news-167448-recording-reveals-existence-of-another-controversial-group.html

a distant region of the world. Some choose to remain blind, deaf and dumb to the real intent of the Ergenekon terrorist organization and the vested interests, economic and ideological, behind it.

But the Ergenekon trial is expected to bring a tradition and a mind-set to an end in Turkey, and it must be so abroad, too. Perspectives on the Turkish Armed Forces (TSK), or more correctly, the coup-loving and coup-making top-ranking generals, and their so-called "secular" elitist accomplices in the state bureaucracy, need to change both domestically and internationally. The "old elite" is no longer the sole ruler of contemporary Turkey. Turkey is not "a special case" where such schemers have to be tolerated.

So far, many from the Western world—journalists, academics, military officers, politicians, human rights activists—have interacted mostly with this small elite due to the public, political and economic resources it monopolizes. This distorts perspectives on Turkish society. In the current state of knowledge, those writing and commenting on democracy and human rights in Turkey would be well advised to reconsider some of their informants and perspectives. Turkish people are growing more confident, and this is a two-way conversation. Observers form and express opinions about the motives and methods of Turkish people; Turkish people are capable of drawing conclusions about the true interests and commitments of those who comment on them.

The Paradox of Judicial Independence and Accountability

June 6, 2009

F or those who seek to consolidate an egalitarian and constitutional democracy in Turkey, legal and judicial reforms are core objectives. An independent judiciary is a prerequisite for the rule of law. It entails checks and balances, prevents the misuse of authority and brings governments to account for abuses of power. However, judicial effectiveness can itself be hampered by a lack of accountability. Therefore it needs to be counterbalanced by restraining mechanisms.

The judiciary in Turkey is superficially similar to an accountable court system. Yet the Constitution in the hands and minds of the top courts, civic bars and certain lodges of acting and retired judges and prosecutors impedes the other branches of government from holding the judiciary accountable for its management, policy decisions and relations with interest groups.[87] Undoubtedly, courts should be independent and have substantial freedom to manage their own affairs. However, they must also recognize that they are part of the government and are thus accountable to the public for their institutional actions.

The Turkish Constitution empowers the legislative branch to determine the judicial branch's structure, jurisdiction and resources. However, any attempt to use this power is turned into a crisis and the government and the Parliament have been paralyzed by judicial impasses and vetoes at the hands of partisan courts. These crises have included recent party closures,[88] the obstruction of Abdullah Gül's presidential inauguration,[89] the vetoing of legislative amendments aimed at accession to the Europe-

---

[87] www.todayszaman.com/news-181064-judiciary-strongly-opposed-to-sharing-of-its-power.html

[88] www.todayszaman.com/news-169446-meps-concerned-over-closure-cases-want-reform.html

[89] www.todayszaman.com/news-120274-mhp-declines-chps-call-to-block-gul.html

an Union[90] and the fines the government has paid in European human rights courts for violations of freedom of conscience and speech.[91] Preventing replays of such crises is critical as Turkey transforms from a closed society into a global player and in terms of enabling honest judges to enact laws and administer justice.

Individual judges and courts face criticism on particular decisions everywhere. However, when the top state courts and the judiciary always act in accordance with a certain ideological stance they fall short in their duties. They undermine the government's capacity to provide the highest quality of service to the public. Therefore all good court systems strive not only to be accountable, but also accept external review and auditing. Such openness presents an excellent opportunity to educate the public and the other branches about democracy, equity, fairness and justice. The judicial branch itself should lead initiatives to identify the core elements of judicial accountability, fairness, impartiality and justice.[92]

Identifying core responsibilities will clear the judiciary of the accusation that it is the product of ideologically motivated judges. It will engender institutional respect for the judiciary and all members of the bar who act with competence and civility and ensure the service to which the public is entitled.

Given the high degree of expected interdependence among the branches of government, each branch should understand and respect the others' roles. The judiciary must strive to work constructively with the other branches of government, but it must not hesitate to speak out when interference with the courts impedes judicial governance and accountability. This requires a sensitive balancing act. However, once the state's court systems develop and abide by the basic principles of judicial accountability, this will serve as a forceful reminder to the legislative and executive branches.

Rather than speaking in multiple and contradictory voices, the state's court system should exert efforts to establish working relationships and

---

[90] www.todayszaman.com/news-175904-former-president-sezers-vetoes-still-blocking-turkey.html

[91] www.todayszaman.com/news-195207-turkey-still-struggles-with-human-rights-violations.html

[92] ww.todayszaman.com/news-175132-tesev-report-law-supreme-neither-for-society-nor-judiciary.html

foster a culture of mutual understanding that reduces resistance, misunderstandings and systemic delays. This can be accomplished by arranging constructive discussions between parliamentary committees and judicial and legislative leaders. As appropriate, in public forums invited judges and legislators may exchange ideas in a continuing dialogue on collective issues. Coverage of such occasions by the media and even inviting foreign experts to these types of inter-branch exchanges on a regular basis would inform and improve the judicial, legislative and executive branches and also the public.

We need a judiciary that is neutral, reform-minded and committed to justice, progress and good governance. Then the legislative branch will have the final word on policy while the independent courts exercise the legitimate role of providing input for collective concerns and the consolidation of democratization and institutionalization. Public affairs offices need to work with the other branches of government and the media to educate them and the citizens about specific judicial decisions, performance and their role in the governmental system. Civic, academic and reform groups are indispensable in developing standards and defining issues. They help to develop long-term strategies to improve inter-branch relations and prevent and manage inter-branch conflicts.

The judicial branch will inevitably be subject to criticism for its actions. However, this should be welcomed in a free and open society. The judicial branch must articulate a clear vision of what it has to achieve to be fully accountable and demonstrate why the courts' ability to meet the public's expectations is dependent on the freedom to control and manage their own affairs. It must take every opportunity to communicate that message to its partners in government and civil society in order to develop a public declaration of the basic principles of judicial governance and accountability so that a just and developed Turkey can share its values, something many throughout the world are longing for.

Democracy: How to Participate and How Not to

June 16, 2009

I t appears that yet another anti-democratic "action plan" has been revealed. This one, it is claimed, emerged from the pen of a member of the Turkish Armed Forces (TSK). It apparently aimed to oust the democratically elected government and divide the ruling party. It also intended to undermine the work of a faith-based civil society movement in Turkey known as the Gülen Movement by making false accusations of terrorism and planting drugs and guns on movement participants.[93]

The evidence is still being investigated; there are claims and counter-claims at this stage. What we know already, however, is that this path is all too familiar to some in the TSK. We, the Turkish public, have become accustomed, though not resigned, to the idea that the military feels a need to protect the "regime" from any government of the day whose taste it does not savor. But this latest plot has an additional edge. In addition to the usual attack on the outer and most commonly acknowledged symbols of democracy, that is, a political party and the government of the day, it also clearly takes aim at a peaceful social initiative known as the Gülen Movement.

Planning a concerted attack on any movement that trains people for peaceful coexistence, a common sense of citizenship and inculcation of mutual respect and compromise means cutting at the root where democracy is developed and consolidated in civil society. But democracy is now the only viable political form in Turkey. People are working to modernize and consolidate democratic institutions in order to build a society where individual rights and freedom are respected and protected. To ensure this, civil initiatives are indispensable; in their activism, they define the limits of a pluralist and participatory democracy.

---

[93] www.todayszaman.com/news-178082-action-plan-sparks-fury-in-business-circles.html

The projects of the Gülen Movement serve society within the rules of the political system. No matter how their worldview or services might affect the political system, they do not disregard or infringe upon the rules of that system. They do not transgress legal and institutional boundaries. Civil society movements like the Gülen Movement contribute to the modernization of a political system and consolidation of civil society and pluralistic democracy. They alert people to the need for institutional reform. They raise people's consciousness of their rights and the definition of what participatory democracy is and can be. They encourage means and ends that are not confrontational, violent or coercive. They are grounded in reliable information and understanding through education and communication, and in freedom, collaboration and peace.

Yet, for the "action planners," it seems that any effort to consolidate participatory democracy is a target now. They are targeting civil and democratic initiatives because such social action reveals the negligence in the "regime" and the shadowy side of its dealings—its misuse of office, authority and resources. Undoubtedly, the action plan would serve the interests of the protectionist minority and subordinate civil society to their single way of understanding of democratic ideas and practice. Opposing any culturally diverse understanding, they aim to rule over all institutional and systemic decision-making processes or to alter constitutionally cot institutional power relationships as they see fit. To achieve this, they will stoop to all kinds of non-institutional, unlawful interventions in the political system. What is being advanced in this new "action plan" is not based on democratic procedure or political consensus. Like all such previous plans from this group, it is to be realized through partisan and violent means. This presents an absolute threat to the very structure of society. It is anti-democratic and anti-egalitarian. It leads to exploitation, radicalization, violent confrontation and corruption in society.

Political participation in a democracy aims directly at influencing the selection of government personnel and the actions of those personnel within the set legal boundaries and separation of powers. Any effort outside this conventional understanding of participatory democracy is exclusionary and ideological and serves ulterior motives and interests. If those behind this latest "action plan" merely intended some form of political participation, then the place to do this would not be from within the military but from within civil society and its representational room, the national Parliament. If military personnel wish to oppose decisions made in Parliament, to defend specific interests, to attempt to shift power relationships within the political system or to acquire influence over decisions, they must do it within the boundaries defined by the Constitution they claim to defend so ardently. They have first to resign from their military ranks and then participate in elections, or set up, head and participate in their own civil society movements. If the people elect them to Parliament, they can hold power and exert control over political decision making, make decisions in the name of society as a whole and impose those decisions, where necessary, through public means or state organizations. If the people work with them in their civil society movements, they will be validated and achieve their aims.

These "actions plans" cannot be reconciled with cultural, political and democratic integrity. They are nothing but residue of the fascist and communist regimes of the past.

The Left Does Not Do Right in Turkey

July 2, 2009

The main opposition party in Turkey has once more given a textbook example of how not to oppose the government in a participatory, liberal democracy. Following the latest legislative amendment passed by Parliament that any military officers planning a coup against a civilian government are to be prosecuted by civilian courts,[94] the opinions and explanations offered by the Republican People's Party (CHP) offer little to the development of accountability in a mature democracy. Democracy can be seen as a history of social struggles over the expansion of political rights, freedom and civil or public space. It is the story of the transformation of human wrongs into human rights. In this transformation, opposition parties play an important role in challenging the constraints of the democratization project. Opposition parties have been instrumental in transforming dictatorial, authoritarian or military reigns into effective democracies. Opposition parties are critical in expanding the space for the rule of law, respect for human rights and accountable governance.

While opposition parties in contemporary mature democracies play these roles, the situation in Turkey is quite different. This is primarily because the leading "opposition" party, the CHP, is so identified with the protectionist, elitist bureaucracy, the legislature, the judiciary and the army.[95] This identification detaches the CHP from the masses and prevents it from gaining and holding power democratically. It condemns the CHP to remain a weak and aggressive minority party, rather than a democratically constructive opposition.

The latest parliamentary event proves the lack of internal democracy in the CHP. It shows how the bosses within the party compromise the party's key responsibility for consolidating democracy. First, CHP depu-

---

[94] www.todayszaman.com/news-208498-constitutional-amendment-touches-untouchable-military.html

[95] www.todayszaman.com/news-180757-appealing-to-constitutional-court-to-annul-civil-judiciary-will-be-end-of-chp.html

ties confirmed a legislative amendment. Later, they claimed that they had made a mistake, that they had been caught unawares and even that the wording of the two lines of the amendment was difficult to understand at first sight. But the opposition leader and members had debated the amendment of the legislation vigorously in Parliament and during the Select Committee process.[96] There can be no doubt that the legislation received their careful consideration. It seems clear now that those high up in the party did not like the way their members voted.[97]

It is important for the leading opposition party, the CHP, to develop and become a champion of democracy, human rights and good governance. It needs to supply policies and viable legislation. As they have not done so, the party has been unable to win power for decades.[98] The party needs to engage in a critical internal debate: How can the party recover when it is viewed so unfavorably by much of the public?

For Turkey to boost democratic governance, the rule of law and respect for human rights, effective opposition parties are essential. However, the parties must take lessons from the experiences of constructive opposition within mature democracies. They do not need to reinvent the wheel. They must not repeat the undemocratic errors they have led Turkey into in the past. Otherwise, they will continue to enable the protectionist elite to dominate the political space and monopolize the administration. This will result in "no fundamental change" from the republican despotism experienced in the '40s and '50s.

Party activism should build institutions and shape public politics, policies and laws that impact the rights and welfare of the community. It is important for leaders to keep their ears open to what the public is saying. Several recent surveys, like that of the Turkish Economic and Social Studies Foundation (TESEV), have indicated that the overwhelming majority of the Turkish public does not want any more military coups or plots.[99]

---

[96] www.todayszaman.com/news-207891-constitutional-amendment-marathon-begins-with-tension.html

[97] www.todayszaman.com/news-179556-european-union-backs-cmk-amendment-on-military-courts.html

[98] The CHP (Republican People's Party) has not won an election outright since 1961, but took part in a number of coalitions in the 1970s.

[99] www.todayszaman.com/news-180336-tesev-report-calls-for-civilian-scrutiny-on-security-forces.html; www.todayszaman.com/news-314685-tesev-report-turkeys-army-police-mit-need-reform.html

Protecting coup planners and makers and backtracking on a constitutional amendment that would enable their prosecution by civilian courts will not do any good for democratization in Turkey or in the CHP itself.

Opposition parties should criticize the ruling party's policies, ideas and programs and offer alternatives. However, they should also recognize and respect the authority of the elected government. This is possible only if the opposition party is committed to the values of tolerance, cooperation and compromise. Democracies recognize that consensus building requires compromise and tolerance. As Mahatma Gandhi argued, "Intolerance is itself a form of violence and an obstacle to the growth of a true democratic spirit."

Good democratic governance is guaranteed by the separation of powers in a modern state—the executive, the legislature and the judiciary. The separation of powers is designed to build institutions that guard against arbitrary rule via a system of checks and balances. The biggest danger to this separation of powers comes from seeking alternatives to these. In the case of Turkey this danger arises from the greed for power and has previously taken form in ideologically motivated military personnel overthrowing the democratically elected government. It is perpetuated by protecting such coup planners and makers from civil prosecution.

The opposition in Turkey should learn that their role is not only to "oppose" by all and any means; they have to learn to play a more constructive role in holding the government to account and causing it to adopt more beneficial, productive and universal projects and proposals.

Turkey from Negarchy to Democracy

November 5, 2009

The junta formation within the General Staff and its relations with self-serving interest groups and the judicial bureaucracy are aimed at negarchy in Turkey.

Negarchy is a form of governance between anarchy and hierarchy in which the self-interests of the separate powers cancel one another out by indirect yet interdependent means. Negarchy maintains the status quo, which serves the self-interest of groups within the system. They negate one another owing to their material interests or their respective privileged resources. They divert democratic and human rights and impose restrictions on others. Restrictions are disguised as legal, judicial or constitutional despite being undemocratic and repressive. They are directed against those who would directly, indirectly or symbolically challenge the group's self-assumed ownership of the state and public resources. If any of the strategies of their own creation that they readily use against others are deployed against them to limit their power or potential affluence, they are unwilling to be subjected to them and come up with contingency plans for smear campaigns, threats, coercion and violence.

Documents sent by an officer who actively took part in the junta formation[100] have stirred civilian outcry across the social and political spectrum.[101] Experts and people of common sense are united in calling for all organs of the state to strictly adhere to the functions assigned them by the Constitution. The overt disrespect and tendency to oppose parliamentary governance that we see among members of the judiciary and military violate the rules and conventions of institutions and the principle of the separation of powers. The dark relationships of negarchy systematically undermine the credibility of judicial and military bodies in the eyes of

---

[100] "Action Plan to Fight Reactionaryism"
[101] www.todayszaman.com/news-191233-the-fulltext-of-informant-officers-letter-over-military-plot.html

the people. The correct conduct of the judiciary and military, inside and outside the bar chambers, courts and military headquarters, is a prerequisite for the smooth and effective functioning of the parliamentary system.

The government and legislators are being encouraged to re-establish the faith of the people in democratic institutions, and the judiciary and military are being urged to purge all members who have taken part in plots and juntas. The members of the legislature and judiciary who have not taken part in the plots and interest schemes should be proactive and exercise control over the military; they should act in unison to achieve the objectives of the Constitution. People now want to see evidence of work and service ethics in the state bureaucracy. Any failure to tame the cunning will allow the contravention of the separation of powers to continue, weaken existing checks and balances and provide for the minority through the oppression of the majority.

The protectionist bureaucracy in the system is difficult to remove completely as they have "friends" nestled in the higher judiciary. A new constitution and reform-minded bureaucrats appointed by Parliament are needed. We need well-functioning parliamentary committees which exercise legally defined regulatory powers.

Keeping the public informed about amendments can help prevent such negarchy. It also prevents interest groups, especially in the media, from interfering with due process in government and the legislature. This sharing of information also keeps the government and legislature somewhat in check. The press thus cannot easily affect public opinion in ways that are contrary to the spirit of separation of powers.

In a system of checks and balances, the judicial branch has the right to say that something is unconstitutional but should not take the place of the legislature and the military. The principle of separation of powers has been most frequently endangered through official misbehavior married to claims of defending the regime or national security. In such cases, accountability is not easy or automatic. However, potential abuses of power may be deterred. In democratic government, when the legislative authority or parliament is united or reaches a consensus by majority, it can legitimately be dominant over other branches. There is an important distinction between constitutional violations—acting in excess of statutory authority—and the violation of the separation of powers in the Constitution.

The principle of separation of powers is problematic and full of statutory and constitutional defects in Turkey. In the latest case of the democratic initiative to resolve the internal strife in southeastern Turkey, interest groups within the judiciary have initiated a legal case against the prosecutors and judges who released the Kurdish militants who surrendered to Turkish authorities.[102] The interest group, the Judges and Prosecutors Association (YARSAV), is attempting to convict and punish the government and supporters of the initiative.[103] This group is usurping the powers of the executive and the legislature. To prevent such abuse in future, the new constitution should give the legislative branch additional powers over the executive, judicial and military so that any individual can be impeached by the legislative branch to consolidate democracy rather than negarchy.

[102] www.todayszaman.com/news-190926-photo-of-the-week34-pkk-members-surrender-amid-enthusiastic-celebrations.html

[103] Shortly after the events on which I comment here YARSAV's top court rapporteur resigned by means of a petition highly critical of the organization: www.todayszaman.com/news-192774-top-court-rapporteur-resigns-from-yarsav-due-to-political-stance.html.

Civil-Military Relations, 'Regime' Stability and Democratization

November 19, 2009

For the first time in Turkish history, an overwhelming majority of civilians and some higher-ranking officers from the military are dismissing the option of military intervention as a viable solution in Turkish politics. This leads to the question: What are the conditions that have either inhibited or fostered the formation of interventionist coalitions so far, that is, the alliances between military and civilian actors that precede a coup d'état?

The Turkish political system has suffered constant instability since the 1960s in almost regular ten-year cycles. Various aspects of civilian-military relations lead dominant groups, political actors and the armed forces to collaborate and carry out military interventions.

There is a plethora of explanations of military interventionism in Latin American countries, but objective research into the causes of similar events in Turkey is lacking. Discussions of civil military relations in Turkey have two main features, both tending to justify military interventions: First, a republican historical scope that focuses only on military preroga-tives, the peculiar authority of the military to "protect" the state and the regime, and second, a one-dimensional analysis of any socio-political con-juncture that ends in a putsch. The latter type of analysis tends to empha-size the "necessity" of the putsch.

Comments often emphasize the necessity of the role of the military in the process of republican state formation and the democratic transition in the 1920s and '30s, as well as new roles assumed because of later armed struggle with terrorists and separatists. But now the most urgent ques-tion is whether the military is re-emerging as a threat to the democratic regime and to political gains made as a result of democratic openings and the government's efforts for accession to the European Union.

Turkey has never experienced an era of military subordination to civil authorities. Civil authorities have come to consider the military to be a political faction—almost an opposition party. All political actors, especially the Republican People's Party (CHP), excluding the periods when Bülent Ecevit led it, have welcomed the military's participation in politics. Thus, the armed forces have exerted significant influence on successive civilian regimes. At certain conjunctures, military participation extended not only to military control of the state but also to binding "suggestions" to governments that were issued through the National Security Council (MGK), an institution formalized in the wake of an earlier coup.

Democracy in periods of civilian rule under the strict supervision of the MGK was far from consolidated. Those periods were characterized by graft, embezzlement, misuse of public resources, persecution and unsolved political assassinations. Rather than a democracy, the regime has become consolidated in the sense that political and economic actors routinely choose to pursue their objectives and interests only in liaison with and with the tacit approval of the military officers.

A historical overview of civil-military relations helps to reveal the conditions linked with military interventions. There are multiple reasons for the peculiar complexity of societal or military-oriented accounts of modern Turkish history, but the prevalent explanations tend to underestimate the importance for the democratization of subordination of the armed forces to civilian authority. Also, they overestimate the interests, perceptions and relevance of the armed forces as an autonomous and primary force in Turkey, ignoring the military's undemocratic and unlawful liaisons with particular interest and ideological groups.

Strategies which might possibly overcome the tendency for coup-making and analyses of the institutional aspects of civil-military relations are rarely or never examined in the public forum. These would include the empowerment of the Ministry of Defense, legislation restricting the role of the armed forces and the building of legislative capacities to oversee defense matters and expenses. There is little attempt to define the political and economic prerequisites that should allow civilian officials to exert control over the military or, in other words, the necessity of military subordination to civilian authorities.

Revelations about the schemes of the latest junta[104] in the General Staff show that institutional mechanisms of civilian control are neces-

---

[104] The military personnel engaged in the "Action Plan to Fight Reactionaryism."

sary but insufficient conditions for the preservation of democracy. For stability and legitimacy in Turkey, the armed forces should be under the institutional control of the legislature. Otherwise, the military interferes with the government's right to rule, its ability to address basic problems confronting the political system and its capacity to implement solutions. However, institutional reform may not produce overnight military officers likely to obey civilian governments for as long as soldiers consider the civilian authorities secondary and unresponsive to "threats" to the nation or regime.

Recent events prove that civilian control must reinforce democracy. Unless Turkey now urgently sets about building a more stable governmental system and Parliament passes constitutional amendments that are equally observed by the ruling and opposition parties, the military will no doubt continue to interfere with the democratic process on the pretext of internal and external challenges.

Turkey's Democratization Knocks at Junta's Bedroom Door

January 7, 2010

Turkey has been going through rapid changes and developments recently. However, defenders of the status quo seem to have been caught in such mental disarray this time that their responses to these developments are beyond any reason or legal bounds. This will definitely not contribute positively to the development of full democracy, the rule of law and civil society in Turkey.

One controversial player in the Kurdish issue, the Kurdish Communities Union (KCK), rather than contributing to stopping the bloodshed, resolving the conflict and speeding up the process of acquisition of cultural and political rights, is blocking peacemaking efforts with further attacks on military posts and personnel and provoking and intensifying violent street clashes with security forces. Yesterday, the KCK leadership gave interviews in which it stated openly that it opposes the probe and searches by a civilian judge at the Special Forces Command of the Turkish Armed Forces (TSK).[105] The searches could shed light on many clandestine dealings and acts of the deep state, the junta and its JİTEM arm, all of which are implicated in 17,000 extrajudicial killings and the escalation of discord and unrest in the Southeast.[106] So how can it be that Kurdistan Workers' Party (PKK) and KCK "rogue elements" from terror bases outside Turkey oppose the probes and searches? Have they something to hide?

Another important element of the status quo, or more correctly, the deep state, in Turkey is the Supreme Board of Judges and Prosecutors (HSYK). HSYK members who have already been photographed and wire-tapped and implicated in plots keep on talking negatively about the ongoing trials and filing complaints against prosecutors and judges who are

---

[105] www.hurhaber.com/karayilan-dan-darbe-plani-iddialari/haber-244169; www.aktifhaber.com/pkknin-balyoz-rahatsizligi-268866h.htm

[106] www.todayszaman.com/news-197808-anti-drug-agency-jitem-dealt-drugs.html

striving to investigate coup attempts and dealings of the junta and terrorists. Their interference in the ongoing trials of Ergenekon and other
assassination efforts are doubtless unlawful and unconstitutional. However, the HSYK's efforts are either hopeless last attempts to protect themselves, their privileges and colleagues, or confident, well-calculated tactics
because they have the conviction that whatever happens they will be
protected by their ideological confreres in the HSYK who are nested in
the judiciary. We will see.

Defenders of the status quo within the media are still publishing stories that aim to distort the facts about the ongoing judicial probes and
searches and mislead the public. They publish or broadcast the most unlikely scenarios, fabrications and conjectures about the trials, arrests and
searches being conducted by the courts. Interestingly, they also oppose
the searches conducted at the Special Forces Command, arguing that this
is the master bedroom of the state and should not be violated by civilian
courts and authorities.[107]

Moreover, while the TSK denies the existence of any unit by the
name of JİTEM,[108] further revelations are being published by its found-
ers, retired personnel, henchmen and assassins.[109] More payrolls, signed
documents, correspondence on official letterhead, guidelines, admis-
sions or confessions are sent to the investigative authorities and press
every day. As the TSK still does not admit its existence and operations,
further revelations seem likely to follow and embarrass the military
authorities who are trying to defend the members and units that are
implicated. Defenses such as the claim that one colonel and one major
know all the state secrets and must not share them even with their commanders or military units are far from convincing.[110] How do these two

---

[107] www.radikal.com.tr/turkiye/kozmik_oda_ozel_yasam_alani-973007

[108] www.todayszaman.com/news-197202-gendarmerie-general-command-also-de-
nies-jitem-existence.html

[109] www.todayszaman.com/news-150942-jitems-existence-finally-exposed.html;
www.todayszaman.com/news-198677-ergenekon-suspect-sacan-confirms-
jitems-existence.html; www.todayszaman.com/news-165245-former-member-
describes-jitems-reign-of-terror; yenisafak.com.tr/gundem-haber/doguda-jitem-
cilerle-birlikte-calistim-14.01.2010-235359; yenisafak.com.tr/gundem-haber/
jitemin-varligindan-suphem-yok--02.01.2010-232640

[110] www.radikal.com.tr/turkiye/kozmik_oda_davasi_yolda-1122580; www.enson-
haber.com/gundem/247008/kozmik-odanin-sirri.html

decide what a state secret is? How can assassinations and plots alleged to have been conducted by the junta or JİTEM be known only by these two officers, who were themselves caught red-handed preparing further plots and assassinations? Why is the TSK still defending such personnel and not handing them over for due investigation and prosecution?

Turkish society and citizens are not the same as they were in the bygone 1950s or '60s. For cultural, democratic and political rights, neither Kurds nor Turks need such people, organizations or heinous plots. We need alternative voices, new peaceful democratic organizations and proper opposition parties to establish and consolidate cultural and human rights, democracy, the rule of law and civil society.

Turkey needs constitutional changes in line with EU accession and a new constitution that can put all the rogue elements in order. We need cultural rights and freedom, proper opposition parties and the supremacy of law to be able to investigate the loss of the precious lives of thousands of people and billions of dollars of state and other human resources for decades. Nothing should remain concealed behind bogus claims of "state secrets" known only to two low-ranking officers and defended by the vested interests and criminal elements in the status quo.

Military-Bureaucratic Shadow Falls over Democratization in Turkey

January 14, 2010

There is a Turkish proverb that says one who falls into water will attempt to clutch a snake so as not to sink and drown. The English proverb, which may be more familiar to some readers, has the drowning man clutching at a straw. Either could describe what we are seeing in Turkey, as those who oppose democratization and changes to the status quo thrash about noisily in the water while sinking beneath the waves.

Their latest cries are complaints of civilian rather than military tutelage, civilian rather than military coup, civilian fascism, institutional clashes, the Putinization of Recep Tayyip Erdoğan, internal civilian threat. The language they use to frame events grows wilder, the last throes of those wishing to maintain their interest in an undemocratic protectionist status.[111]

No one disputes the skill in their language use. However, the quality of the argument reveals the true intentions of the defenders of the protectionist, undemocratic status quo. The overwhelming majority of the people, journalists and intellectuals do not believe there is any clash between government or state institutions. They do, however, see a clear clash between democratic and despotic principles, a clash between civil society and governance and an authoritarian, class-based military-bureaucratic tutelary regime.

In the recent past, we heard these same opponents of democratization talk of threats to the regime, national security or state security; they spoke of fundamentalism, Shariah, neighborhood pressure, of examples from Iran and Khomeini or Malaysia. Now they are bandying about words

---

[111] www.todayszaman.com/news-198774-civilian-tutelage-arguments-found-groundless.html; www.todayszaman.com/news-200227-ilicak-civilian-dictator-ship-debate-is-unsubstantiated.html

like coup, fascism or Hitler. Their examples reveal how desperate they feel faced by likely European Union amendments, a civilian Constitution and further democratic developments. Rather than discussing the process of democratization and establishing the rule of law in Turkey or presenting constructive opposition for the betterment of projects, public services and governance, the defenders of the status quo are coming up with self-contradictory ideas and discourse.

Political power is generally understood to mean the capacity of certain groups to exert privileged control over the processes of political decision making. Groups with political power make normative decisions in the name of society as a whole and impose those decisions where necessary. Political participation comes in the form of political demands: the first kind of demand is about how exchange is regulated between particular groups within the society; the second kind calls for the modification or adaptation of the rules of the political system so as to widen or restrict access to it; the third kind of demand is about maintaining or changing the mode of production and distribution of social resources. Political participation is also the defense of specific interests, an attempt to shift power relationships within the political system, to acquire influence over decisions.

The defenders of military tutelage and the status quo in Turkey know full well what political power is and how to use it but need reminding of the desirable properties of democracy.

Generally, if a political party comes to power through a democratic election, it is given the right to run and modify certain things within the law and Constitution in line with the majority vote and interests. However, in the case of the Justice and Development Party (AK Party) government and the election of President Abdullah Gül, the defenders of the military bureaucratic regime opposed the majority's choice expressed through the vote and pushed Turkey into crises and a waste of time, energy and resources. In the current legal investigations of the formation of a military junta and the preparation of plots against the public within the Turkish Armed Forces (TSK), concerted efforts by opposition parties and deep-state elements in the judiciary and the media to block the investigation run completely counter to any democratic norms.

These elements oppose change through individuals nested in the bureaucratic cadre and through their voices in the media. For example, the latest remarks from the head of the Press Council about the legal intimidation and sentencing of a journalist who was investigating the Ergenekon and Cage plots are beyond all reason. Incredibly, in a national radio interview, he argued that journalists avail themselves of too much freedom in investigating and writing and that journalists are transgressing their boundaries.[112]

While Turkey is trying to pass to democratic civilian rule, establish a new Constitution and recognize the cultural and human rights of all its communities and groups, trying to break the shackles which have made it an authoritarian and inward-looking country, trying to play an appropriate role in a volatile region and offer intellectual, academic and cultural richness to global society, we have only one request. Like Diogenes speaking to Alexander the Great, we ask the defenders of the military and bureaucratic exclusivist regime to remove their shadow from us and allow the people a place in the sun.

---

[112] Oktay Eksi, a member of Parliament at the time of going to press, in an interview on Samanyolu Haber.

To Reform the Judiciary in Turkey

May 20, 2010

R ecently released voice recordings of a discussion between two members of the Supreme Court of Appeals reveal more about the mentality of the judicial and military bureaucracy.

The two judges talk about their plan to free Erzincan Chief Public Prosecutor İlhan Cihaner, Colonel Dursun Çiçek and several others on trial for being involved in a criminal deep-state gang. In the recording, one judge tells another that he will become the head of the Supreme Court of Appeals if he ensures that the two cases against Cihaner and Çiçek are merged and that they are freed from prison. They label some members of the Supreme Court of Appeals as "cowards" for not acting to save Cihaner.[113]

The newly revealed voice recordings provide yet more evidence for the Turkish people of the contradictions that prevail among the state bureaucracy; how inconsistently the judiciary deals with different groups and the reasons for that inconsistency. These events show once more that in a situation of lawlessness it is hard for any administration to pursue successful judicial reform. No judicial reform with such officials in place could establish an independent and effective judiciary.

During the latest debates on constitutional amendments there appeared a real chance that, due to the opportunities brought about the social and political movements and changes in social settings, judicial reform will succeed. If not a fully independent, at least an effective judiciary is a reasonable expectation for 21st century Turkey.

This has not come to pass so far for many reasons—previous military interventions and constitutions drafted under military tutelage changed administrations but not the relationship between the state, civil society

---

[113] www.todayszaman.com/news-211101-ergin-investigation-into-voice-recording-ongoing.html; www.todayszaman.com/news-211598-judges-in-recordings-should-withdraw-from-cihaner-case.html

and individual. Due to political dilemmas in subsequent periods and some politicians' lust for power and eye for short-term gains, the reform-minded have not been able to reach the goals they set for themselves. This was not because governments did not want to carry through on their promises, but because of structural problems and obstacles installed after each military intervention. Judicial reforms became piecemeal, producing an ineffective and partial judiciary. Reforms did not amount to positive action for rights and freedoms, consolidating civil society, but were organized and interpreted in such a way as to protect the interests of powerful actors taking advantage of the political process. Public and academic discussions of the judicial process and the execution of parliamentary decrees or amendments in Turkey often touch on the problem of "double sovereignty" and the dualities of the republican elitists vs. reformists, Kemalists vs. religiously conservative, secularists vs. religious. But the dilemmas of judicial reform which are central to the discussion attract no serious or formal consideration by the bureaucratic judiciary and their friends in the media.

Yet the complexities and contradictions of incremental and systemic reform must be confronted. For example, reform-minded civil society groups, academics and journalists have drawn attention to the lack of finality in the litigation process, and the resulting weakness of incentives to settle. In addition, ethics training for judges will do little to obviate underlying motivations for receipt or solicitation of bribes and promotion in a corrupt system, as is discussed by the two judges in the voice recording. The appointment of a few new judges to the Supreme Board of Judges and Prosecutors (HSYK) and other courts will do little to alter the corporatist culture of a career judiciary.

Currently, our legal system in Turkey lags far behind developments in the global arena in technical standardization, professional rule production, human rights, intra-organizational regulation in multinational enterprises, contracting, arbitration, and legal pluralism. These legal frameworks have worldwide validity independent of the law of nation-states. But the Turkish judiciary, in the grasp of ideological and power-hungry judges and prosecutors, as we have just witnessed, has blithely ignored the consequences of globalization in the legal and judicial arenas.

Reform will involve considerable investment of money, time, social capital and non-partisan political efforts to increase the efficiency, accountability and independence of the judiciary, at least to the level of the developed democracies of the EU or other developed democracies of the indus-trialized world. Legal NGOs and local, national, and international legal institutions of legal professionals must be encouraged to contribute to discussions and amendment of legal practice. In addition, there needs to be adequate study of why and how judges and prosecutors' sense of jus-tice becomes ideological and how this can be avoided, and of how judi-cial corruption and the disenchantment of the masses with the judiciary can be prevented. The current effective immunity of high-level officials must be removed so that any irregularities open the way to suspension and early retirement or even due punishment. Society needs to be orga-nized in accord with individual rights, majority rule, and the rule of law. The rule of law must be a true guide rather than a mere hindrance, illu-sion or myth.

Above and Beyond the Law: No Reform for the Turkish Judiciary

June 17, 2010

Many intellectuals, scholars, jurists and legal professionals have called on Constitutional Court member Fulya Kantarcıoğlu to resign after the content of a telephone conversation she had with former Justice Minister Seyfi Oktay was revealed.[114]

Oktay's conversations were being monitored legally, and he was briefly detained two weeks ago as part of the investigation into Ergenekon, a clandestine gang charged with plotting to overthrow the government.

Former Republican People's Party (CHP) leader Deniz Baykal called and told Oktay to "do something about" the reform package before Parliament. Oktay then called Kantarcıoğlu to intervene in the court hearing initiated by the CHP about the reform package. Kantarcıoğlu, as a Constitutional Court member, should not have discussed a case that would come before her. In the conversation she also made reference to the Constitutional Court's annulment of a law that would have lifted a headscarf ban on university campuses. The language both speakers used indicated their clear bias about the case and about the possibility of the court issuing a stay of execution on the amendment package.

Kantarcıoğlu's colleagues and others called on her to withdraw from the case and resign to preserve the principle of a fair trial, to maintain the dignity of the judicial office, to avoid impropriety and the appearance of impropriety, and to preserve the ethical conduct that allows public confidence in judicial independence, impartiality, integrity and competence. Kantarcıoğlu retorted that she has been a jurist for 40 years and a member of the Constitutional Court for 15 years: "Do you think I cannot evaluate what constitutes an appearance of impropriety?"

---

[114] www.todayszaman.com/news-213243-jurists-call-on-controversial-high-court-member-to-resign.html

This is not the first time the Turkish public has come to know about such unlawful, unconstitutional interventions in serious cases. The actions of some bar associations, the Supreme Council of Judges and Prosecutors (HSYK), the Judges and Prosecutors Association (YARSAV), and their associates, individually and collectively, have been seen to contradict the principles of justice and the rule of law.

Many of the same issues occur in judiciaries throughout the world. However, our top judiciary has not become part of full or partial reform and resists learning from the reform and development in Central and Eastern Europe, Asia, the Far East and South America.[115]

The crisis in our legal system can be partially but not wholly attributed to court operations being stifled by rising costs and caseloads, declining productivity, an inequitable distribution of resources or lack of modern management mechanisms. In fact, in recent years, court budgets have increased, Turkey's judicial complexes have improved, and the government has promoted more judges to reduce the workload. We can now make the ambivalent boast of having the single largest court complex in Europe and super judges who can pass judgment on 1,500 cases a day.[116]

The real crisis, however, is caused by judges who place themselves above and beyond the law. News coverage is replete with the cases of individuals, with the content of wiretaps ordered by courts dealing with cases of plots and coups, and with stories of judges and prosecutors acting in a wholly unaccountable and unjust manner. Under the guise of judicial independence, but concealing patronage and cronyism, these judges have often unduly influenced government authorities, political parties and the passage of the amendments aimed at EU accession. We are overly dependent on ideologically motivated judges who are often used as instruments to advance the interests of the protectionist elite and military bureaucracy.

Many challenges will remain as long as procedural delays or idiosyncratic interpretations undermine the administration of justice, as exemplified in Kantarcıoğlu's remarks that we cannot know and practice law

---

[115] www.todayszaman.com/news-233827-high-judiciary-does-complete-about-face-on-reforms.html; www.todayszaman.com/news-221276-judicial-overload-clogs-system-judges-want-no-change.html

[116] www.todayszaman.com/news-231760-draft-bill-to-reform-cumbersome-high-judiciary-finalized.html

better than she and her cohorts. However, the passage of the latest constitutional amendment,[117] albeit limited, is a significant step toward overcoming these problems. With adequate judicial education, advanced training, sufficient emphasis on judicial ethics and by learning from the professionalism and effectiveness of judiciaries throughout the developing world, we may continue to promote the rule of law and full democracy instead of the present juristocracy.

We should establish a strong framework for an independent, accountable and effective judiciary. Otherwise, judges who act as if they are above and beyond the law will continue to diminish public trust in the fairness and efficiency of the judicial system, and society will be further plagued with corruption. Without an independent judiciary and improvement in judicial ethics, the right to a fair trial and other fundamental rights, democratic governance, economic development and social equality will remain illusory.

---

[117] www.todayszaman.com/news-207070-constitutional-amendment-package-will-result-in-changes-to-107-laws.html

Crises and Accountability: Civil, Military and Judicial

July 22, 2010

I t is not news that Turkey is at present going through many crises. However, we still see little sign of individuals or institutions being held accountable for the incompetence, incapacity, malfunctions and dysfunctions within the system that are causing these crises and failures.

While ostensibly ironing out the dysfunctions, imbalances, paralyses and blockages in the system and subsystems, the authorities themselves always manage to end up less affected and less accountable. Meanwhile, society pays the price. We can offer several clear examples of this process.

Increasing terrorist attacks on military units and posts and all the lives lost indicate that commanding officers lack the skills, qualities and ability to protect their own soldiers and the nation. If they have what it takes to complete their task, then it means that they are not doing their job conscientiously.[118]

As for the executive, that is, the government and Parliament, the crises indicate that with the authority granted to it by law, the Constitution and the public, the executive branch does not have or does not exert the necessary power to supervise or run the military and the chief of General Staff. So the government and Parliament lack the ability, character or strength required to govern the nation and the system and its subsystems such as the military.

Turning to the judiciary, we see that even when the executive attempts to exert its power, it is blocked by the ideological judiciary. Thus, the executive remains unable to perform adequately, properly or normally. As we see in the latest cases, the higher judiciary and courts characteristically interfere to protect the tutelage system and their fiefdoms established around the Supreme Board of Judges and Prosecutors (HSYK) and

---

[118] www.todayszaman.com/news-214268-army-announces-new-border-units-amid-negligence-allegations.html; www.todayszaman.com/news-216260-professional-units-should-serve-along-border-says-erdogan.html

the Judges and Prosecutors Association (YARSAV). And so crises arise from the system's failure to function properly or normally because of a fault or bad design or an irregularity in the functioning of its parts.[119]

With every passing day the public learns more about incompetence, negligence, misdeeds and abuse of power and position, especially by military personnel. The latest revelation of the wire communications between two air forces officers and an admiral may be the last straw. An air forces officer was recorded asking a pilot to shoot down their Herons (unmanned aerial vehicles) or change their flight plans because they were causing too much damage to a group of Kurdistan Workers' Party (PKK) terrorists, whom he referred to as "our men." For three years, despite being informed of the event by the National Intelligence Organization (MİT), the chief of General Staff seems to have done next to nothing about this except cover it up.[120] It is an open case of treason and collaboration with terrorists, but for years no one has been held accountable for this or similar events. In any other country, a much lesser event would have led to investigations, resignations and prosecutions.

The financial and economic dealings of the Turkish Armed Forces (TSK) are also problematic. Tomorrow, the case of the Turkish Armed Forces Assistance Center (OYAK) will be raised before Parliament. OYAK, the largest pension fund and the third-largest conglomerate in Turkey, is still unaccountable for its investments in many sectors, such as steel, logistics, automotive, trade, cement, insurance and banking. It benefits from state subsidiaries, has certain privileges and a monopoly on certain fields and tender bids, but is still unaccountable to and even unmonitored by civilian authorities.[121] OYAK does not accept a recent court verdict that stipulates it has to comply with the Law on Public Procurement and has therefore turned to Parliament to request a renewal of an exemption from the legislation. It has enjoyed this exemption for the last 50 years. This case highlights the imbalances and breakdowns between the parts of the

---

[119] www.todayszaman.com/news-181540-all-eyes-on-hsyk-as-deliberations-continue-over-appointment-list.html

[120] www.todayszaman.com/news-216178-air-forces-officer-asks-to-down-herons-to-save-pkk-terrorists.html

[121] www.todayszaman.com/news-218447-turkish-military-nurtures-an-economic-leviathan.html

system and will show which is superior—the law or hidden agreements between the government, other parties and the TSK.

All events like these, similar disaggregation of the system, all break-downs of the functional and integrative mechanisms of relations in one sector of the system or another, and paralyses or blockages therein, pro-voke crises. In all cases, we the public pay for the crises while the highest authorities maintain their status and privileges. This provokes a reaction, disgust and dismay in those who seek to correct the imbalance that has taken place in the system.

However, the public never forgets the wrongdoers, injustices and atrocities it witnesses in so much loss of human life and state resources and in such malfunction within the system. Sooner or later the public calls to account the culprits and teaches them a lesson. In their arrogance and willful neglect some authorities may delude themselves that they will escape the repercussions of their abuse of power and position. But history is full of examples of the fall from grace and power of heedless rulers.

Civilian and Military Readiness after the Referendum

August 12, 2010

T hree recent events preoccupy the Turkish public and politicians: The Supreme Military Council (YAŞ) meeting over the promotions of generals[122]—some of whom are suspects in plots and coup cases, the referendum about the constitution, and increasing violence from the terrorist organization PKK (the Kurdistan Workers' Party).

These developments prompt the question: Are our civilian authorities and the new military bodies ready and equipped for the socio-political implications of these developments, or will they only start to think about remedies and solutions for any undesired and undesirable consequences once the life and destiny of the whole nation has been badly affected?

The result of the September 12 referendum will be constitutionally binding. As the ideologically motivated members of the Constitutional Court did not allow the legislature to enact the amendments, they are being submitted directly to the popular vote as an alternative to adoption by the legislature. The referendum's socio-political effects will be powerful because changes to the constitution will affect the future policy and action of any ruling party and opposition.

The referendum is a measure to stop the adversaries of constitutional reform and democratization from slowing politics and parliament down. It is an invitation for citizens' direct participation in building stability, democracy and prosperity. The constitutional amendments will pass if there are more yes votes than no votes. A "yes" vote promises to reduce political stagnation, systemic blockages and conflict. Certain decisions will be taken out of the hands of the legislature and judiciary. They will be determined by the people's will, directly expressed. Voters are

---

[122] The August reshuffle period is when military officers are promoted or retire. Around this time, so-called national security threats, and faith-inspired movements or communities are always made headlines by some likely-to-be-retired generals.

already giving the impression that they are less driven by transient whims than by careful deliberation of the common good.

Although the three opposition parties have asked their voters for a blanket "no" vote, seeing dissent, resignations and counter arguments coming from among the ranks and leading figures of those parties,[123] many voters seem likely to make a "yes" decision, despite the parties' campaigns of propaganda and personalities. The combined attempts by the opposition parties and the members of Judges and Prosecutors Association (YARSAV) to convince citizens' groups to reject the amendments[124] have degenerated into a sloppy and desperate mishmash of poor argumentation and tactics.

Meanwhile, terrorist attacks on military and security personnel and outposts and attempts to foment ethnic clashes[125] in various regions are not coincidental. They indicate that deep state forces, the Ergenekon terror organization, putschist generals and their PKK subcontractor intend to sabotage the referendum and the elections that should come a year later. The hand of the putschists in the military has not been weakened: the general who worked with websites spreading propaganda against the government and civil society, propaganda later used as 'evidence' in the closure case against the AK Party, is still a force commander.[126] The traditions of the military are still defiantly claimed to be superior to the law, parliament and the civilian administration.

Although it is an important stage in Turkey's democratization, the referendum is not a cure-all. The military is still not accounting for failing to act against terrorist attacks in July despite intelligence provided by Her-

---

[123] www.todayszaman.com/news-215978-mhp-leader-kicks-off-no-campaign-for-september-referendum.html; www.todayszaman.com/news-215649-stances-made-clear-ahead-of-sept-12-referendum.html

[124] www.todayszaman.com/news-221495-news-analysis-referendum-results-to-have-dramatic-impact-on-higher-judiciary.html

[125] www.todayszaman.com/news-198078-rising-discrimination-in-society-rings-alarm-bells.html; www.todayszaman.com/news-217611-11-arrested-in-inegol-after-suspicious-ethnic-clash.html; www.todayszaman.com/news-213923-strategist-nihat-ali-ozcan-ethnic-clashes-possible-in-turkey.html

[126] www.todayszaman.com/news-208960-propaganda-websites-used-defense-ministry-ips.html; www.todayszaman.com/news-294759-general-says-basbug-knew-about-propaganda-websites.html

ons to 30 security units throughout every moment of the attacks.[127] Those who have planned and condoned coups have still to be called to account. The torture, abuse, rights violations and extra-judicial killings surrounding past and present plots are still an issue for democratization, freedom and accountability.

In addition, there is a clear lack of sincerity in the PKK's strategy of simultaneously calling a cease-fire and claiming autonomy and independence in a part of Turkey. This will ensure not peace but more ethnic tension and military intervention in the region. It is an invitation to escalate the conflict rather than pursuing a civilian and democratic solution based upon the wishes of the majority of the Kurdish citizens of Turkey. This can only result in the further meddling of generals in politics.

We await the imminent hand-over speeches by the generals. Will they promise accountability and the protection of borders, military outposts, soldiers and civilians? Or will they brag and harangue about guarding the Republic, Kemalism, and so forth as they have for the past 50 years? Is the Interior Ministry ready with multiple strategies and measures for the pre- and post- referendum period and for the claims of autonomy and independence and more? Or will the Minister stubbornly insist on his former instructions to the military coterie, "Go and clean all those mountains of terrorists?"[128] It is high time that civilian oversight in Turkey became so active and efficient that no institution or authority can escape its scrutiny.

---

[127] www.todayszaman.com/news-262797-report-herons-broadcast-hantepe-attack-live-but-general-staff-slow-to-react.html

[128] www.todayszaman.com/news-218800-prospective-military-chief-highlights-respect-for-law.html

5
Conflict and Its Resolution in Southeast Turkey

A Brief History of Turkey's Conflict in the Southeast

October, 9, 2008

At Ankara University in 1978 leftist student Abdullah Öcalan formed the outlawed Kurdistan Workers' Party (PKK) and led a separatist conflict and terrorism in the southeastern provinces in Turkey. After the 1980 military coup, the Turkish army opened a new front against separatist Kurdish terrorists that gradually escalated.

In 1989, then-President Turgut Özal used his position to redefine Turkey's role in regional and world politics. Especially after Iraq invaded Kuwait in 1990, Özal saw in this the potential for a political solution to the "Kurdish problem." Although initially his efforts paid off, the first Gulf War left Turkey in a complicated relationship with Iraq and the Kurds. The Kurdish autonomous zone in northern Iraq, seen from the Turkish perspective then, constituted a potential incitement to the Kurds of Turkey. Since 1989, Özal had been seeking a non-military resolution to the conflict and advocating greater cultural liberty for Kurds. The end of the Gulf War in 1991 seemed a propitious time to carry that project forward.

Özal directed the Cabinet to repeal a law that had been passed in 1983 forbidding the use of languages other than Turkish. Two prominent Iraqi Kurdish leaders met with Turkish Foreign Ministry officials, twice with the Turkish military and later with President Özal. In October 1991 Süleyman Demirel came to power in a coalition government with the Social Democratic People's Party (SHP), the party the Kurdish groups supported.

Since the 1980 military coup, Turkey's civilian politicians have never succeeded in gaining control over the military's actions in the Southeast.

Through the mechanism of the National Security Council (MGK), the generals have repeatedly intimidated politicians, including Özal and Mesut Yılmaz (the prime minister in 1991).

When, during demonstrations in 1992, more than 90 Kurds were killed by security forces, the Kurdish deputies in the SHP resigned in protest. The chance of a negotiated solution receded. Meanwhile, the number of "unsolved" murders in the Southeast climbed. These killings were carried out by clandestine paramilitary groups, some of whom probably operated independently, but evidence began to mount of their being funded by the state, or, more correctly, by the "deep state."

The conflict escalated in 1992 and 1993. Nearly 250,000 troops deployed to the region destroyed some 2,000 villages, displacing an estimated 2 million people, and themselves suffering more than 23,000 casualties. Local people fled to major cities all across Turkey. The Turkish army conducted a number of military operations across the border in northern Iraq to wipe out terrorist bases used against Turkey.

In 1993, Öcalan announced a unilateral ceasefire. Some were surprised, but President Özal had been directly involved. The military, however, interpreted that ceasefire as a sign of the terrorists' weakness and, assuming final victory was close, intensified operations. Negotiating with President Özal through Jalal Talabani, Öcalan renewed the ceasefire. At this critical juncture, Özal died suddenly in April 1993, while still serving as president. To date, most still hold the idea that he was poisoned by dark forces within the deep state as he tried to resolve the conflict. After Özal, Turkey struggled to reconcile the changes of the 1980s and 1990s—the legacy of the late president—with the traditions of the republic and the requirements of modern democracy. Turkey was beset by economic difficulties, political scandals, corruption, the ongoing battle against terrorism and Kurdish separatism.

Within a month, Demirel became president and Tansu Çiller prime minister. The Kurdish ceasefire broke down and military operations against the PKK resumed as before. The PKK ambushed a bus and murdered 33 off-duty military personnel. Heavy fighting erupted and hope of a political solution to the conflict seemed lost. Neither Demirel nor Çiller was capable of opposing the wishes of the generals or prepared to risk a civilian–military confrontation by challenging some generals' assumption of a free hand in dealing with southeastern Turkey.

After the Susurluk case in 1996, newspapers published reports, based on police and intelligence documents, showing that state organizations had been hiring death squads to murder Kurdish terrorists and "other enemies of the state" since the mid-1980s, and that these death squads had evidently received a strengthened mandate in 1991.[129]

The ugliest aspect of the conflict is that the murderous gangs were able to operate with the acquiescence of the Turkish military and bureaucrats then, who found them useful against the separatists and other political dissidents. These gangs included not only ultra-nationalist groups and leftists, but also marginal fundamentalists. A police shoot-out with an illegal Kurdish fundamentalist group called Hizbullah in eastern Anatolia in early 2000 led to the discovery of huge caches of weapons and the remains of dozens of people murdered by this group, which had received state support for its opposition to the PKK.

What have we gained and what progress has been made since 1980? The ongoing struggle has brought nothing but more killings of citizens, soldiers and terrorists, serious economic problems, forced displacements, societal tensions and polarization, estrangement from the EU and alienation and hostility between us and neighboring countries. It has also compromised the integrity of the state through the influence of organized crime—the Turkish Gladio-equivalent, known as Ergenekon, and its pawn, the Kurdish Ergenekon.

[129] For an account of these events with all academic references see Çetin, *The Gülen Movement: Civic Service Without Borders*, 35, 38, 44–45.

The Robber and the Merchant

May 14, 2009

T he more ammunition caches and assassinations plans are found, the more restless and aggressive coup lovers and Ergenekon supporters become. The usual strategy is to accuse all who want to end social and political turmoil and terrorism in Turkey of plotting against them, the "guardians of secularism," the regime and the modern world.

But this group, the "guardians of secularism," clearly contains some strange actors. Remarkably, as the Milliyet daily has reported, Murat Karayılan, the commander of the Kurdistan Workers' Party (PKK) terrorist organization, now claims to be one of these "guardians of secularism." Like the coup lovers, he claims that the Gülen Movement, a civil society movement, is "trying to take over the state" and—oddly for an organization that has spent years trying to bring down that same state—he and his friends are now "protecting" the state and the Southeast from "Islamic fundamentalism." To put it mildly, the self-proclaimed "guardians of secularism" are an unconvincing bunch.[130]

Their concerted efforts remind me of the story of the merchant and the robber I heard in my childhood:

Once, a merchant with his caravan was carrying merchandise to a destination. Journeying down the trade route, he met a helpless, lone wayfarer. Out of pity, the merchant gave the man water, food, new clothing and also took him into his caravan, offering him companionship and protection. One night, during a stop, the wayfarer attacked the merchant, incapacitated him and stole all his merchandise. As the robber was about to leave, the merchant came to and said: "I don't mind losing my goods. Let them be yours. However, you've robbed me of my goodness, my willingness to help other needy people. I can forgive you for what you have

---

[130] siyaset.milliyet.com.tr/karayilan---fethullahcilar-gelecege-donuk-bir-risk-/siyaset/siyasetdetay/08.05.2009/1092197/default.htm; todayszaman.com/newsDetail_getNewsById.action?load=detay&link=174801

stolen, but I cannot forgive you for what you have stolen from inside me and from humanity. From now on, I will be wary of helping the needy along caravan routes. Besides, when they hear about this, all the other caravan owners will not be willing to help people, either. For that, I, all those will no longer offer assistance and all those who will not be helped can never forgive you."

During the February 28, 1997 coup and afterwards, coup makers and supporters jointly fabricated news and threats. They accused civil society actors such as the Gülen Movement of seeking to overthrow the regime and presenting threats of reactionary fundamentalism. But while the events revealed the extent of unlawful, undemocratic practices in Turkey, they also suggested a will for renewal in society. The Gülen Movement accommodated the new situation and responded positively and peacefully.

Now the terrorist Karayılan has joined the chorus. As the Gülen Movement's peace-building educational and service initiatives have grown in strength in the Southeast, they have become a "threat" to his band of brigands, and he is now the unashamed ally of his erstwhile opponents in the "state." We must confess that we are little surprised by the facts, only by the open admission of this alliance.

In 2009 Turkey, Ergenekon participants are still not listening to society at large. As though nothing had emerged about their schemes and as though they were thoroughly innocent, they rehash the tactics they deployed during the February 28 coup. They attempt to mislead the masses about their own true identity and nature and about those who oppose their schemes. They are still perpetuating their alienating and conflicting interests and ideologies. While some perpetrate terror in the mountains and the Southeast, trapping the population between opposing military forces, the more "respectable" are ordering tailored "research" and academic workshops, dispatching new groups to Europe, the US and especially to the Caucasus, Russia and Central Asia. But it is too late: they have already been caught red-handed in their heinous schemes and plots, on their own voice recordings and in their own statements to the press.

Once, a Turkish politician went to a Central Asian country to give the president a dossier of prefabricated misinformation about Turkish entrepreneurs and philanthropists working in that country. The intention was to manipulate public opinion there about certain civil society initiatives inside and outside Turkey so that a new onslaught could be unleashed against such initiatives in Turkey and elsewhere. The president ridiculed the Turkish politician, saying: "Don't assume that we are all fools except you and will buy into your false arguments. We are able to tell who is good and beneficial. You cannot persuade us not to host peaceful educational and cultural efforts that are for the good of all humanity and not only of this country." No doubt Karayılan has spoken up now because he is getting the same response from the people of southeastern Turkey.

They will not be allowed to do what the caravan robber did—discourage third parties from coming to the aid of the needy in society at large and destroy all goodwill and trust between people. The caravan will continue to assist.

Talking Conflict Resolution in Southeast Turkey

August 20, 2009

Many people in Turkey are occupied with the latest government initiative, the peace and fraternity project to bring further democratization to the country and alleviate the problems and issues experienced by the nation's Kurdish population. From the parents of serving and fallen paratroopers to businesspeople, journalists and government authorities, all are involved, making their own suggestions about the project's name, content, form and outcomes.

Yet, to date there is no concrete, formally outlined project. So the discussion, which goes on, can to a certain extent be likened to the story of people trying to pull a large but unidentified animal from a deep, dark cistern. Some grasp the animal by the tail, some by the leg, the belly, the ear or the tusk. The helpers all advance strategies to save both the cistern and the creature from destruction, but it remains where it is.

Needless to say, all efforts are valuable, and they should be encouraged and supported, rather than letting the rescue be stalled by ideological interest groups. Any potential plan needs to have both short and long-term strategies and goals and will certainly have short and long-term implications. This is not a matter for one party or a single government. Successive governments should also be able continue the project. The Ergenekon trial in Turkey gives rise to some specific concerns about the security aspects of the plan.

The project, wrongly termed "the Kurdish initiative," is a matter of civic, cultural and political rights and wrongs in the Southeast. If the people concerned turn to the courts with details of crimes perpetrated in the Southeast in the name of the state, are we prepared to watch cases dealt with by the judges of the Judges and Prosecutors Association (YAR-SAV) or Supreme Board of Judges and Prosecutors (HSYK), organizations which attempt to replace any judges or prosecutors who try to resolve cases of torture, kidnapping and extrajudicial killing by deep-state elements? When the people subjected to forced displacement into large cities during martial law return to their former villages and homes, how will the system provide services, security and funds for them so that they will not be exploited by terrorists or other forces again?

How can the people in the region, village guards and terrorists, be disarmed? What will happen to the arms that are collected? The Ergenekon case has already revealed that the same weapons frequently changed hands between terrorists and military units. So, how can it be made sure that weapons will not be sold to terrorists who do not accept the project?

The attitudes of the Republican People's Party (CHP) and the Nationalist Movement Party (MHP) are not helpful. Likewise, the insistence of the Democratic Society Party (DTP) on Abdullah Öcalan as a main source of the solution to the conflict promises little. Many people doubt the thoughts and ideas supposedly coming from Öcalan because he can only speak through his lawyers from a military prison. There are deep misgivings about how much his words are tailored by his lawyers, party members or the deep state. There will need to be other Kurdish or pro-Kurdish leaders talking and negotiating freely for the sake of both Turkish and Kurdish people. They must come forward freely to stop the bloodshed and injustice. They must also be assured about their security and that their perspectives will be evaluated fully and properly and not silenced or eliminated by the deep state. Fallacious claims that ethnic and religious minorities will make more demands and claim more rights which will lead to the division of the state should also be handled with care. The opposition and counterarguments to the project should also be given proper responses from respected community leaders and academics without turning events into a short-sighted investment in their careers.

Turkey already has top scholars who have spent years on this issue, proved to be sincere, rational and unbiased and are already acknowledged both inside and outside Turkey. Experts such as Dr. Doğu Ergil,[131] and others of similar caliber, need to be consulted regularly. The demands of other communities for independence, self-rule or partial autonomy in local, financial and administrative affairs and reconciliation efforts that have been

---

[131] Sociologist and author of a groundbreaking survey on the views of the Kurdish population in 1995, as well as many significant later publications on the topic. See www.nytimes.com/1995/10/29/world/in-turkey-open-discussion-of-kurds-is-casualty-of-effort-to-confront-war for a report of his early survey and its political impact.

made in Europe—the Irish and Scottish cases for example—and in Africa and other parts of the world should be thoroughly studied, and the outcomes should be shared with the public and authorities in an unbiased way.

Groups that do not wish to be part of the project and any solution cannot be allowed to derail the project with their confrontational efforts. They can freely have their say in public—the project is, after all, about extending democratic rights and freedoms to ever-greater numbers—but attempts to agitate families of fallen soldiers and particular ethnic or religious groups in the community with ultranationalist discourse and provocations should be ignored and treated with the contempt they deserve. Citizens of Turkey of Kurdish origin need to beware of manipulation by organizations already acknowledged to be terrorist and clandestine by the US, the European Union and other international communities and maintain their resolve to end the clashes and suffering in the region. The solutions and discussions are intricate, sensitive and require short and long-term strategies, sincerity, patience, mutual respect, empathy and commitment. In the end, the beast wants to get out of the cistern, and the people want the beast out of the cistern, so while there may be some squeezing and struggling, in the end cooperation will be the only way.

Conflict Resolution in the Southeast:
A New Kind of Listening Post

August 27, 2009

The recent initiative by the Turkish government in the short run aims to end violence, and limit suffering and the loss of lives in the Southeast. In the long run, it aims to establish stability, peaceful co-existence and respect for human rights throughout the country. However, it is still unclear what kind of conflict resolution and human rights approaches they will choose to achieve these goals. As far as state-minority relations are concerned, there is no perfect option. If there were a perfect solution, the world would be much less conflict-ridden. However, though we may not know exactly which options are "right," we do know that there are obvious wrong options: segregation, oppression, ethnic cleansing and genocide. Unfortunately, despite claims of enlightenment, civilization and new world orders, many governments still consider brutal strategies among their choices. They fail to recognize, or choose to ignore, the fact that these are not solutions, but the very core of the problem.

Turkish military authorities have openly admitted that military aggression in southeast Turkey is largely ineffective, costly, destructive and time consuming. The government has seized the opportunity to initiate the latest democratic process before the clashes can spiral into the destruction of the country and nation. If the parties to the ongoing clashes commit themselves sincerely to overcoming biases, to settling their differences in ways which are mutually satisfactory and socio-politically integrative, previously unconsidered options can be visible and feasible. However, if the situation is not handled properly, attempts at resolution could actually worsen the conflict.

The government is seeking to use the influence and leverage of outsiders to the conflict, and its interactions so far have proved helpful and integrative. The government seems to be listening to people from all walks of life in an unbiased and non-aggressive way. This helps the government and its constituencies understand what makes the parties to the conflict hostile toward each other. However, the hawkish discourse from the opposition parties, the Republican People's Party (CHP) and the Nationalist Movement Party (MHP), has shown them to be intractable, biased and limiting.

These attitudes are important because in conflict resolution, how effectively we listen is at least as important as how effectively we express ourselves. It is vital to understand other people's and groups' perspectives, not just our own, if we are to come to a mutual resolution. Good listening also helps to bridge the gap between the conflicting parties and understand where the societal disconnect lies. This can channel negative emotions and energies toward the causes of conflict rather than toward individuals and groups. The alternative, the elimination of "the other" through violence, may temporarily lessen the intensity of a conflict, but does not end it permanently. On the other hand, it is simplistic to believe that enhanced communication alone will be sufficient to resolve a conflict. Studies suggest that more accurate communication sometimes actually widens, rather than narrows, differences between protagonists.

Conflicts vary. They can involve struggles for inclusion, recognition, development, allocation and control of resources. When all of these are pertinent, it may seem extremely difficult for parties to the conflict to find a solution to satisfy all the needs of all sides. The role of regional and global interest groups and lobbies that benefit from the continuation or intensification of the conflict makes things even more complicated.

In any major conflict, there are always some leaders or factions on both sides that turn to hawkish, fanatical and violent means and ends against the wishes of the majority. To deal with those who do not wish to compromise, both sides need to cooperate to the advantage of the majority without encouraging any further negative feelings or a new front in the conflict. It can be almost impossible to resolve some conflicts if particular groups on each side are not willing to work toward resolution. Nevertheless, we should leave the door open for individuals who decide to leave the uncompromising group to change their behavior; they should be provided with emotional and legal safety on their return, any consequences should occur in a non-punitive environment and those who are uncompromising should be held accountable for their own behavior. Where little agreement can be achieved, the important thing is to come to a place of understanding and try to work things out in a way that is respectful and beneficial to all involved.

Interests, meanings and values overlap at every level in all types of human relationships, including in societal and ethnic conflicts. Peaceful and mutually satisfactory ways to manage or end conflicts are therefore complex. Psychological, historical, economic, political, ideological and global factors all contribute to the resolution of conflicts or their escalation. Studies indicate that conflicts occurring at the individual, organizational, national and international levels have common features. So lessons learned from resolving conflicts at one level will be applicable to others, although conflicts may take many different forms and require different resolution strategies and outcomes cannot be generalized.

The interior minister's meetings with the luminaries of the arts, business and media are praiseworthy but not adequate in themselves. He would be well advised to form and meet with a team of conflict analysts now as well.

The Kurdish "Issue": Trapped between Two Deep States

July 1, 2010

T he recent intensified attacks and killings by Kurdish terrorists[132] and the ineptitude of the Turkish Armed Forces (TSK) against Kurdistan Workers' Party (PKK) terror have led to much discussion of the tutelage of Turkish democracy by the deep state.

In some coverage, the army is on the point of eradicating the PKK, the latest attacks being the terror group's last throes. According to others the PKK is on the very cusp of victory and there is no other option but to agree to their terms and conditions. There was even a panicked call for emergency rule in the Southeast—a type of rule for which the people paid very dearly in the past and which is one of the causes of our current problems.[133]

But isn't the root cause of our troubles right now the same for all "sides" in this conflict? On neither side can the leaders be held accountable.

The government has no operational authority in military operations and yet is ostensibly responsible for the circumstances. Meanwhile, some in the Armed Forces High Command pass their time concocting coup plans and plots instead of putting forward solutions to the conflict. If any doubt the advantages for the terrorists from the officers' pastime, why has the PKK opposed taking military personnel into custody during the Ergenekon probe?

Still, to some, the government is guilty simply because it is under the tutelage of the deep state embedded in the military and judiciary. But this

---

[132] todayszaman.com/news-213283-two-soldiers-martyred-in-clashes-with-terror-ists.html; todayszaman.com/news-213459-four-terrorists-killed-in-iraq-opera-tion.html; todayszaman.com/news-213478-turkish-military-kills-2-terrorists-in-clash.html

[133] todayszaman.com/news-213938-mhp-leader-devlet-bahceli-blames-govt-for-terror-calls-for-ohal.html

seems like blaming the victim. If such critics want to bring the military under the control of the government, what are their proposals for concrete steps to achieve this?

From the other angle, the PKK speaks as if it were the sole representative of all Kurds and Kurdish issues. However, while the Peace and Democracy Party (BDP), the political wing of the PKK, has 23 deputies in Parliament, the ruling Justice and Development Party (AK Party) has 75 deputies of Kurdish origin. Many Turkish citizens of Kurdish origin do not want separation from Turkey. More Kurds live in the West of Turkey than in the Southeast, and this group has not voted overwhelmingly for the BDP.

Take the latest threat from the BDP to their "own" Kurdish community. They are "'telling" all Kurdish people in the Southeast to remain in their homes and not go out at all on the day of the referendum.[134] In other words, the BDP does not trust their "own" people to vote as the party tells them to. So, if Kurdish people dare to leave their homes, will the BDP mark, intimidate or kill them?

It seems the BDP is offering the Kurds a choice between a Turkish deep state or a Kurdish deep state, a new deep state or the old deep state. Not much of a choice, many Kurds will think.

Is it any wonder that the PKK is being described as a "subcontractor" of foreign powers, the deep state and the Ergenekon gang?[135] These, too, have shown a very similar distrust of referenda and civilian rule.

And how will the Turkish state guarantee its citizens' safety to come to the ballot boxes and vote? Do we need something like the Australian solution to voter intimidation, in which all are obliged to enter the polling booth and vote? Spoiled ballot papers or "none of the above" gauge the voters' dissatisfaction with politicians' efforts.

Other polarizing elements at work are the Kurdish parties' insistence on Abdullah Öcalan as the sole decider and arbiter of the conflict, while they give little or no importance to the banning of their party from Parliament, and the arrests of members of the Kurdish Communities Union

---

[134] Post-referendum reports indicated that threats and boycott calls had some impact: www.todayszaman.com/news-221508-boycott-followed-in-kurdish-areas-reducing-yes-votes.html

[135] www.todayszaman.com/news-217518-former-pkk-leader-ocalan-controls-pkk-deep-state-controls-ocalan.html

(KCK), which seems to be an urban reorganization of PKK. The attitudes and commitment of all these involved in these events to the democratic values of peaceful dialogue, justice and the rule of law will eventually become clear.

Many "solutions" and policies are being suggested, from professionalizing the military, extending more cultural rights to the Kurds and establishing further dialogue. Ninety-nine civil society organizations in the Southeast have united to call on the PKK to stop its use of violence as this only brings the Kurdish issue to an unsolvable point.[136]

It is essential now to interact without resorting to "otherizing," demonizing and killing the children of Turkey, whether Turkish or Kurdish. We need proposals for viable solutions that the state and civil authorities can implement, proposals from a greater variety of voices, proper discussions and valid arguments, especially from the Kurdish people and civil society leaders, regardless of intimidation. The overwhelming majority will support them to solve a problem that has gnawed at us for decades.

Solutions need to be comprehensive, practical and based on sociopolitical projects for the future of all peoples of Turkey. They should be institutionalized so that whoever comes to power in the future must support them. The first topic could be "How are we going to save ourselves from the tutelage of both the Kurdish and Turkish deep states?"[137]

---

[136] www.todayszaman.com/news-214525-kurdish-civil-society-calls-on-outlawed-pkk-to-stop-violence.html

[137] On the Kurdish "deep state", see www.todayszaman.com/news-209322-can-kurds-confront-pkks-ergenekon-by-orhan-kemal-cengiz.html. On the variety of developing views among Kurds in Turkey, see www.todayszaman.com/news-228118-pkk-tutelage-over-pro-kurdish-politics-under-question.html

PKK Cease-fire: Unmapped and Unverifiable

August 19, 2010

The Kurdistan Workers' Party (PKK) terror organization has announced a unilateral and conditional cease-fire until September 20 [2010]. It claims to have suspended all its hostilities and military operations "inside Turkey only" but that it will "defend itself" if attacked. It says the cease-fire could last longer if "Turkey satisfies certain conditions." However, the PKK's conditions do not seem so much peace terms as excuses for either side to "accidentally" start fighting again.

Bozan Tekin, a PKK spokesperson, told reporters from a base in Iraq that a lasting cease-fire is possible if Turkey stops military operations, releases some 1,700 "political" detainees and starts peace negotiations directly with the separatist group, with imprisoned PKK leader Abdullah Öcalan actively involved in the process. Tekin cited the holy month of Ramadan as a reason for the move. At the same time, news emerged that the PKK has threatened to kill religious and community leaders encouraging people to vote "yes" in the upcoming referendum.

Also, while contending that a cease-fire might lead to a peaceful, political solution, Tekin confirmed that the PKK has, in "self defense," blown up a pipeline in southeastern Turkey carrying Iraqi oil.

In the past the Turkish state has rejected the PKK's cease-fire declarations, saying a cease-fire assumes it is two legal parties in conflict. The PKK has also scrapped previous cease-fires due to continued Turkish military operations. The PKK is classified as a "terrorist" organization by the US and EU and other countries, and PKK violence has undermined the present government's attempt to enhance Kurdish minority rights and end the 26-year separatist conflict. The PKK is now under pressure to keep its popularity in the southeast of Turkey, for it has not contained its senseless violence.

But a cease-fire is more than simply not firing or stopping hostilities. It has to include mechanisms to ensure that neither side violates the agreement and mechanisms to ensure that those who do violate it are investigated, exposed rapidly and, if necessary, condemned and sanctioned. A cease-fire has to be designed in such a way that it can build confidence between the opposing forces. Each side needs to know what the other side is doing, either through direct observation or through the reports of trusted third-party intermediaries. Each step that one side takes that might make it militarily vulnerable to the other needs to be matched by a step taken by the opposing party. Cease-fire documents are usually accompanied by a map, and also by an exercise in mapping and verifying the positions of the opposing forces.

A cease-fire fails partly because it is a weak agreement with no map, partly because two different versions with extra demands exist, partly because no trust at all exists between the opposing forces and partly because the mechanism set up to guarantee the cease-fire is not given the mandate or force necessary to complete its task. The negotiating teams should come to the table determined to improve on past attempts. The PKK's cease-fire until September offers an inadequate timetable for what will be a complex set of actions. Experts propose that 90 days would be more realistic for completing these activities, and it is the PKK's claim that it can be done quicker that really causes doubt about its sincerity.

Nevertheless, some argue that the cease-fire is worth pursuing but add nothing to this abstraction. This view is creating a secondary controversy over the efficacy of efforts to reach a peaceful solution. But rather than wasting energy defining the indefinable, we need to sincerely and persistently get down to developing strategies that can really work. Consistently and explicitly we must insist that societal peace, accord and prosperity come through civil, diplomatic, educational, cultural and economic engagement and empowerment, human rights and the consolidation of democracy, equity and justice, rather than through uncontrollable, unsupervised military force or armed struggle and coercion.

The greatest obstacle to a cease-fire is that hostilities are continuing in Turkey and across the border. As sovereign, the Turkish government has a right and responsibility to protect its people and borders. The PKK cannot infringe upon this right. While instability continues in the Southeast due to PKK violence, protection rackets and other impositions, while the PKK maintains cross-border terrorist and clandestine activities, the cease-fire cannot be implemented. The cease-fire, albeit only tacitly accepted by both sides, should have a strong enforcement mechanism, but very little can be done to enforce its provisions. A political resolution to the conflict, a very sincere and robust mechanism for enforcing the agreement on societal peace and then some important gradual steps are needed for a comprehensive cease-fire to become a reality on the ground.

The Education Boycott and Pseudo-Civil Society in Turkey

September 23, 2010

The Peace and Democracy Party (BDP) and affiliated associations, including the Movement for Kurdish Language and Education, have called on the Kurdish-speaking citizens of Turkey not to send their children to schools in the Southeast between September 20 and 25 [2010].

The Education Ministry has released a written statement saying that "education is a constitutional right and [violating this right] is a misuse of parental rights."

Pro-Kurdish-language groups are demanding that children be given the right to be educated in their mother tongue, especially since the recent campaign for "democratic autonomy." The campaign envisages such powers being granted to regional Kurdish municipalities as to make them "governments," including establishing local parliaments in the regions and having a separate flag. Signs promoting an education system in the Kurdish language were posted on billboards around Diyarbakir in a number of Kurdish dialects.

Pro-separatist and other more moderate Kurdish groups and critics consistently complain about the unprecedented unemployment in the region, lack of teachers, resources and systems to train qualified teachers, the inability of those who are already teachers in the region, the "inhuman working conditions" in the education sector and the local population's being deprived of work and security. The separatist groups now add to this the claim that "these rights can't even be discussed because of the paranoia and excuses of the existing political situation of the country." While they do not make it clear how children who are educated exclusively in Kurdish will be able to compete on equal terms with those who receive education in Turkish, they point out that children who do not receive education in Kurdish "will have difficulties in understanding, perceiving and expressing themselves in a seriously unequal system. They assert they "will certainly not accept that." While being forced to admit that the democratic initiative in Turkey is not progressing as they had hoped, they also, somewhat undemocratically it must be said, reject any discussion of or comment on the motives behind their call for a boycott.

Journalists and intellectuals are divided and politicizing the issue. While some defend the right of citizens to be educated in their mother tongue, others state that by law public schools in Turkey can only educate students in Turkish, the country's sole official language.

Reports from the region and in the national media on the results of the boycott are unclear. While many dailies report that people are sending their children to schools, BDP-affiliated news agencies and organizations claim that "pro-Kurdish school classes were almost empty as the campaign to boycott education solely in Turkish began." BDP representatives and supporters represent the boycott of the first five days of the new school year as "civil disobedience." In line with the politics of the party, they add that they also oppose the existence of private schools and the examination system because they are all "closely associated with [and] supporting the market mentality."

However, whatever democratic and civil-society credentials pro-separatist deputies, organizations and activists claim for themselves, the reality is different in the region. In addition to the children obliged to "boycott" their schools, the rate of children who never enroll at all is inordinately high in the region. Many also drop out to join in the violent activism in the region. The Kurdistan Workers' Party (PKK) affiliated Firat News Agency has broadcast another shocking press release from the boycott-backing Movement for Kurdish Language and Education that publicly threatened: "Those who send their children to private educational primary and secondary schools, tutoring programs, university preparation courses and other associations established in the region by the civil and local sector will severely be punished. Those who are affiliated and support such educational institutions and services along with all [Justice and Development Party] AK party representatives in the region will be our target."

Of course, mother-language education is and can be possible in Turkey as in many other places in the world, but issuing threats aimed at exactly those who might want it and benefit from it is antipathetic to any true notion of freedom and democracy. Yet this is exactly the same tactic used in the referendum period, when separatist groups threatened to punish those who voted in the referendum.

But this does not only concern Kurdish people. Citizens of all ethnic backgrounds are able to judge who is working to remove the obstacles which prevent people from all identities and cultures in Turkey from seeing and expressing themselves as equal citizens. They can see who is working for and who is trying to obstruct the new, democratic and pluralist constitution that the majority of society demands. It doesn't take a school teacher to show them that.

Kurds and Turks: No Singular Solution

December 23, 2010

We have seen many improvements and positive developments taking place in Turkey in terms of human rights, democratization and the development of a civic society in the last few years. Media coverage has been plentiful on many such issues, especially on the successful strides taken by the current government or the system recently.

However, news of such improvements must not be used to blinker us to our remaining problems, or to produce a self-congratulatory discourse of complacency. We now need to innovate valid strategies and policies to help resolve long-term and vital issues related particularly to the diverse ethnic and religious groups and communities in our country.

Although there are in fact many diverse groups in Turkey, the current debate about the representation and wishes of Kurds is once again dominating the public space. At one extreme are Turkish nationalist extremists. In the face of all evidence, they attempt to deny or wipe from public view the reality of the existence of differing ethnic and religious groups within Turkey. On the other, some Kurdish separatists would have Kurdish as the second official language, autonomous governance, a separate flag and even a separate defense force. Political, militant, separatist groups, who claim without any strong evidence that they represent the majority of Kurds in Turkey, seem to be willing to take on the whole of Turkey to suit their own interests and those of the suspect ideologies that underpin their cause.

Separatist Kurdish groups and their representatives and ideologues are undoubtedly well organized. They are capable of producing an incessant stream of new demands, proposals, refutations and disputations. They swiftly initiate new discussions, cause agitation amongst their opponents, escalate tension in wider society and then just as rapidly backtrack and give up on their claims. By the time they do that, they have of course already dumped a residue of problems and ill feeling into the lap of the incumbent government or the system for them to deal with.

Most tellingly, separatist groups act as if they were the only victims of ongoing injustice, conflicts and clashes in the region, particularly in southeast Turkey. Their discourse is highly exclusivist. They talk as if they were the only ethnic group, people and language in the region; as if there were no non-Kurds there; as if a Kurdish identity were singular, unmixed and easily defined; as if all Kurds wish for the independence of the whole population and region; and as if all in the Southeast and among the Kurds support them in their claims, actions and terrorism.

This delusion leads to their attempts to impose "the" resolution of the problem—the single roadmap of their ideologues and terrorist leaders—on our mutual problem, country and people. In this they resemble the Turkish nationalists, who would also like to impose a "pure" and singular identity on a population and a simplistic and conclusive resolution.

It is ironic that, having benefited from the struggle of many other cultural, religious, civic and political groups to break the shackles of the few elitist protectionists and their cohorts in the Turkish system and bring human rights and democratization and recognition of diversity in Turkey, the political wings of Kurdish separatist groups have been so emboldened that they attempt to impose "the" roadmap and "the only viable" offer of engagement with governmental and nongovernmental institutions and the wider Turkish society. A further clue to such groups' lack of respect for civic society and democratic governance lies in the fact that although they claim to be representative of Kurds, they can abruptly change their demands and discourse at the behest of their "chieftain" behind bars on İmralı.[138]

However, nothing has been resolved yet. Ankara needs to behave more intelligently and efficiently. It must not postpone democratic initiatives until after the forthcoming elections.[139] Security for all in the region must be improved. There must be more civic committees and initiatives with a high degree of public participation in the region, so that all the different segments of society are represented.

---

[138] Abdullah Ocalan, founder member of the PKK, sentenced to life imprisonment and held in isolation on İmralı island, in the Sea of Marmara.
[139] June 11, 2011.

This is not a case of "either/or," but it is possible to quickly resolve the issue of using local languages in some official settings. The government needs to produce more viable, valid and effective policies and channels rather than remaining a mere critic of initiatives coming from the Kurdish parties. People need to see the positive fruits of the democratic and cultural initiative, which is in danger of being stillborn in the region. There should be not only private meetings, but more publicly visible, concrete efforts that will not be sacrificed for fear of losing votes in elections. Brusque retorts and calling on state prosecutors to act against the discourse and action of Kurdish is not the solution.

6

International Perceptions

Foreign Policy Rankings and Fethullah Gülen

June 26, 2008

F ethullah Gülen, a Turkish Islamic scholar, has come first on a list of the top 100 living public intellectuals in a survey organized by the British magazine *Prospect* and *Foreign Policy*, a US publication.[140] The results apparently surprised the organizers: The top 10 individuals in the poll were all Muslim intellectuals, two of whom were Turkish citizens. The rankings are already generating discussion and their implications are relevant to many people from different backgrounds, cultures and societies, whether they are Muslim or not. Here we should acknowledge the editors of the journals and those who conducted the survey for permitting the selection of these nominees, for not interfering with the voting process and for sharing its results with the whole world.

Even a cursory reading of what has been written about the rankings reveals several points about the winner of the survey, the other highly ranked individuals and the reactions to their ranking.

Prospect's editor, David Goodhart, admits to not having heard of Gülen before and feels Gülen's supporters "made a mockery" of the poll, but that the result "flagged up significant political trends" in Turkey. From this, we might conclude that the results of the poll and the reactions to it "flagged up" a regrettable gap in Western journalists' and editors' knowledge of Turkey and the Middle East.

Nevertheless, since Gülen was included among the nominees by the editors, it must mean that he was already known at least to some and

---

[140] www.prospectmagazine.co.uk/prospect-100-intellectuals/; www.prospectmagazine.co.uk/magazine/amodernottoman

acknowledged for his contribution to faith, dialogue, education, culture and peace.

The fact that he is still not known among certain spheres in the West could be attributed to several causes. Until 2004, there was not much interest in Gülen and the movement academically. Since then, there have been a number of conferences and hundreds of academic articles written on the Gülen Movement and its contribution to global societies. Another factor is the lack of acknowledgment given to him by "enlightened" intellectuals in his own country. They would like to see Gülen as just a preacher or an ordinary "mosque imam." They can no longer, however, deny Gülen's immense contribution to the thought and action of the movement. So, to see him only as "religious leader," rather than as a prolific writer, a social initiator, a promoter of interfaith dialogue, an intercultural reconciliatory opinion-maker, an activist, a peaceful progressive civil society mentor and an authentic Islamic scholar is an injustice to Gülen and the public.

Western commentators' analyses of the results and the voting process also show a further lack of understanding of the Middle Eastern context. For example, while the organizers attributed the results to "a sustained campaign by Gülen's followers" after the Zaman newspaper publicized the poll, could that ever account for the position of Orhan Pamuk at No. 4? Pamuk's views on faith and Sufism, for example, do not seem to sit easily with those of Gülen.[141] Are Pamuk's supporters also reading Zaman? The Iranian human rights lawyer Shirin Ebadi came in 10th. Are Zaman readers supposed to have organized a stream of voters for Ms Ebadi? Why?

The high rate of return to the survey in Turkey and the Middle East can be accounted for by a number of factors. Within the Gülen Movement, for example, the rate of computer literacy and access to computers is very high. Yet another reason for the high return rate is that the movement's participants are educated members of the urban middle class: they have technical and cultural competence and a strong economic-functional position, which make them more likely to mobilize. The participants prioritize individual achievement in the private sphere and expansion of the freedom of expression, democratic participation and self-government in the public domain.

---

[141] See interview with Orhan Pamuk at www.artsci.wustl.edu/~archword/interviews/pamuk/interview.htm. Accessed on 10 October 2013.

These days communication through information networks in social movements is strong and participants in such networks are often more committed than those who have formal membership in political parties.

But the cases of Ebadi, Pamuk and the seven other Muslim intellectuals remain inexplicable to the poll's organizers. Could it be that a certain view of the Muslim world as "backward," "downtrodden," and "stuck in the Middle Ages" is being challenged? The results show that the Muslim world is not on the wrong side of the great "digital divide." It has embraced this branch of modernity with zeal and competence. It is clear from these results that Muslims will gladly, enthusiastically and fearlessly participate in all kinds of open voting, given half a chance. This is not the time for onlookers and poll organizers to lurch into a half-baked conspiracy theory and refuse to heed what the Muslim world is telling them: that the people prefer peaceful and even democratic influences and are eager participants in all kinds of civil society activities.

The use of certain words in hasty analyses by journalists may lead to a cross-cultural failure in understanding or even to misunderstanding Gülen and his movement. For example, "Gülen is both revered and reviled in his native Turkey." We know how the protectionists "revile" him, but terms such as "revere" also have some connotations and implications inappropriate for a faith-inspired civil society initiative coming from a Muslim background. The participants in the Gülen Movement appreciate Gülen for his knowledge, scholarliness, sincerity, integrity, commitment to altruism, profound concern and compassion for others. It should not be ignored that all these qualities come from his Islamic education and upbringing. However, they do not result in any sacred celebration of Gülen or any others in the movement.

In spite of the slim knowledge of the poll's organizers, so far the Gülen Movement has been better—that is, more objectively—studied abroad than in Turkey. Because a protectionist elite prevails in Turkey's academic institutions, free scholarly discussion within Turkey still seems a rather distant ideal. Freedom of speech in Turkey, especially in academia, is not what it is in the West. Nevertheless, the great majority of people in Turkey know and appreciate Gülen and the movement despite the polemics of the protectionists. This fact is often overlooked. Commentators would do well to turn their attention to the results of surveys and research on the movement done by independent scholars and institutions.

President Obama's Inauguration, the Great State and the Deep State

Thursday, January 22, 2009

Barack H. Obama became the 44th president of the US on Tuesday[142] in a state ceremony. His inauguration was conducted before a massive crowd in Washington while millions in other parts of the US and in communities throughout the world followed it via live coverage.

The difference in the way Americans inaugurate their president and his cabinet and the way we select and inaugurate our president, prime minister and/or cabinet reveals the gap between the cultures of a great state and a petty (deep) state.

The first thing that strikes viewers is that the inauguration was a joyous celebration for the whole nation and its executive and legislative administration. People of all shades, colors and races, people from across the spectrum of political thought, people of different faiths and creeds or of no belief were all there celebrating. They were smiling, hugging one another and trying to capture that historic moment among their peers, colleagues or political opponents with their cameras. Whether they voted for President Obama or not, from noon on Tuesday onwards, Obama was their president, and they celebrated the people's choice regardless of their partisan interests or political ambitions.

Let's flash back and remember how people acted during and reacted to the presidential election Abdullah Gül won in Turkey.[143] Certain people in the political, judicial and military administration were not happy at all about Gül being elected by Parliament and the popular vote. They accused the people of idiocy and folly, and they claimed on TV that 10 or 100 votes from "ordinary people" were not worth one of their "white Turk"

---

[142] January 20, 2009
[143] www.todayszaman.com/news-120679-gul-is-the-fifth-civilian-president-of-turk-ish-republic.html

votes.[144] They did not accept the popular or parliamentary verdict and did whatever they could to prevent President Gül and Prime Minister Erdoğan from coming to power. A majority vote in Parliament, the Constitution and the elections meant little to them if they brought to power someone outside their ideological grouping. They caused political and financial crises to further their petty ambitions. So our inaugurations always foretell some kind of crisis of state or regime, and we all feel very tense and agitated rather than joyous and celebratory.

State dignitaries, the new cabinet and their families all fittingly joined and enjoyed the inauguration in America. Obama's two little daughters were right there with their parents and relatives. It was an occasion to be rightly shared and celebrated among family and friends, in addition to being a great state's formal procedure. Behind President Obama, we could see an African-American woman wearing a traditional white head-scarf. Contrast this with Turkey, where we remember the arguments of supporters of the deep state that President Gül could not take his wife into the presidential palace because she is not permitted to wear a head-scarf in a public space, that she cannot join or host state or foreign dignitaries at receptions within the palace and that Gül and Erdoğan should divorce their wives if they wished to take up their positions.[145]

On the west portico of the US Capitol building, all except former and future presidents and vice presidents sat on simple chairs, and people were there from dawn so as to be closer to the portico and podiums. Then let's remember the tension and conflicts in Turkey's celebrations, where all state dignitaries and bureaucrats sit on thrones fit for sultans and quarrel about where they sit, and let's remember the heads of the military—who, as officers of the Ministry of Defense, are supposed to be serving the government and public—acting like rulers of a country with a

---

[144] www.hurriyet.com.tr/english/domestic/11102495_p.asp; www.hurriyet.com.tr/magazin/haber/8565854.asp; youtu.be/VhrcqeXowBI

[145] These arguments were maintained into the second year of his presidency: in.reuters.com/article/email/idINIndia-52555620101029; www.hurriyetdaily-news.com/default.aspx?pageid=438&n=chp-not-attending-presidential-reception-cites-headscarf-issue-2010-10-14.

military regime and even ordering the removal of certain civic and political leaders from the celebrations.[146]

President Obama was inaugurated with his full name, Barack Hussein Obama. Now, what if a parliamentarian of Armenian or Kurdish ethnic origin were appointed to a state position using a name which clearly expressed their ethnic identity? Would we not, all of a sudden, start discussing Turkishness and the indivisibility of the Turkish state and how such ethno-religious identity is a threat to the Turkish Republic?[147]

However, the United States of America, with its great state culture, conducts the inauguration ceremony with a sense of purpose and civility. President Obama said, "As for our common defense, we reject as false the choice between our safety and our ideals." Yet, contrary to our common defense, the marginal group of "white Turks" of Turkey, or the deep state, always put their petty interests, ambitions and ideology before the ideals of democracy, the rule of law or civility.

President Obama said the United States is "ready to lead once more" in the world, but people in our deep state have even failed in their attempt to lead their murderous gangs within Ergenekon. Obama said greatness is never a given but must be earned. Those in Turkey's deep state seem to think they can earn their greatness though bombings, killings, plots and coups against democratically elected presidents and governments. Unlike a great state culture, our deep state culture chooses fear over hope and conflict and discord over common unity of purpose. Is there any need to wonder why the US became a great nation and a world power, while Turkey languished under the dark influence of Ergenekon?

[146] www.zaman.com.tr/gundem_torende-padisah-tartismasi_1021909.html; www4.cnnturk.com/2010/turkiye/08/30/aydinda.vali.ve.chpli.vekil.arasinda.gerginlik/588266.0/; www.sabah.com.tr/Gundem/2010/08/30/torende_padisah_tartismasi

[147] www.todayszaman.com/news-161910-chp-deputy-aritman-unapologetic-as-gul-denies-armenian-roots.html; www.todayszaman.com/news-176580-ethnic-diversity-is-cultural-wealth-says-court-in-aritman-case.html; www.todayszaman.com/news-162236-aritman-should-apologize-or-resign-say-european-leaders.html

The Turkey-Russia Rapprochement and Its Implications

February 19, 2009

S etting aside uneasy political issues of the past, Turkey and Russia are exploring further rapprochement to improve sociopolitical and commercial ties, to enhance the prospects for regional energy development projects and to have a broad stabilizing effect, especially around their borders; however, this positive move has been read by some as a shift from the West to the East or, exaggeratedly, as witnessing the "imminent" rise of Turkey as a "regional superpower."

Russians and Turks have lived side by side for centuries. As nations, states or peoples, they have been interacting since long before many modern nation-states were even established in Europe. Both nations were filling the pages of history in peace or conflict long before the Americas were discovered, colonized and divided into contemporary nation-states. So, after the collapse of the Soviet Union and the emergence of independent states in Central Asia, if these two old neighbors were not to seek dialogue and cooperation, who would?

Geographical proximity and ethno-cultural background provide a resource for both countries to forge closer ties with the Central Asian republics. Both Turkey and Russia share substantial ethnic, linguistic and cultural ties with Central Asia. The populations of Central Asian countries are mostly Sunni Muslims, like those of Turkey. The ancestors, heroes and literary and scientific luminaries are the same in all Turkic countries. Turks share their culture and aspirations through massive educational exchanges and investments in Turkic nations formerly in the Soviet Union. People in the region listen to Turkish music and watch Turkish TV stations, and Turkey draws many artists, musicians, qualified workers and tourists from Russia as well as Central Asia.

Turkey's relationship with the region was exaggerated in the late 1990s. Turkey was fallaciously introduced as the "elder brother," an obvious role model for the newly independent republics. This was supposed to promote democracy, to make them follow the laicist model of national development and espouse pan-Turkic ideas. However, the Central Asians no more wanted a Turkish elder brother than a Russian one. So Russia and Turkey met with similar reactions to their cultural and political impositions.

Economy-wise, besides the oil and gas industry, Turkish companies benefit from major investments in Russia and Central Asian countries, such as the construction of airports and pipelines and operating hotels and supermarkets. Russia's economy is now reeling from the sharp fall in oil prices, and its stock market is down 75 percent since last summer as the world economy collapses into recession. This accentuates the need to re-evaluate existing trade and commerce between Turkey and Russia. Both need to export Russian and Central Asian gas and oil via Turkey to other countries. From ordinary citizens to regional experts and political authorities, all want dialogue and cooperation between the two countries in order to improve prosperity, peace and stability in the region.

Politically, this rapprochement may improve the situation in the conflict-ridden zones in the Caucasus. It may further contribute to normalizing diplomatic relations between Turkey and Armenia, Georgia and Russia, and especially to a Nagorno-Karabakh settlement between Azerbaijan and Armenia. Also, as Russian Prime Minister Vladimir Putin noted, it may help Russia to "develop economic ties with Turkish Cypriots" and to contribute by "acting exclusively as a mediator and guarantor of future accords."[148] Russia is no longer viewing Turkey as a subcontractor of policies Russia disapproves of. The Caucasus is no longer a source of discord. Russia also wishes to increase its investments in the countries whose economies could be reinforced by expanded trade with Turkey. The short-term fluctuations in Russian-Turkish relations arise from issues such as commercial land transit, customs regulations and the use of the passageway of the Turkish Straits. Along with curbing human and narcotics trafficking, these were undoubtedly on the agenda.[149]

Peaceful ties, based also on shared security considerations, will not shift Turkey's foreign policy inside or outside the region, nor will they have

---

[148] www.freerepublic.com/focus/fr/1319433/posts; www.turkishweekly.net/news/1877/russian-leader-putin-isolation-of-turkish-cypriots-is-not-fair.html

[149] www.todayszaman.com/news-166595-primakov-turkish-russian-ties-will-take-on-new-momentum.html

a negative impact on Turkish–European Union relations. A main purpose of Turkey's foreign policy is to ease tension in the region, which will certainly improve Turkish–Russian, as well as their global relations. Both countries seem determined to avoid any scenario that could escalate into major political conflict or military confrontation in the region, especially given Iran's troubled relations with the United States and Israel. Turkey holds that the atmosphere of mistrust needs to be eliminated and all sides must exercise self-restraint in this volatile region.

This rapprochement between Turkey and Russia is to consolidate a long period of peace and stability and to address their current economic problems. Continuing tensions and conflicts and their possible escalation will surely not serve their long-term national interests. The Turkish president's visit should be interpreted as expanding relations in the political, economic and cultural fields rather than as a minor political gesture or a shift in Turkish foreign policy. This rapprochement does not threaten Turkey's ties with the United States, Europe, other countries in the region or Turkey's NATO membership. Turkey still functions as a bridge between continents and cultures, not as a barrier to the common good.

Who Is Radical Anyway?

March 19, 2009

L ast week the international magazine *Newsweek* featured a striking cover. The main headline was in Arabic with an English translation in smaller type below: "Radical Islam is a fact of life. How to live with it." Fareed Zakaria's article and editorial argued that not all groups that find support in Muslim communities advocate jihadist ideologies and not all Muslim communities host terrorists—in fact, most do not. The managing editor, Daniel Klaidman, also emphasizes, "We must be smart about distinguishing between true threats and irrational fears. What we need is more analysis and less anger." As he hints, different readers see such covers and topics in different ways—deceptive with a twist, or menacing—and the graceful Arabic calligraphy is beautiful, but commercially catchy, too.

Such media analyses deserve attention in many respects.

While approaching issues related to Muslims or Islam, the naming and framing of issues is mostly erroneously misconstrued or used falsely, and specific terms are used with ideological motives. For instance, many Muslims rightly object to the phrase "radical Islam" and refuse to accept or use it. Individuals or people can be radical, the interpretation of certain principles of a religion by some of its followers can be radical, but not the whole faith or religion itself. Expressions such as "radical Islam" imprint themselves and mold people's minds even before they start reading and thinking about the religion and Muslims.

This deepens communication problems. Any individual follower of a religion, male or female, can be radical, extremist or even terrorist, but not the religion. The term "Islamic terrorist" is used so often and in such a slack or even ill-intentioned way, whereas the media and politicians never refer to "Christian terror" or "Christian terrorists," or "Jewish terror" or "Jewish terrorists" or any other religion or faith, for that matter. At most they become "Christian rebels," "the far right" or some other dignified term, but never terrorists for their faith. Yet, the Lord's Resistance Army (LRA), which claims to be guided by the Bible's Ten Commandments, has wreaked havoc in the regions bordering Congo, Uganda and Sudan for two decades.[150] The LRA is notorious for cutting off the limbs, lips, ears and throats of civilians, torture, executions, rape, forced displacement and forcing thousands of children to serve as soldiers or sex slaves.

A second issue is the visual imagery used to depict Muslims. While discussing violence and terrorism, the Western media use pictures of mosques, people praying or reading the Qur'an or innocent children and women in traditional clothing. Even as it argued against stereotyping Muslims, *Newsweek*'s March 9 edition itself fell prey to this error. It showed children in traditional white gowns walking down the stairs of a modern mosque, young girls and women wearing headscarves at a university during Friday prayer and children reading the Qur'an in an underprivileged, remote area of a country. The reader is not brought to understand that these people have nothing to do with "nihilistic philosophies and expansionist aims," as the *Newsweek* editor put it. Instead, this associates all Muslims, man, woman and child, all their resources and institutions, the Qur'an, the mosque and their universities with fear; they are all seen as potential sources of radicalism, fundamentalism or ideological violence.

So even when people start with the right diagnosis of the issues, if they pursue the discussion with the wrong language and imagery, it does not help to resolve any ongoing dehumanizing of another group, especially of Muslims in this case.

The range of issues to confront, and they are many—various sociopolitical and economic backgrounds, dysfunctional systems or regimes, disruption or disorientation of modernity in traditional societies, imposed cultural alienation, the negative effects of globalization, the role and weight of authoritarian regimes or militaries, media or judicial systems, transnational corporate and international agencies intervening or interfering with the domestic and international affairs of a country, regional conflicts and wars, the backlash produced by a colonial past or former or present foreign military interventions—are all experienced and resolved differently in the varied and vast lands in which Muslim communities or societies live. So it is misleading to talk about "global Islamic insurgency." The different interests, issues and conflicts facing a particular society are rep-

---

[150] www.warchild.org.uk/issues/the-lords-resistance-army

resented by a range of political, ideological and sectarian groups. None of these stand for all Muslims, Islam or Islamic teachings, meanings and values. They are not part of a single global movement. Groups, motives, interests and movements are far more local or regional than that. They each have their own specific issues and grievances. Many do not have much in common in terms of tactics, strategies, reactions or positive responses. Thus, so-called radicalism, extremism or fundamentalism in various parts of the world cannot be resolved by bombing, killing, capturing, torturing, dehumanizing and demonizing individuals, people, communities or countries, as *Newsweek* also points out.

The problems are not the same in every society, and neither are the people. The same medicine cannot be used for all patients. As modern, educated and sophisticated people, we should demonstrate our political, moral, intellectual and spiritual superiority to extremists and radicals by sustaining civic, educational, philanthropic and altruistic efforts and projects. We need to bring people into our fold, not repel, stigmatize or compartmentalize them with artificial ideological labels. In the end, we have one world and one life to live. The world is not the property or responsibility of only a few.

The Unbearable Lightness of Media Being

June 25, 2009

I n a globalized world nothing is truly particular or local. Gains and pains are both general and universal. But if various transnational lobbies, political entities, other countries and outside attention get involved in a particular issue, how much say can local people have in their own resources and destiny?

Also, how far do we perceive other people's local issues through our own particular interests? To what extent are we spoon-fed one-sided coverage of local issues by transnational networks and media? Whether it is intellectual, political or military meddling, whether it is done through new or relatively old means of communication, does this interference help to disseminate accurate information, and thus equip people with the means to bring about peaceful coexistence? Let's consider two current cases and try to deduce our own and others' interests in them.

In the first case, on June 12 [2009], Ahmadinejad officially won the Iranian presidential election by a margin of two to one against Mousavi. Mousavi's supporters claimed the election was rigged and organized demonstrations. A partial recount did not help, and protests and a crackdown, both resulting in injuries and fatalities, ensued. A young woman was shot during the skirmishes and at lightning speed became a symbol of the opposition via a cellphone video recording. Much of the media coverage of events seems to have been gleaned from Twitter.

In the lesser known case, for two months native Indians have been clashing with police in Peru. The Indians are demanding the repeal of a government decree that allows further oil exploration, commercial farming and logging in the indigenous people's lands. In the clashes, 34–40 natives and 23 police officers have been killed. Sixty more indigenous people are missing. An indigenous leader of the protests fled the country to Nicaragua, from where he continues the struggle. There has been no Twitter campaign for him yet.[151]

The media coverage and political involvement in the Iranian and Peruvian cases exhibit stark differences. It is important to examine how the particular and local becomes general and transnational and binds our emotions and intellects. How do the pervasive pictures and discourse affect our attitudes on the issues? Is this intellectual and emotional invasion bringing solutions to our common problems or proving more problematic in the long run?

Western governments are recalling their ambassadors from Iran. International intervention in Iran is discussed as if it were an option. It seems that when any political group which does not please the West wins an election in another country, Western powers feel free to cut political ties or intervene in the other country's domestic matters. Yet, when the killing of a female protestor is enough to bring talk of intervention by super powers in Iran, does Peru face international intervention? Far more people have been killed there so far.

In the run-up to the election, Western media, governments and NGOs supported Mousavi against Ahmadinejad.[152] They were bold in their estimates that Mousavi would win by a wide margin, claiming, for example, that he was widely supported by women.[153] In the event, Ahmadinejad won more women's votes.

But my focus here is the meaning of the global, not the local, action. Intellectuals are now asking if all the external support for Mousavi in fact helped Ahmadinejad win. The next question must be whether that was the intended outcome or not. That is, were Western and Eastern minds manipulated by the Western media and discourse, and if so, to what extent? Could it be true that Western power lobbies do not really want Ahmadinejad replaced by an alleged reformer?[154] Why are the expec-

---

[151] www.nytimes.com/2009/06/06/world/americas/06peru.html; www.nytimes.com/2009/06/10/world/americas/10briefs-Peru.html

[152] www.pbs.org/wgbh/pages/frontline/tehranbureau/2009/06/who-voted-for-ahmadinejad.html

[153] www.theguardian.com/commentisfree/2009/may/05/iran-elections-women; www.theguardian.com/world/2009/jun/15/zahra-rhanavard-iran-elections-presidential

[154] drezner.foreignpolicy.com/posts/2009/06/15/whats_next_for_us_foreign_policy_on_iran. Accessed on 28 October 2013, behind paywall.

tations of the millennialists in both East and West so attached to Iran and to belligerent theocratic leaders? How different did analysts assume Iran under Mousavi would be compared to the previous government? Could the revolutionary forces and theocratic leaders allow Mousavi to act in accordance with Western alignments? These are serious questions for the media.

I am offering no support for any leader or regime here. My point is how people have been misled by the media coverage of the Iranian elections. Whether or not media agencies share ulterior motives of vested interests, media coverage too often works against moderation and developing effective and non-violent solutions to problems in the Middle East and other parts of the world. The coverage of these elections, with their protest banners in English sending messages to Western powers, as if the media has a duty to overthrow a person elected by the people, further isolates Iran and encourages polarization locally and globally. The current regime will use the coverage to affirm its own ideology and grip on power. The coverage will not help the reformists in Iran.[155]

To conjecture about future developments based on Twitter messages or unverified cellphone coverage of partisan activists may not be sensible. We must ask why Peruvians killed by police bullets or assaults with spears and machetes by indigenous people are not at all iconic and pervasive in our minds and monitors. Perhaps if the indigenous Peruvians were given electronic gadgets to post on Twitter, we might expect future interventions there, too. But I won't hold my breath while I'm waiting.

---

[155] For a later analysis of Western media organs responsibility and participation in various "covert actions" see consortiumnews.com/2013/06/17/ahmadinejad-won-get-over-it.

Knowledge and Accountability at Home and Abroad

July 16, 2009

The knowledgeability of citizens and the availability of information to voters has a great effect on policy, politicians' actions and their accountability. Informed voters are able to name, rate and dismiss public officials by popular vote. In addition, representatives who keep their constituency informed of their work are more likely to testify before congressional hearings, to serve on committees and to vote against the party line for the benefit of their constituency or the general public. So it has long been recognized that voter information is essential for effective democratic governance and for holding elected officials accountable for their policy decisions.

However, in weak democracies most people can only get information from or about their representatives indirectly. Reporting becomes more selective and superficial. Corrupt governments are reluctant to share information with the public and the press. They have strong incentives to silence active political coverage. To counter this trend, regulations or laws must oblige the content, timing and programming of information sharing by politicians and representatives.

Citizens' interest and engagement in politics increases the close monitoring of politicians. It prompts representatives to work harder and produce better policies for their constituencies. This benefits all voters; it affects voting outcomes and increases participation in elections and the tendency to support successful incumbents. As a result, voter information also draws more funding to services and investment in local constituencies. The opposite case, a lack of information for voters, affects representatives' behavior negatively. Representatives who share less information with their constituents vote in a more partisan manner, rather than being responsive to the needs, expectations or understanding of their constituents.

Freedom of information improves accountability. It reduces the chances of voters casting ballots for the wrong candidate, for poor policies or for corrupt political interests. Less public access to information leads to distorted policy outcomes in favor of narrow interest groups. In a pluralistic world, this then affects the welfare of all citizens. Here, of course, the proliferation of technology and global information networks have wide-ranging implications for voter information and political accountability.

Two recent events are illustrative of this discussion. The first concerns Dick Cheney, the former vice president of the United States. Word has leaked out that Mr. Cheney kept the US Congress in the dark about several clandestine operations, pushing the limits of legality. Former and current intelligence officials also indicate that plans to assassinate certain people in other countries without the knowledge of other US authorities existed, and the foreign governments concerned may seek criminal prosecution. This news has led to further discussion about whether the CIA was involved in making or carrying out such plans, and whether the CIA is still running other such efforts that Congress has not been briefed on and whether the US military participated in these operations or not. It is alleged that one particular assassination in Kenya has already proved a severe embarrassment for the US government.[156] It is the US government's job to resolve this issue thoroughly. The point here for us is that nothing remains secret in the globalized world of information, and nothing affects one constituency or nation alone. Whether Cheney was right or wrong is again another issue, and not the scope of this column. The point this US story illustrates is that information equips voters to monitor and hold their representatives accountable, and that poor or reduced access to information may lead to clandestine decisions which have wider implications for all the citizens of a country or countries concerned. We hope that the accusations prove false and do not lead to any further moral ambiguities or blemish the high values and legal norms American democracy purports to represent.

The second example is from the Turkish Gladio, or Ergenekon terror organization. So far, no one knows exactly how many plots, assassinations and killings this amorphous organization and its clandestine members have carried out. No one can reckon the valuable time and opportunities Turkey has lost in its economic and democratic modernization as a result of Ergenekon's false flag terrorism, chaos and discord, not to

---

[156] www.theguardian.com/world/2009/jul/13/cheney-cia-al-qaida-assassinations

mention the deaths of 17,000 people in southeastern Turkey. All these events were plotted within exclusivist salons and secret society organizations. Now the Turkish people have learned about them and would like to hold accountable all those who took part. Although the culprits are attempting to conceal themselves and escape prosecution and legal sanctions with various political, "medical" and judicial schemes, the people are now equipped with enough information to pursue the case, and Ergenekon cannot cover the sun with mud.

Information and knowledge empower ordinary people and constituencies. Knowledge brings about accountability and liability. Shared knowledge consolidates the public's wisdom and status. When it is not shared, knowledge may serve ulterior motives. Whoever assumes that things could be concealed from the public is self-deluded. Sooner or later the truth prevails over falsehood, "for falsehood is by its nature bound to perish."

Torture: Breaking the Breaking Wheel

August 8, 2009

Military and police activities in the Middle East and the public debate in the US over who should be held ultimately responsible for events in Guantanamo and Abu Ghraib raise many new and old questions about the ethical boundaries between interrogation, punishment and torture.

Widely accepted definitions of torture encompass both physical and mental pain and suffering. Torture or exposure to torture has long-term psychological or physical effects. It is regarded as one of the most extreme forms of victimization human beings can experience. Against all moral principles and religious teachings, torture has persisted from ancient times and been used to punish, coerce and extract information. In spite of the ingenuity and cruelty of past torture methods, the 20th and 21st century can seem the most ruthless and savage of all times because of the way pain, suffering and damage of all kinds have been inflicted on the masses. Torture is not only used to force a person to yield information but also to break down an opponent's integrity so that that person can then be used to spread terror throughout the community.

Nowadays, definitions of torture are becoming increasingly varied, even though international law defines it very clearly.[157] Contemporary administrations show a regrettable ambiguity regarding the definitions and prosecution of torture.

The overwhelming majority of the parents of my generation in Turkey were not schooled to any great degree. They did not receive higher education but had the decency to raise their children well. We grew up listening to events and morals within the prophetic tradition of Islam; we learned, say, that when a woman confined her pet in her house without food and water and the pet perished painfully, as a punishment she deserved hellfire. We were all warned not to make any threatening ges-

---

[157] www.hrweb.org/legal/cat.html

ture with a sharp object because to do so is forbidden and punished in religion, not to give a knife, a pair of scissors or any pointed household objects to a person with its pointed tip turned toward the other person as it is not only dangerous but also intimidating and so punishable according to Islam. So we grew up knowing that we should not frighten or harm people and that for any act that may be perceived as frightening or harmful we are accountable. In this context, it is easy to see how falsely recently emerged radicals interpret religious elements while defending their own violent ideologies and atrocities.

Alarmingly, with the advent of the 21st century, we see contemporary people and administrations growing more subjective and less civilized in terms of the definition and effects of torture. From the Nazi and communist camps of the past to recent events in Bosnia, Congo and Rwanda, administrations have become more cunning and cruel but less accountable in the foreign and domestic spheres with respect to the full range of physical, psychological and social suffering they have inflicted on their own and other peoples. In their rhetoric, torture becomes "aggressive interrogation techniques" or "detention procedures." Some dire acts and methods are simply never recognized in their political theory and jargon as torture. Torture is all too often not truly about eliciting information but about breaking an individual's humanity and dignity. Enduring such ill treatment makes individuals feel there is no meaning in living or life in general.

Empirical research shows that psychological manipulation, including different forms of deprivation and sexual humiliation, causes as much mental distress and trauma as physical torture.[158] They also cause distress and trauma at similar rates and to similar extents. The empirical evidence defies the vague distinctions and labels of the jargon used in endless and inconclusive political discussions to obscure the truth.

The cases of innocent people who are held and subjected to harsh treatment under authoritarian regimes which fail to prove that such people have been engaged in any terrorist activities is also a serious matter hurting the common conscience all over the world.[159] Whether the victim is innocent or not, torture is inhumane, unethical and immoral. Further-

---

[158] www.eurekalert.org/pub_releases/2007-03/jaaj-pap030107.php
[159] news.bbc.co.uk/1/hi/uk_politics/8179373.stm; news.bbc.co.uk/1/hi/uk/7906842.stm

more, torture survivors rarely get the mental and medical health treatment they need. Moreover, torturers are themselves at increased risk of post-traumatic stress disorder. They also need care and treatment afterwards. The latest example of this is the confession of an officer from a Central Asian country carried by the BBC this week.[160]

Again this week, on a CNN program about the ongoing war in Afghanistan, some war correspondents made the point that younger generations witnessing all this war in Afghanistan and elsewhere ought to be provided with a sound education so that they will not engage in violence and terrorism and fall into the hands of extremists and radicals afterwards. In the same way, some journalists and authorities in Turkey, as a remedy to the ongoing conflict in southeast Turkey, are arguing for the provision of a sound education for young people and advocating for the involvement of peaceful civic initiatives like the Gülen Movement against violence, radicalism and fundamentalism.[161] Instead of going round and round again, every cycle worse than the last, it is time to break the breaking wheel.

---

[160] news.bbc.co.uk/1/hi/programmes/newsnight/8195906.stm
[161] www.todayszaman.com/news-181543-observers-say-boldness-a-must-for-addressing-kurdish-issue.html

Pre-emption and Presumption:
Blair and Turkish Juntas

February 4, 2010

T he Chilcot Inquiry into the Iraq war, which is currently under way in the United Kingdom, provides an interesting point of comparison for Turkey, where press and prosecutors are pursuing with some vigor inquiries into activities involving the military.

Testimony to the Chilcot Inquiry has indicated that then-UK Prime Minister Tony Blair was repeatedly advised that the invasion of Iraq would be illegal and that the security service informed him that Iraq did not possess "weapons of mass destruction" but only some battlefield weapons that could not be fired at the UK "at 45 minutes' notice"—one of Blair's claims at the time. It seems to have taken a lot of finagling by more "amenable" advisers to create a political context in which an invasion might possibly be seen as legal.

However, as we know, even with this engineering of the truth, many nations and people failed to be convinced of its legality at the time of the invasion or afterward.[162] The more information that emerges, the more difficult it is to avoid concluding that Blair lied to his people and to parliament or that he is self-deluding in his grandiose desire for power and influence and his presumption that, no matter the evidence, he knows "better" than the common throng. His testimony to the Chilcot commission made it clear that he adheres to the doctrine of pre-emption, that is, one can commit an illegal act against a person or persons now in order to prevent a potential illegal act by the other later. So, for example, it becomes feasible to invade a country just in case it may become dangerous to you at some later date.

---

[162] www.bbc.co.uk/news/10463844; www.independent.co.uk/news/uk/home-news/lord-goldsmith-blair-did-not-reflect-legal-advice-on-iraq-war-2187031.html; www.telegraph.co.uk/news/politics/7885629/Iraq-inquiry-Government-intentionally-and-substantially-exaggerated-WMD-threat.html

Blair's *post hoc* justifications are just as unreal as those advanced prior to the war. He cites Iraq as dangerous because it is a center for al-Qaeda and other similar terrorist entities. He "forgets" that such groups had no place in Iraq prior to the invasion, so the invasion actually increased opportunities for both local and global terror. He presumes that his skill in self-presentation will somehow lead the general public and the world as a whole to overlook this most appalling fact.

The illegality of the Iraq invasion does not justify the general conduct of its former government, but without doubt the invasion and its aftermath have caused the violent deaths of a greater number of innocent civilians than Iraq's previous regime ever did. That is in addition to a huge breakdown in society and an enormous surge in criminality, including the crimes of some British soldiers for whose presence there Blair is responsible.

As a Turkish citizen, what am I reminded of?

We also seem to suffer from a discomforting excess of those who wish to enact illegal "regime change" just in case the current incumbents might later do something they do not approve of. Our "regime changers" differ in that they are working internally, but are similarly self-deluding in their presumption that illegal means can be used to defend a nation and its values and that they know best what those values are. Other hallmarks the power-hungry in Turkey share with Blair are their love of secrecy and their inability to benefit from or modulate their conduct according to consultation with others of different views than their own.

In 2003 Blair rejected the advice of the pope at the time that the Iraq war was not morally justified.[163] He has since converted to Catholicism, but still stands by his regrettable decision. Perhaps he should now cut down on his speaking engagements in the United States, profitable though they may be. With a little more time on his hands, he might ponder the story of Pharaoh. Pharaoh was also a powerful man with great self-belief. When troubled by those who were apparently ungrateful for his rule, he also had a tendency to overreact. Like Blair (and our own coup-plotters in Turkey), Pharaoh went through the motions of consultation without heeding any advice that went counter to his own wishes. Pharaoh tried to contest with Moses in front of his ministers and men of knowledge, and was

---

[163] www.nytimes.com/2003/01/14/international/europe/14POPE.html

infuriated when his advisers agreed with his opponent but refused to change his course. Opponents or naysayers fall like skittles around such "leaders." The Chilcot Inquiry and investigations into coup-plotting in Turkey say the same.

In events in the UK and Turkey we see that dishonesty, arrogance and power-seeking are not qualities inherent to particular tribes and nations, but are evenly spread, a part of their human nature individuals must strive to overcome.

"Leaders" with such presumption do not lead their people to success. Far from it, robbed of the strength of sincere consultation, or in the modern world, the democratic process and the rule of law, their nations crumble, and such leaders finally earn nothing but scorn and contempt in this world and the next.

Diplomacy, Diplomacy and Diplomacy

June 3, 2010

T he assault on the Gaza aid convoy[164] by Israeli commandos and the events and criticism unfolding in its aftermath are likely to dominate the news for some time. It has drawn a wide range of views from diverse commentators.

Israel's attack on the aid flotilla is viewed as unnecessary, ill-conceived and disproportionate. However at a deeper level, arguments concentrate on the Israeli military and its past botched operations, the blockade of Gaza, the plight and future of Palestinians and the complicity of the wider international community in the treatment of Gaza.

In the Turkish media, some columnists are demanding that the Israeli government be made morally, legally and financially accountable for the attack in accordance with international law and UN regulations. They see the assault as Israel shooting itself in the foot and avoid connecting it to any religious issue. Others in the media are, however, using provocative arguments to galvanize the prime minister into taking drastic military action against Israel.[165] This is now leading to infighting among journalists as some criticize their colleagues for having no intention of contributing to the resolution of the conflict but aiming to get the ruling party bogged down in an international conflict.

The tenor of the criticism in the European media is different. They see the attack as an error-ridden operation. They support their arguments with the remarks of prominent figures in Israel who question the wisdom of the operation. They quote from Israeli papers that describe the operation as a "fiasco."[166] They denounce the use of force to stop the flotilla and blame the "political echelon" for the decision. They quote Israeli media criticism that the operation was "deeply flawed and incorrectly prepared";

---

[164] www.bbc.co.uk/news/10210949
[165] www.bbc.co.uk/news/world-europe-14791210
[166] www.haaretz.com/print-edition/news/fiasco-on-the-high-seas-1.293415

that it was "a cardinal mistake" that the military did not plan for the possibility that some people on the ship were willing "to risk their lives"; and that military intelligence had overestimated the ease of the operation. They ask why Israel did not use the most effective tactic of disabling the vessels before they even entered the bloody confrontation.[167]

Some journalists are discussing the capacity of Israeli soldiers. They are enumerating the military interventions that have ended in failure and disgrace since 1973: the 1982 invasion of Lebanon, permitting the Christian militias to massacre the Palestinians in the Sabra and Shatila refugee camps; a long and unsuccessful guerrilla war against Hezbollah; the bombardments of Lebanon in 1996 and 2006; and the attack on Gaza in 2008. All of these are interpreted as failures, as they did not weaken but strengthened Hamas and Hezbollah in the region. The Western media are also reminding readers of what General David Petraeus, the top US military commander, warned—that the failure to resolve the Israeli-Palestinian dispute is damaging America's security interests across the Middle East.

One European journalist also warns that "the fluency and mendacity of Israeli spokesmen ... distort Israelis' sense of reality."[168] As their spokesmen portray failures as successes, Israelis are led to believe that their leaders have never made a mistake. They gain an inflated idea of their own abilities. In this way, their failure to see mistakes is a major cause of the same errors being repeated time and time again at ever greater cost.

However Western commentators are now openly discussing the fact that so many countries have been complicit in the policy of isolating Gaza and seeking to turn its population against Hamas. The hope of undermining Hamas that has been lingering since 2006 is now failing. Such tactics are now being interpreted as the collective punishment of Gaza's population[169] and hence politically counterproductive, further radicalizing people in the region and elsewhere.

It is widely accepted that the blockade is hurting the civilian population much more than Hamas. Opening routes for humanitarian aid to

---

[167] online.wsj.com/news/articles/SB10001424052748704366504575278621338138694

[168] www.independent.co.uk/voices/commentators/patrick-cockburn-pr-dangerously-distorts-the-israeli-sense-of-reality-1988977.html

[169] www.amnesty.org/en/news-and-updates/feature-stories/trapped-collective-punishment-gaza-20080827

Gaza will reduce smuggling and illicit diversion of goods. Internationally supervised projects and infrastructure must be given priority. Independent international monitoring of traffic and exchange would be an important step toward peace in the region. All sides implicated in this ongoing conflict, especially the international community, need to re-examine their tactics and policies. Even Hamas supporters need to be won over and engaged peacefully in a two-state solution.[170]

Provocative acts must be avoided by all parties, whether transporting aid or controlling borders. All conflicts and clashes, including world wars, have been initiated by a few individuals and their reckless actions. If the aftermath is handled coolly and responsibly by all sides, this latest incident, even with its casualties, could provide an opportunity for peace-making, coexistence and prosperity in the region rather than further escalation of conflict, so that people can stop killing Palestinians, Arabs, Israelis and Turks, or Europeans, or Americans.

---

[170] www.csmonitor.com/Commentary/Opinion/2009/0624/p09s01-coop.html/ (page)/2

Cutting through the Fog over the Golden Horn: Perspectives on Turkey

October 7, 2010

In recent years, more and more Turkish citizens have been traveling abroad to pursue postgraduate studies in the social sciences. Such courses often entail discussions about the modern history of the Turkish Republic, the nature of Turkish democracy and politics, and the concurrent factors that have led to intermittent plots, coups, assassinations and extrajudicial killings.

This also often requires an academic battle against misinformation and an unfortunate lack of accurate perspective on the part of non-Turkish researchers and supervisors.

Like many of my Turkish colleagues in the social sciences, I was initially stunned at how non-Turkish readers and researchers on Turkish politics remained ignorant of the separation between the state and government in Turkey. This limited knowledge is a persistent impediment to proper public discussion or comprehension of many issues, especially democratization, Westernization, civil society and the engagement and empowerment of faith in Turkey.

The second factor is mostly related to resources—that is, the authors and literature emerging from a Turkish background. Because only until very recently the authors of most such academic papers were employed by universities under the control of the Higher Education Board (YÖK), they were mostly drawn from a very limited group of people adhering to a tightly constrained ideology. Needless to say, under the strict, ideological and undemocratic governance of YÖK at the time, the pressure academics felt to keep their position or get promoted forced them to hold distorted stances; they became uncritical of issues related to the system. There are honorable exceptions, of course. However, many academics and their writings were either very biased or did not investigate events within Turkey truthfully or thoroughly.

The third influential factor was the dominant source of knowledge about events and personalities in Turkey. This factor still applies today. Unfortunately, many in the rest of the world get their understanding of Turkey from popular magazines, dailies or TV channels. Viewing coverage by those media, Turks easily see that the journalists seek sensationalism and that correspondents usually end up speaking to a small clique of ideologues and political activists, those with marginal perspectives. The elitists—people whom the correspondents seem to feel close to—are in fact from the minority of what is called "republican" defenders of the authoritarian, statist, elitist and laicism-based bureaucracy of the military, judiciary and academia. These groups have always opposed true democratization, civil society and other pluralistic developments in Turkey.

This state of affairs has served certain ends: While Turkey was being politically pressured for particular political gains by some interest groups, the mostly inaccurate and biased perspectives of political activists could be aired unchallenged both inside and outside Turkey as if they were the perceptions of the mainstream or majority. Even a cursory look at the coverage by, for example, the *Economist* and *Newsweek* can illustrate how often the marginal perspectives of ethnic and ideological activists are presented as actual reality or as the views of the overwhelming majority of people and intellectuals in Turkey.

Then comes a problem familiar to many Turkish students, researchers and academics. While discussing matters related to Turkey, they stumble into being misperceived as a new kind of political activist, or an ardent subscriber to wild conspiracy theories, or an over-excited and unreasonable zealot because many of the issues; events; plots; killings; abuses of power, rank or position; corruption; and plots in Turkey's recent history do strike outsiders forcefully as outlandish tales, something from the movies, or events in a contemptible "banana republic." They do not square easily with the images propagated by the elite and marginal groups that cluster and chatter around foreign correspondents.

Even well-meaning and honest onlookers and commentators about Turkey have to cope with an ever-swirling confusion of events. There are the trials of those accused of extrajudicial killings, the wiretapping of members of Ergenekon, investigations of hidden caches of weapons of Turkish military origin, information from unmanned aerial surveillance vehicles about terrorist attacks and now a debate about the assassinations of General Eşref Bitlis and former President Turgut Özal.[171] Concealed in the fog creep the schemes and ghost writers of sensational books that are working a strategy of tension.[172]

But now, as the swathes of fog start to be driven back by daylight, both inside and outside Turkey, we are gaining a better perspective on events. So, if researchers, academics and the media can free their vision of the dark clouds of bias and misinformation from marginal and elitist resources, we should start to be able to discuss, from more enlightening perspectives, constitutionalism, pluralism, democratization, freedoms and rights, civil society and faith in the past, present and future of Turkey.

---

[171] www.todayszaman.com/news-224253-parliament-plans-to-investigate-deaths-of-turgut-ozal-esref-bitlis.html; www.todayszaman.com/news-327112-esref-bitlis-case-will-not-be-shut-down-under-new-order.html

[172] www.todayszaman.com/news-219888-avcis-claims-in-new-book-lack-any-evidence-experts-say.html

A Long and Dishonorable European Tradition

October 21, 2010

Comments by German Chancellor Angela Merkel—that attempts to build a multicultural society in Germany and for communities to live side by side have "utterly failed"—occurred in the context of many debates around anti-immigrant feelings in European countries.[173]

Merkel's remarks seem to be an attempt to counter recent comments by German President Christian Wulff, who said Islam was "part of Germany" just like Christianity and Judaism.[174] It is obvious that Merkel has been facing pressure from within her conservative party and its allies to take a tougher stance against immigrants in German society.

But her remarks cannot be taken at face value as a good description of reality. Almost 50 years ago Germany first invited foreign workers to come to help build its economy, to do the dirtiest and heaviest jobs and live in Germany without enjoying the full rights of citizenship; they were, for example, excluded from certain jobs, such as teaching. There was no attempt to "integrate" them, but rather to keep them on the margins of society. So, if multiculturalism has been a failure, that failure is not just attributable to the behavior of the "guest workers." The "welcome" offered to the "guests" must have had something to do with it. The gap in Merkel's powers of analysis and grasp on reality shows up again in her assurance that all the workers whose arrival they once greeted with bands "soon will be gone."

It is too easy in Europe to say almost unchallenged that "immigrants from different cultures like Turkey and Arab countries, all in all, find it harder" to integrate. The claim that Turks, Arabs and others who are mostly Muslims are in some way "inassimilable" or indigestible is easily disproved

---

[173] www.bbc.co.uk/news/world-europe-11559451

[174] www.spiegel.de/international/germany/the-world-from-berlin-should-muslims-be-treated-on-an-equal-footing-a-722065.html

by taking a look at other societies, such as the United States, South Africa and countries in South America, where these groups seem to be having no such problems. If incoming groups are unwilling to share all your values, it just might be that there is something wrong with some of your values. Merkel's remarks are better understood as the reflection of expressions of the neo-nationalism that has emerged in Europe and that peaks during election campaigns.

Most nationalists utilize exactly the same arguments: They believe that their own particular country or Europe consists of people who would rightfully defend themselves against people from non-Western countries, and particularly against Muslims; those non-Westerners choose spouses and a way of life from outside Europe; they therefore pose a risk by virtue of their traditions and religion; and they are a source of mischief and crime in Europe. Immigrants, and particularly Muslim immigrants, are clearly portrayed by some politicians and others as a threat to "European" values and society.

However, the argument that Muslimness is essentially "un-European" stands in clear contradiction to the historical facts and indeed the map of Europe. Apart from the long history and contribution of Muslims to European society,[175] unless the EU intends to contract back so as to become a small rump—perhaps the "Western European Union"—Merkel and her allies in argumentation haven't got a leg to stand on. While in Turkey we know that some EU figures reject our "European-ness," and apparently cannot locate the Bosphorus on a map, where do they think Bosnia is located? What about Kosovo? Are they in the Middle East? It is tempting to send Merkel a map. Wulff's view is more historically accurate, and less "mythologized" and emotional than Merkel's.

The irrational nature of the attack on Muslim immigrants is exposed by the refusal to even acknowledge the existence of, and let's be frank here, white Muslims in Europe, and the paroxysms of rage that engulf such nationalists when forced to face them. Whether these Muslims are of Eastern European origin or converts and the children and grandchildren of converts, they unnerve the racists and expose their real and foolish fears and motives. These "white Muslims" pose a huge psychological

---

[175] frontiersmagazine.org/washington-irving-and-the-rediscovery-of-the-lost-centuries-of-knowledge/; www.huffingtonpost.com/craig-considine/overcoming-historical-amnesia_b_4135868.html

threat to the European racists' system of categorization. Just like European nationalists' refusal to accept as "native" citizens of color and different religions, no matter how many generations they have lived in the country, this is pure racism, a long and dishonorable tradition in European history of fearing the "other," a tradition to which an immigrant cannot adhere without becoming self-hating and psychologically disturbed, and thus a danger to all around him or her. So, if Merkel sees immigrants as a "danger," perhaps it is because some of them have in fact sadly integrated the receiving culture's hatred of themselves. This may be the paradox of integration into a racist culture.

If Merkel and her ilk truly wish to solve the "problem of immigration," they will need to do a little more self-accounting. They must develop some education around tolerance and universal values so that their own "native" EU citizens should learn how to live and coexist with those with whom they are not identical.

The Lion's Share, the Wolf's Fate and the Arab World

February 3, 2011

T he shift in the fortunes of the Tunisians and Egyptians, their challenging the efforts of their countries' autocrats to divide national interests between internal and external interest groups and the growing signs of division between autocrats and external powers contrast with the unity of the people and their aim. All of this reminds me of the story of "The Lion's Share" told by Rumi, one the greatest exponents of the Islamic spiritual tradition. It is a tale about the inability to recognize true power and ownership.

In the fable from the "Mathnawi," Rumi illustrates through the lion and his hunting companions a lesson about the annihilation of dualism and unity with God. However, as with many fables, it can illuminate events in this world as well as the path to the next.

Three animals—a lion, a wolf and a fox—go hunting together. By the end of the day they have caught an ox, an ibex and a hare. When it is time to divide the spoils, the wolf and the fox expect the lion to share the abundance with them, being unaware of who they are dealing with.

The lion tells the wolf, "Divide up the catch between us in any way you like." The wolf deals the spoils into three parts. He gives the largest part, the ox, to the lion; he claims the ibex for himself and hands the hare to the fox. The lion, seeing the wolf's failure to recognize that all the lands and all the bounty they contain rightfully belong to him, roars, "How dare you talk of 'mine' and 'yours'!" With a single swipe of his mighty paw, he tears off the wolf's head. Then the lion turns to the fox and says, "Divide up this abundance between us in any way you like." The fox humbly declares straightaway that all the catch rightfully belongs to the lion alone. Then the lion asks the fox where he learned to divide the spoils in this way, and the fox replies, "From the wolf's punishment and fate."

The fox sees clearly that the only way to avoid death is to abandon all greed. Some may think how much better it would have been to have shared in a friendly spirit. However, today we should recognize, as the fox did, that the bounty cannot be divided or possessed when the true owner of the lands and the bounties they contain is the people.

Rumi concludes that we are lucky if the examples of past generations guide us. Through the unfolding events, in particular in Egypt, we see that people are not after a partisan or ideological revolution or the rule of a single person, group or party. They are seeking their freedom and dignity. They have grasped an opportunity to break the shackles clapped on them by a despot who has ruled them for the past 31 years. This collective uprising cannot turn into and should not be interpreted as, "Either you accept Hosni Mubarak or you need to get prepared for another Hamas or Taliban in power." This uprising cannot even be attributed to the Muslim Brotherhood, which is now acknowledged by many to have renounced violence years ago.

Many interest groups and outside arbitrators might be worried for a multitude of reasons. However, this should not divert us from the main course: People should be allowed to enjoy rights, democracy and freedom. They will no longer live with harassment, coercion and torture imposed by a dictator, his puppets and his ruthless intelligence service. Like any people anywhere in the world, the population aspires to progress, welfare, safety and security for themselves and for their children. We don't expect them to bother developing hostilities towards their neighbors and other nations. They have had enough of such events and policies.

Some may have presumed that that they are the lion and that the Egyptian people can be beheaded like the wolf or must cringe like the fox. But now the true owner of the land and its bounties will be revealed in Egypt and other countries concerned—countries which have already started to feel the spasms of new developments in and around them and have so far only come up with some window dressing, a few symbolic changes of ministers and governments that resemble each other.

Let the fate of wolves like Egypt's Mubarak or Tunisian Zine El-Abidine Ben Ali be a lesson that people cannot live forever under the yoke of authoritarian rulers. May the people be themselves, enjoy their freedom and decide for themselves. Let them enjoy their lion's share. Human beings are our first concern. We ought to understand their grievances and support them in being able to pick their next leaders peacefully so that they become a center of stability in the region. The opposite would not serve anyone's interests, not the lion, the wolf or the fox.

European Security and Islamism: Planks and Splinters

February 10, 2011

E uropean leaders met at the Munich Security Conference on February 5 to discuss extremism and terrorism. UK Prime Minister David Cameron delivered a speech[176] focusing on radicalization and Islamist extremism.

Cameron controversially claimed that multiculturalism can foster Islamic extremism and that the biggest threat the UK faces comes from terrorist attacks, some of which are carried out by their own citizens. Although he stressed that "terrorism is not linked exclusively to any one religion or ethnic group," he also claimed that "the threat comes in Europe overwhelmingly from young men who follow a completely perverse, warped interpretation of Islam" and from the "the existence of an ideology, Islamist extremism." He urged Europe "to wake up" to what is happening in their own countries.

Cameron had given the impression he was about to focus on the security aspects of the European response: tracing plots and stopping attackers before they strike, counter-surveillance and intelligence gathering as well as the social exclusion of the overwhelming majority of peaceful Muslims, the discrimination and oppression suffered by their communities within Europe and the spread of neo-Salafism or Wahhabi Islamism owing to British, European and even American societies' long failure to recognize or diagnose the root of the problem.

Alas! Cameron only managed simultaneously to single out Muslims for blame and offer further economic cuts in educational support. Thus he succeeded in feeding the hysteria and paranoia about Islam and Muslims in Europe, without referring even once to the agenda, plans and activities of such anti-Muslim and fascist groups as the British National Party (BNP) and the English Defence League (EDL), which are another source of violence, discrimination, isolation, radicalization and tension.

---

[176] www.gov.uk/government/speeches/pms-speech-at-munich-security-conference

Cameron marshaled all the cliché arguments about Islam, Islamism and Islam and the West. He distinguished between Islam as a religion observed peacefully and devoutly by over a billion people and Islamist extremism as a political ideology supported by a minority. But immediately thereafter he made the strange assertion: "At the furthest end are those who back terrorism to promote their ultimate goal: an entire Islamist realm, governed by an interpretation of Shariah. Move along the spectrum, and you find people who may reject violence but who accept various parts of the extremist worldview, including real hostility towards Western democracy and liberal values." He admitted the contributory factors to radicalism, such as the West's lumping all Muslims together, and a list of real political grievances like the Palestinian conflict and Western foreign policies that prop up authoritarian leaders across the Middle East. His conclusion suggested that Europe must turn the page on the failed (multicultural) policies of the past, stop ignoring the extremist Islamist ideology and confront it in all its forms. Also, instead of encouraging people to live apart, we need a clear sense of shared national identity that is open to everyone.

Cameron's wish for "a much broader and generous vision of citizenship" seems attractive. However, his "muscular liberalism," which appears to threaten freedom of speech and belief, combined with his "blame game," are likely to cause any such vision to fail. Many respected Western academics have exhaustively analyzed the elements of "Islamism"—a modern and post-modern excrescence in the history of Islam—and how such extremist ideologies are constructed out of a set of *Western* philosophies, such as Marxist-Leninist ideologies, in the face of unrelenting economic, cultural and military assaults and impositions on the Muslim world. They have a thin veneer of Islamic vocabulary but no religious content. When Cameron blames the Muslim community, saying, "Some organizations that seek to present themselves as a gateway to the Muslim community are showered with public money despite doing little to combat extremism," he is refusing to acknowledge the fact that the origins of "Islamist extremism" are as much the responsibility of his community as any other. He is dumping the blame.

Cameron notes but fails to grasp the import of the fact that many "Islamist extremists" are second or third-generation Europeans, born, bred and educated in their system for decades. Their thinking, dress and speech are pure Hackney, Scouse, Mancunian or Glaswegian. Their rhetoric is the discourse of individualistic rights, racism, unfettered freedom, class, anti-imperialism and self-determination. This is not the language of Islam.

Certainly Muslims can help in combating extremism of whatever ilk. But it will be easier to do so if we confront all its manifestations in the same way, whether expressed by disenchanted white racists in the EDL (and indeed the Conservative party) or angry, misdirected youth from minority communities. Let all the parties extract the splinter from their own eye so we can all see clearly.

7

Faith in the Public Sphere

Madrid Dialogue Conference: How Can Interfaith Dialogue Make any Progress?

August 7, 2008

Recent internal issues, such as Ergenekon—the deep-state terror organization—and the Justice and Development Party (AK Party) closure case, have distracted us from discussing an international interfaith conference organized by King Abdullah of Saudi Arabia in Madrid on July 16–18 [2008]. The conference's final statement was comprehensive[177]; yet the real question still remains to be answered: How can the principles and recommendations agreed upon by the elite social and political leaders and selected academics lead to commitment and action among ordinary people?

Almost 300 invitees from different faith groups convened in Madrid to advance interfaith dialogue. The final statement, the Madrid Declaration, highlighted the importance of dialogue in achieving mutual understanding, cooperation among the adherents of religions and cultures, peaceful coexistence among nations and the rejection of extremism and terrorism. They came up with a broad list of principles that they agreed on and adopted recommendations to which no one can object.

The conference had admirers and detractors. On behalf of knowledge, learning and humanity, we appreciate such educational, cultural and peace-seeking efforts. Yet what was declared in Madrid is nothing new. It has all been said by many and done by few before. The real question then should be how the recommendations expressed can lead to commitment

---

[177] susris.sustg.org/2008/07/19/the-madrid-declaration/

and action. Can any initiative which is not internalized and practiced by the grass roots, by the ordinary believers of faith communities, lift off and contribute to local and global wellbeing? We know that past efforts at dialogue on the part of political entities, governments and organizations have often not taken root as expected. When governments and politicians change, support and attitudes toward these actions also change in tune with new policies, priorities or conjunctures. The global ethics initiative, for example, financed by the World Bank, drew sharp criticism, was received with cynicism and skepticism and is no longer pursued by all or discussed except as an intellectual pursuit. But dialogue cannot be a short-term project. Sharing panels and conference halls is short term, but true dialogue takes a great amount of time, sacrifice, empathy, compassion and dedication.

Some faith leaders and believers have worked quietly over the past two decades to achieve true dialogue, arguing that it is the best way for people to move beyond stereotypes, develop mutual respect and combat the exploitation of religion in the name of political, ideological, financial and racial interests. Many faithful volunteers and civic organizations have dedicated themselves to finding common grounds and shared values. I cannot talk on everyone's behalf. However, I can share my experience in one interfaith dialogue organization which has developed and been joined by many leaders, academics and volunteers from diverse faith communities over the past six years—the Institute of Interfaith Dialog.[178]

The Institute, like many decentralized interfaith institutions, is run by volunteers from local Turkish communities in the US. It was inspired by the peaceful teachings and the example of the scholar, intellectual and dialogue activist Fethullah Gülen. The institute, with all its branches, listens and responds with openness and respect and advocates ways that acknowledge genuine differences but aim to build on shared hopes and values, particularly among the grass roots of diverse communities. By being in constant interaction with other people from different traditions than their own, the institute's volunteers prepare the venues and opportunities in which the basic feelings, thoughts, aspirations and spirituality of all individuals can be heard in a space that is free of dogmatism and criticism. In contrast to the Madrid conference, which is closed to the press

---

[178] www.interfaithdialog.org

and the grass roots, the institute's activities and events are open and free to all.

Apart from IID's academic workshops and conferences, the most effective events are the interfaith meals, especially the breakfasts and dinners organized by individual families at their homes for the families from other faith communities, most of whom have never met each other before. I know many families that have given several dinners to groups of three or four families in their homes, sharing their traditional home-made dishes. What they do is in the Abrahamic tradition, sharing food with "strangers." These table fellowships have produced such deep friendships between people of diverse backgrounds, cultures and faiths that many people have reciprocated in the same way and are encouraging many others to do so, too.

They thus share the message that we are all worshippers of the same almighty Creator and that we are indeed no different from one another in hopes, values and aspirations for our own families, communities and humanity. With such inter-family gatherings, the volunteers demonstrate to society the idea that people can live together regardless of group, faith or indelible differences. Rather than the professionalized approach of the special guests of the Madrid conference, the grass roots have embarked on discovering the great deal there is to learn from one another so as to coexist in respect, peace and harmony, and are already profiting from good examples, like the volunteers of the institute.

The UK's Official Shariah Courts and 'Us'

October 16, 2008

T his is the first time ever that many columnists from a wide political spectrum have openly questioned the Turkish generals' competence and ability to compromise to produce any civic solution to terror: What else could there be as a solution to the Southeast problem other than military campaigns?[179] If we resist bias and prejudice and impulsive reactions to alternatives, there are many good examples from the contemporary world that might resolve blockages in the system and societal conflict.

One recent and "scary" example for many protectionists and self-described secularists in Turkey is the UK's "Shariah courts."[180] The disclosure that Muslim courts already have legal powers in Britain comes seven months after Rowan Williams, the Archbishop of Canterbury, suggested that the application of Shariah in Britain in the future "seems unavoidable."[181] Subsequently, the head of the judiciary, the Lord Chief Justice, said Shariah could be used to settle marital and financial disputes.[182] In fact, since August 2007, long before the public debate, the British government had officially allowed Shariah courts based on the Arbitration Act 1996.

The courts are classified as arbitration tribunals. Their rulings are binding in law provided both parties in the dispute consent to the tribunal's rule on their case. The tribunals and judges can rule on civil cases ranging from divorce, inheritance, neighbor nuisance and financial disputes to cases involving domestic violence. Rulings are issued by a net-

---

[179] For the damage done by militarization in southeast Turkey, see www.todayszaman.com/news-155295-expanding-military-authority-does-more-harm-than-good.html

[180] www.telegraph.co.uk/news/uknews/2957428/Sharia-law-courts-operating-in-Britain.html

[181] news.bbc.co.uk/1/hi/uk/7232661.stm

[182] www.theguardian.com/uk/2008/jul/04/law.islam

work of five tribunals in London, Birmingham, Bradford and Manchester, with headquarters in Warwickshire. Their rulings are enforceable with the full power of the judicial system. Two more tribunals are planned for Glasgow and Edinburgh. This method of regulating community affairs is called alternative dispute resolution and, in some cases, works in tandem with police investigations. It will also handle "smaller" criminal cases in the future as more Muslims approach the tribunals. So far the Muslim tribunals have passed judgment on more than 100 cases.

The existence of these proceedings and their enforceability have been debated in a civilized fashion in the UK. It has been asked whether they represent a parallel legal system, whether British law is absolute and must remain so, whether the tribunals might favor men or women, whether the mentoring by community elders suggested by the tribunals is as effective as intervention by professionals, how right it is for police to stop an investigation when a complaint is withdrawn and whether the state should enforce its law between two parties if they both prefer religious arbitration.

In fact, in the UK, the Jewish Beth Din courts, also religious tribunals, have been allowed to flourish under the same provision. These courts have been resolving civil cases, ranging from divorce to business disputes, for more than 100 years, and previously operated under a precursor to the current act.

Overall, Shariah tribunals are allowed to decide civil matters in the same way as can any other framework of mutually accepted binding arbitration, such as industrial tribunals, university courts and even the FIFA courts for recalcitrant footballers. This arbitration poses no threat to UK law, which allows it in many circumstances when parties do not want to go through normal court proceedings. Having inclusive and flexible ways of handling civil law is deeply democratic, not an erosion of a democratic institution or a threat to sovereignty.

The British are unperturbed by Muslims being able to settle civil disputes in a way more friendly to their faith. However, there is concern about anti-Muslim sentiment being stirred up in the public by opponents of this innovation. To the British nowadays, it seems, allowing people the right to rule themselves by the laws of their religion is civilization, true liberty and freedom of religion. Good law should help raise those less powerful to a position to fight injustice, not further institutionalize their position of relative powerlessness. Furthermore, this alternative legal system eases the workload of the judiciary. Muslims do not have to participate in a tribunal unless they want to and, in fact, Shariah requires Muslims to follow the laws of the country they live in.

If the British arbitrate civil disputes their own way, it is up to them. Clearly, Britain can synthesize the different cultures living within its borders. Their small island is shared by people of various backgrounds. What about us? Or, more correctly, what about the modern, "progressive" dominant elitists of Turkey, who never accept criticism from others? Why can they not accept the rights of their compatriots to share the same public space, and to hold governmental, judicial and military authority and positions? We are not asking for Shariah courts here. We are asking how it is that peaceful, lawful and substantiated criticisms or suggestions to the current authorities still make critics "enemies of the state." Can't we speak and question openly yet? Can't we have democratic parliamentary committees at which officials can be called to public account? In Turkey, the public can scarcely dare to suggest such a process, let alone Shariah tribunals. Absolutely not! For ours is a nation that has seen so many "traitors" hanging silenced on the gallows of Independence Tribunals and military coups.[183]

---

[183] See page 2.

Business, Faith and Freedom

October 23, 2008

[In the previous article], I wrote about Shariah courts in the UK and how its alternative legal system eases the workload of others in the judiciary and keeps Muslim citizens content with their own family and community affairs. Continual mass migration, the welfare-state, globalization, and its own multi-ethnic and multi-religious composition, are making the UK's population more diverse and its labor market multi-faith rather than, as they once were, predominantly Christian. It is acknowledged that in London alone, there are almost 50 nationalities with communities of more than 10,000. As a consequence, people are used to being in workplaces with people from other religions and ethnic backgrounds.

In the past people perhaps used to keep faith and work fairly separate, but more and more they are being intertwined. Employers and business managers are building faith-based networks, and providing activities and office space to cater for employees' religious beliefs. Probably the times when the relationship between faith and work are most visible are on religious holidays, when believers take leave according to their own religious calendars.

I arrived in England from Turkey at the beginning of the 1990s, after having lived and studied in Ankara where we were unable to find any prayer rooms or masjids, let alone mosques then, except for the few passages amongst the shops in the Kızılay area. In the UK, we were able to pray at chapels specifically allocated for Muslims at universities and, to our utmost surprise, in government buildings like the Home Office when we were applying to renew our visas. These were eye-opening and life-changing experiences for us and for many other Turkish citizens. Now, prayer rooms, once only found in hospitals, airports and colleges or universities, are increasingly common in private and government offices.

Furthermore, these days in the UK and Europe, alongside the diversity of faiths in the workplace, more top directors, chief executives and other higher ranking personnel in international institutions and government positions feel able to express their various faiths. So the modern workplace has become an unintentional but natural meeting point for interfaith encounters. Believers who are part of the rank and file show greater willingness and desire to integrate faith and work. Whether a matter of dress, dietary requirements, prayer or personal one-to-one business contacts, European institutions, companies and governments are becoming more sensitive to the faith-specific needs of their employees. One-third of companies are developing explicit policies to manage religious beliefs in the workplace. In this way, business and management become more faith-friendly or responsive to faith. They share best practice on faith-related issues, and provide prayer services, educational programs and festive celebrations, luncheons, dinner events and various other activities. They have faith and ethnic networks and through these they tend to manage the practical issues sensibly and fairly. This trend is, as in the case of the UK, partly encouraged by new legislation introduced in 2003 on religious discrimination at work.

Subsequently, we have seen another indicator of a healthy understanding of the faith and work relationship in the modern workplace in the legal issues and the number of media reports highlighting instances of religious discrimination at work. From March 2007 to April 2008, six hundred cases of workplace discrimination on religious grounds passed through the courts. There are many examples of individuals laid off by their companies, who were eventually compensated and decisions reversed.

Being faith-friendly increasingly proves to be good business sense. It improves productivity and turnover, and increases profit and mutual contentedness. The best examples are in finance, labor, environmental and other relevant company policies which are nowadays being modified to be compatible with religious traditions. Banks, faith-based investments, and financial stocks compatible with specific or diverse faiths are capitalizing on opportunities, especially in the Islamic banking and mortgage markets.

However, things are not all rosy. There are of course contentions about business conduct and ethical behavior. Many people across the globe still find it hard to hard to reconcile ethics and trade with the illegal activity, shady bids, or corrupt dealings of transnational companies, moral dilemmas related to child labor, work-slavery and lack of arbitration against big companies. The point is that now business and managers have to take ethical considerations and corporate responsibility into account more than they did before. Ethical business and the "criticism of ruthless capitalism" are not on the agenda of only religious leaders or ideological actors. They are everyone's concern.

Managers and companies are well aware that faith, ethical conduct and successful business, especially in the modern workplace, reinforce each other. So they respect and allow religious or spiritual practice. Let this be a lesson to the "enlightened" professors of Boğaziçi University who recently have started not admitting female students with headscarves to their lectures.[184] As the professors can speak English, they can refer to and benefit from the many surveys and reports about these matters, like the one by the UK's Chartered Institute of Personnel and Development from 2007.

---

[184] www.todayszaman.com/news-157148-newcomers-to-bu-face-pressure-to-conform-to-scarf-ban.html; www.todayszaman.com/news-154365-reaction-reminds-rector-of-bogazici-ethical-principles.html

Obama's Olive Branch

June 11, 2009

P resident Barack Obama's Cairo speech[185] has been analyzed line by line. Some journalists have commented on the speech as if Obama is their own president. They are demanding all the needs of their own culture and country be met by a foreign country's president. They direct the harshest and most undue criticisms at the president and the message he delivered and fail to see the potential good in his message. President Obama came to Cairo with the same message he advocated during his election campaign. It is senseless to expect anything else. Commentators need to recognize that the basic politics, the running of the state and the objectives of foreign policy do not change with different administrations in the US. Only in some particular areas might differences be observed between the Democrats' and the Republicans' management of events.

From the very beginning President Obama has been consistent. He has not denied his background or the Muslim elements in his family. He has never been embarrassed about his middle name, Hussein. His openness and integrity make him consistent and trustworthy. He has shown that he does not need to appear different from what he is. He openly declares that he is a Christian, attends and contributes to a church. So his attitude towards other religions is between God and himself. He does not attempt to conceal that he grew up hearing the call to prayer during his childhood spent in other countries, and this multicultural upbringing gives him the comfort and ease to meet with other cultures and religions. He is not one who hates or despises other cultures, races or ethno-religious backgrounds. Being judgmental about Obama's ease at switching between various cultural issues in his Cairo speech, some commentators doubt his sincerity and integrity. This is where they are seriously wrong.

---

[185] www.whitehouse.gov/the_press_office/Remarks-by-the-President-at-Cairo-University-6-04-09

Even if we assumed that what he said in Cairo was because of ulterior political motives and just for the sake of managing the masses, he has in any case given the message that the US is a land where people need not conceal their racial, religious, cultural, and political beliefs and backgrounds. Rather than the staging he was accused of, his presence was a meaningful embodiment of the message that the US is a land of freedom, equality, democracy and opportunity.

What is more, the peaceful majority in the Muslim world has been waiting for this message. Those who failed in the past to deliver a message of peace, cooperation and just world leadership did wrong. Instead of delivering peace they delivered bombs, bloodshed, hostility and hopelessness to a vast area of the world, not only the Middle East and Afghanistan. President Obama offers hope that people can forgive and forget past mismanagement and bad policies so as not to be engulfed in further discord and destruction.

The message of support for mutual respect, diplomacy, negotiation and cooperation was received very well. The satisfaction shown by Muslim scholars, administrations and the public, in the hall in Cairo and on the streets across the world, along with Obama's own pleasure at seeing the people's contentment, proved that this was an extension of what he said in Turkey. So Obama and his administration have bound themselves with these promises and have also helped the US to regain its world leader status. With such messages and promises, it is certain that neither the US nor Muslim populations will lose out or be harmed, contrary to what some columnists argue. The US, the Democrats and world communities stand to gain from the message of this administration.

The references to dialog, tolerance, and peace, taken from the Talmud rather than the Old Testament, and from the Qur'an and the prophetic tradition produced empathy among people. Love, mutual respect, trust and peaceful cooperation can work against extremism and exploitation. This is what we have been striving towards for years. What is wrong with this being expressed by a US president? Now the only obstacles are ignorance and the lack of just distribution of resources. The arms, oil, and drug lobbies will no doubt scheme to protect their interests all over the world, so the new US administration should be wary of such groups and the extremists they will utilize. World history is full of examples of the dangers to those who poke a stick into the hives of such interest groups.

Lastly, the remarkable message from the head of a superpower about the injustice of the secular assimilation imposed on observant Muslim women at educational and state institutions and in public spaces cannot be ignored. So the significance President Obama and his administration attach to this human rights and democratic issue, which has become gangrenous in countries like Turkey, Tunisia, Algeria and France, may lead to further peaceful developments in the countries concerned. Such change will transform Muslim attitudes towards the US and Americans, a process in which all would be winners. Many people in our communities have not taken President Obama's message as empty and cynical as some commentators falsely assume. The Obama administration is on the right track. It is to be hoped that the protectionist minority and interest groups in Turkey will grasp this olive branch too.

Testing Times for Muslims, Americans and Believers the World Over

November 12, 2009

T he recent murders of American service personnel at Fort Hood, Texas,[186] have once again raised the potential for enmity between the different segments of US society, and between different nations.

The upsurge of anger and enmity will undoubtedly be a setback for many who have been working hard for peace and understanding in the years since stories of international terrorism started to spread. At that time people started asking where peaceful Islamic voices, the voices of moderation and tolerance over extremism and radicalism, could be found.

After September 11, 2001, there were calls around the world to listen to the moderate Islamic voice. At that time many other groups changed their rhetoric. In contrast to those groups, the Gülen Movement's participants (also known as the "volunteers' service") were well placed to speak up because the Gülen Movement had already been teaching and practicing peace and tolerance for 30 to 40 years. Fethullah Gülen and the supporters of the services the movement provides did not need to change their language and attitude to become acceptable. This was one of the most significant factors that drew the attention of community leaders and authorities the world over.

Just before the execrable events at Fort Hood, I was in Baton Rouge, Louisiana, for the annual Community Prayer Breakfast of the Interfaith Federation for a talk about the volunteers' service. Federation members were especially interested in how the Turkish scholar and preacher, Fethullah Gülen, encouraged people inside and outside Turkey to offer apolitical and altruistic services to humanity. What we shared was not an idealized picture of a particular individual but the meaning of his message and the achievements of the people inspired by it. Federation mem-

---

[186] www.nytimes.com/2009/11/06/us/06forthood.html

bers were eager to learn how a scholar's ideas had changed the direction of youth, how Gülen helped Turkey through a time when political and religious strife threatened to pull it apart and how he convinced the masses about Islam's demand for mutual respect, caring and cooperation.[187]

At the heart of the message of the volunteers' service lie education, sound morality, altruism and inner transformation. This understanding and practice have convinced people to avoid violence, ignorance, moral decay and corruption. The movement has aimed to inculcate peaceful, non-violent thinking and attitudes in people through conversation, interaction, compassion, education and collaboration. Gülen argues that "only if they receive a sound education can individuals and their society respect the supremacy and rule of law, democratic and human rights, diversity and other cultures," and this is why the services provided by the movement's participants are recognized and welcomed by various nations and people. Gülen has convinced many to fund new schools, where children from various segments of society not only learn, but also become friends. The education at the schools and institutions accepts differences and renders them valuable.[188]

The organizing committee of the breakfast wanted to hear how the movement's participants had worked to establish a progressive and prosperous society without violence, terror and destruction during the turbulent Turkey of the 1980s. Together, we looked at the fruit that brings recognition of the tree. The volunteers' service demonstrates to people that we may be powerless as individuals, but when we work together, we have the power to shape our community and history; we can all leave our mark for good because we can all serve humanity. It contributes to the creation of common public spaces in which an agreement can be reached to share the responsibility for a whole social field. In this respect, through the process of interfaith dialogue between groups such as the Interfaith Federation and the volunteers' service, people can grow deeper in their own faith while practicing the common virtues and accomplishing the shared goals that faith commends.

---

[187] Çetin (2009).
[188] Kalyoncu (2008).

A few days after the Community Breakfast, the shootings at Fort Hood and then the execution of the Washington, D.C., sniper took place.[189] No one can condone the despicable crimes of those two men. Although their motives are not yet fully known, such incidents show that we are indeed in dire need of the type of sound moral and spiritual education, and beneficial services, given by the volunteers' service and other similar groups.

Some in the press and media are already playing with fire by covering the views of extremist individuals from both sides about these particular incidents and individuals. This, too, confirms once more that we need men and women of common sense who will not galvanize the enmity caused by such incidents but will work to prevent further hatred, polarization and clashes in and between societies. We need to work hard together to disseminate the messages and teachings of academic, moral and spiritual authorities to avoid further ignorance, violence and decay.

---

[189] www.washingtonpost.com/wp-dyn/content/article/2009/11/10/AR20091110 01396.html

Elections, Religion and the Opposition Parties in Turkey

November 25, 2010

I n about seven months Turkey will hold a general election. In the meantime it seems that the opposition parties are attempting to capitalize on religion. They know in most surveys of public opinion that opposition politicians rank lowest for honesty, integrity and dependability.[190] So, how will the oppositional parties try to use the religious communities to advance their own political ambitions and maneuvers?

Religious persons and faith-inspired communities have considerable influence on any nation's political life. Faith played a significant role in the 2000 US presidential election. Religion affects how American people think about a wide range of socio-political issues, from domestic to foreign affairs, from the scope of government to matters concerning the environment, race and defense. While most Americans believe in the separation of church and state, in the way they express their take on many issues, they do not sound as if they are in favor of the separation of religion and politics. They mostly seem to favor the idea of religion playing a prominent role in public life and even speak of the necessity of a "public religion" for the health of the republic. While the American constitution forbids the establishment of a state religion, Americans do have a public ethic of religious tolerance, as well as this proud tradition of religious influence on politics. Many American electors hold that religious individuals, motivated by the strong conviction of their beliefs, contribute constructively to public dialogue. They bring an unmatched moral vision to political affairs.

Religion influences politics through religious individuals and congregations, and through voluntary associations. Just as everywhere in the world, religious communities and faith-inspired associations in Turkey

---

[190] www.todayszaman.com/news-212263-forces-working-to-dent-support-for-ak-party-ahead-of-2011-elections.html

bring to the political arena passion, money, media savvy, organizational skill and drive. Ethno-religious groups are already working together across denominational lines on issues ranging from religious freedom to cultural and human rights. The strides made by the ruling Justice and Development Party (AK Party) in weakening the strangling grasp of the military/ bureaucratic tutelage system in Turkey have created space for many other groups, including religious leaders and faith-inspired communities to play an important role in the public arena.

However, most Turkish voters do not want a specific faith or religious view imposed upon them. Nor do they want the government to tell them how to worship. A great many voices have already spoken out against the idea of government interfering in the freedom of church, synagogue, or mosque, or promoting one religion over another. Many people believe that religion has no application at all to politics, or argue that religion does more harm than good in the political arena. We have top religious scholars who point to the fundamental difference between the absolute divine and compromising politics, who argue that religion is grounded in certainty and truth, while politics addresses issues that are not clear-cut, but are circumstantial and temporary. They remind people that religion lifts our eyes to high and lofty ideals, while politics deals with messy everyday problems.

Given the huge variety of views and the important constitutional limits to what religion can offer to Turkish politics, we might assume that when they enter the political arena politicians would do well to leave behind their religious beliefs or their intentions to support partisan ambitions by exploiting religion. However, the latest maneuvers by the opposition parties in Turkey remind us that this is not to be expected. Opposition parties may be approaching religious communities only in order to increase their vote and pass the 10 percent threshold.[191] However, there are also suggestions that they would attempt to utilize that rapprochement to give a signal to the incumbent government that the religious communities are now cutting their support for it and thus cause a rift between the AK Party and its "natural" constituency.

---

[191] Turkey has a system of proportional representation; the number of seats of each party in a district is based on its share of the local vote. In addition, to gain a seat in parliament, a party must receive a minimum of 10 percent of the national vote to gain any seats in parliament—an obstacle for new or smaller parties.

Whatever the underlying motivation, opposition party leaders should bear in mind that religion and religious communities are not to be used for partisan purposes. Instead, they should teach everyone to reach out beyond personal interest with a constructive and compassionate concern for others. They should encourage everyone to care for the welfare and dignity of all people, including our enemies, and to seek for them justice and freedom. Religion can help provide a moral framework for political debate. Public decisions involve and reflect moral values, and help us all to separate the trivial and inconsequential from the serious and important. Religion can encourage us to work together to meet our national challenges and further international peace. If party leaders ignore these facts, Turkish voters will bury those politicians and parties in history as they have done with many politicians and parties in the past.

8

The Hizmet or Gülen Movement

Gülen-inspired Schools and SMOs

July 8, 2008

I n an attempt to distract the public from Fethullah Gülen's acquittal by Turkey's top court and perturbed by his top ranking in *Foreign Policy* magazine's poll, elements of the Turkish media are using a lawyer's wording in an attempt to engineer a setback for Gülen.[192]

In the brief submitted by US Citizenship and Immigration Services (USCIS) lawyers on the appeal filed by Gülen about his residential status, the lawyers used the term the "Gülen schools." In a display of adversarial journalism a few Turkish correspondents seized on the term and claimed that Gülen now "admits" in the US that the schools "belong" to him, while he has always denied it in Turkey. The adversarial coverage has brought the schools, their financial accountability and leadership to the fore, displaying them in a negative light.

Further, some journalists have begun attempts to smear the 27 US community leaders and scholars who have written letters to the court in support of Gülen's application. The leaders and scholars have described Gülen as "an extraordinary educator."

Once again we see a media cartel transforming information, instead of transmitting it objectively.

In fact, as yet there is no consensus among writers on what to call the Gülen-inspired institutions; this is as true for American lawyers as it is for Turkish correspondents of all political colors. The use of terms like

---

[192] www.todayszaman.com/news-146072-gulen-attorney-dismisses-deportation-claims-as-baseless.html

"Gülen schools" can arise from ignorance or disinformation. If the term "Gülen schools" is equated with, for example, Montessori schools (where a particular training and qualifications are required for personnel and a specific methodology is used), it leads to misunderstanding. Gülen Movement participants have their own perspectives on terms used for the movement and the social movement organizations (SMOs) it has inspired. However, many outsiders seem oblivious to these perspectives or choose to ignore them.

Because of its brevity, outsiders tend to use "Gülen schools" rather than "Gülen-inspired schools." But the shorter term seems to imply some sort of central control of activities and even an ideology, while the second makes it clearer that there is no centralization in the movement. Gülen Movement participants tend to use the Turkish term *hizmet* (volunteer services) for the projects and services they provide. This is a solution for the inconsistency in naming the Gülen Movement and the institutions it inspires and in clarifying their identity for outside observers.

Probably because of its transnational growth since the 1990s, the financing of the Gülen Movement is occasionally queried in newspaper and journal articles. There has been little detailed study of the finance issue, but all academic research on this issue so far has made clear that each institution and project network in the movement is legitimate and transparent in book-keeping and accounting and that all financial management is done at the local level and subject to local regulatory inspection. The movement might be well advised, however, to present clearly a number of studies of how projects are financed so as to remove any suspicion of that backing by vested political interests.

Some allege that it is impossible for the movement to have achieved such great accomplishments and such rapid expansion without "other financial resources." Accusers do not seem to be self-conscious enough to see the contradictions or improbability in such lurid and circular imaginings.

Those who are really interested in this topic will need to take insider perspectives into account. Firstly, attitudes to donating time and money to charity vary across cultural traditions. In Islamic and therefore Turkish tradition it is often considered more blessed to give some donations anonymously. Onlookers need to be aware of people's sensitivities about such matters. Secondly, in attempting to account for the scale of the movement's activities in relation to funds available, it is necessary to take note of how much of the movement's resources consist of voluntary, unpaid work, rather than money.

Questions about Gülen's role usually center on what will happen after him. Could there be a change in direction if there are no prominent figures after him able to exercise the same moral, spiritual and scholarly influence? Gülen and movement participants have already answered these and similar questions to the extent possible in public forums.

The extensive training and professionalization within the SMOs, the clarity of their goals and the collective ownership of projects are sources of stability. The movement's well-established use of collective reasoning and consultation should prevent any sudden changes of direction. Moreover, looking at the long history of faith-inspired initiatives in Islamic culture, we see that the understanding of great scholars like Rumi did not cease abruptly or diminish over time into sectarian groups. The disapproval of aspirations for power and leadership expressed in the Islamic tradition must also be a factor in any examination of this question. It is likely to prevent any sudden change in direction led by a new "charismatic" figure. This is all of course conjectural. The future cannot be known before it happens.

Now, however, those who have for years belonged to the privileged group still enjoy financial and status benefits from the political and economic status quo in Turkey. They are determined to hold on to their privileges by any means (including association with organized crime) and whatever the cost to the people or society. The adversarial journalism seen in recent weeks is all symptomatic of the refusal of the protectionist elite to loosen its exclusive grip on the institutions and economy of Turkey.

They interpret the Gülen Movement and its services as a symbolic challenge to their control, because the movement educates the periphery (the masses), forms the public space and consolidates civil society and democratic consciousness. They produce new meanings, new social relations and services that point out failures and inadequacies in the protectionists' policies and worldview.

The services the Gülen Movement offers are worlds away from any physical or political challenge that directly confronts the legitimacy of the authority of the state or its agents. Nonetheless, those agents will no doubt persist in the dubious task they have been paid to perform.

An Example to Curb Terror and Violence

July 31, 2008

Following the explosions on July 27 in Istanbul,[193] police arrested three suspicious individuals between the ages of 16 and 17.[194] The suspects' ages reminded me of my teenage years before the 1980 coup, during which ideological clashes between rightists and leftists resulted in the deaths of 30,000 people in addition to immeasurable social, psychological and physical damage and loss.[195] Up until the 1980s, all families and their children lived amid that turmoil. Political leaders and the milieu offered the youth nothing but clashes, bombings, assassinations and polarization. These memories led me to reflect on how terrorism might be curbed in contemporary societies. During my own soul-searching in the 1980s I came to hear about a preacher, scholar, writer and peaceful civil society leader, Fethullah Gülen, a series of whose lectures, attended by thousands of people and in which he preached against violence, anarchy and terror, were [first] made available on audiocassette in February 1980.

Throughout that period, Gülen strove to draw people out of societal tension and conflict. His message reached the masses through audio and video cassettes, as well as public lectures and private meetings. He appealed to people not to become part of ongoing partisan conflict and ideological fights. He analyzed the prevalent conditions and the ideologies behind societal violence, terror and clashes. He applied his scholarship and his intellectual and personal resources to convince university students that they need not resort to violence, terror and destruction to establish a progressive, prosperous and peaceful society. He maintained that violence, terrorism, ignorance, moral decay and corruption could be over-

---

[193] www.todayszaman.com/news-148691-2-bombs-in-istanbul-kill-13-and-injuring-around-70.html

[194] www.todayszaman.com/news-149245-turkey-suspects-in-deadly-bombing-arrested.html

[195] See Military Coup III, p. 22.

come through forbearance and compassion, through conversation, interaction, education and cooperation. He reminded them not to expect everything from the system, because of its backwardness in some respects, its stifling bureaucratic, partisan and procedural stagnation and its lack of qualified personnel. He urged people, instead, to use their constitutionally given rights to contribute to and serve society constructively and altruistically. And he convinced them that such service is both the means and the end of being a good person, a good citizen and a good believer.[196]

Gülen has always seen education as being at the center of social, economic and political modernization, progress and welfare. Individuals and society can only be respectful of the supremacy and rule of law, democratic and human rights and diversity and cultures if they receive sound education. Equity, social justice and peace in one's own society and in the world in general can only be achieved by enlightened people with sound morality through altruistic activism. Therefore education is the supreme remedy for the ills afflicting Turkish society and humanity in general.

To Gülen, a higher sense of identity, social justice and sufficient understanding and tolerance to secure respect for the rights of others all depend on the provision of an adequate and appropriate universal education. As so many people are unable to afford such an education, they need to be supported by charitable trusts. For these trusts to function well needs the right human resources—dedicated volunteers who would enter and then stay in the field of service. The volunteers should not be making a gesture (however worthwhile) but a long-term commitment rooted in sincere intention—their motivation should have no part in it of racial or tribal preferences, and their effort should be both patient and persevering, and always lawful.

Gülen spoke to people from all walks of life in Turkey. He visited individuals, groups, cafes, small villages, towns and metropolitan cities. From peddlers to industrialists and exporters, from secondary school students to postgraduates and faculty, from the common people to leading figures and members of the elite, he imparted the same message to all: sound education and institutionalization, and to achieve that, altruistic contribution and services. He appealed to values that are present in all tradi-

---

[196] Çetin, *The Gülen Movement*, 166.

tions and religions: duty, moral obligation, disinterested contribution, voluntary philanthropy and altruistic services.

Educational institutions established by charitable trusts inspired by Gülen present solutions to areas with ethnic-territorial problems.[197] These institutions accept differences and render them valuable, rich and negotiable. This invites students and others to coexist peacefully in diversity. It calls for tolerance, dialogue between different spheres of society and different nations of the world, peace and love, and firm commitment to openness of mind and heart. Students work to achieve this civilized disposition through the sound education offered them. With the sponsorship of movement supporters, hundreds of such successful institutions have been set up in over 100 different countries.

Gülen holds that "all human beings are one's brothers and sisters. Muslims are one's brothers and sisters in religion, while non-Muslims are one's brothers and sisters in humanity;" and also that "Human beings are the most honorable of creatures. Those who want to increase their honor should serve this honorable creature."[198]

In this and similar ways Gülen encouraged people from all walks of life to a non-political, non-conflict-ridden and non-violent of life and altruistic services to people. If the perpetrators of the acts of terrorism in Istanbul, or anywhere else, had had the chance to listen to and take heed of the teachings of the Gülen Movement, they would surely not commit such atrocities.

---

[197] Çetin, *The Gülen Movement*, 167–8.

[198] Here Gülen reminds people of a well-known teaching from Ali, the son-in-law of Prophet Muhammad, peace and blessings be upon him, and encourages them to apply it in daily life.

Infiltrating or Contributing?

October 14, 2010

Over the past few days Muslim scholar and social activist Fethullah Gülen has given a measured and straightforward response to accusations that the Gülen Movement, or as it is often called, the "volunteers' service" or Hizmet, is engaged in a conspiracy to infiltrate state institutions. Gülen replied that all citizens have a right—in accordance with the law—to be employed in their own country within the ranks of state institutions, including the police and military.[199]

Indeed, it seems to me that since the participants and supporters of the movement number in the millions within Turkey, their presence within such institutions is a statistical certainty given that the movement is not a clandestine organization or cult.

This latest public discussion first started to develop around Police Chief Hanefi Avcı's accusations against the movement. Apart from accusing the supporters of the Gülen Movement of having infiltrated top state posts, Avcı, who is currently in custody, claimed that ongoing criminal investigations of illegal activities within the state—such as the clandestine criminal network Ergenekon that plotted to overthrow the government—lack evidence and are based on illegal wiretapping. However, recent legal probes show Avcı himself not only wiretapped illegally but also tortured dozens of individuals. Avcı was arrested last month on charges of aiding and abetting a terrorist organization. [200]

As these events were progressing, researchers taking part in the Mapping the Gülen Movement Conference in Amsterdam, were presenting their research findings to the academic world.[201]

---

[199] www.todayszaman.com/news-224140-gulen-citizens-do-not-infiltrate-state-posts.html

[200] www.todayszaman.com/news-223910-avci-complained-of-wiretapping-but-tapped-dozens-of-lines.html; www.todayszaman.com/news-224321-hanefi-avci-confessed-to-illegal-wiretapping-in-interview-with-author.html

[201] www.fethullahgulen.nl/mapping-the-gulen-movement

A number of Turkish and non-Turkish academics inside and outside the movement contributed. Most of the speakers were completely independent of the movement. Yet not one of them produced a shred of evidence that could be used in support of Avcı's accusations.

Thomas Michel, an academic who has years of experience observing the movement, spoke of the centrality to Fethullah Gülen's thought and teachings of *ikhlas* (purity of intention). He pointed out this concept includes honesty or freedom from dissimulation and that Gülen stresses "pursuing nothing worldly."

İhsan Yılmaz and Sammas Salur presented a joint paper on the compatibility of Islam, democracy and secularism in Gülen's thought. *Today's Zaman*'s own Doğu Ergil, in his capacity as an academic at Ankara University, pointed out that while participants in the movement may have their own political views and even party political affiliations, these are not allowed to affect the activities of the movement.

Pim Valkenberg of Loyola University Maryland made a study of Gülen's publications over the years and concluded that there has been no change in Gülen's message. From the beginning of his career as a preacher he has expressed concern for humanity as a whole, not just selected parts of it such as a community or a nation. Only Gülen's sensitivity to the widening of his audience has developed, as the movement has grown and become transnational, so that later works can be understood by a wider range of people with different educational and cultural backgrounds.

Helen Rose Ebaugh of the University of Houston reported her research on the finances and fundraising of the movement. She investigated 11 major institutions and found the accounting practices were straightforward and transparent and that institutions were very willing to let her inspect their accounts.

My own paper about the structural dimension of the movement described how the movement functions without centralized control. Papers by Johan Leman, on the efforts for social integration by Gülen Movement volunteers in Belgium, and by Maria Curtis, who wrote about women's goals in the movement and how they strive to contribute to society in the United States, also confirmed the characteristics of service to others and decentralization.

None of the academics in attendance reported finding any sign of attempts by movement members to overthrow democracy or even to "grab a bigger share of the pie" for a new elite, shady or otherwise.

Turkish people nowadays are almost used to wild and inaccurate conspiracy theories and weary of the existence of the very real plots of the deep state that have marred the life of the nation for years. We can now spot the use of smoke and mirrors on the stage, while the villain attempts to exit unseen stage left.

The fact-based, peer-reviewed world of academia, though dry to some people's tastes, has a contribution to make to Turkey's future. In contrast to the drama and fiction of politics, the requirement for balance and credibility in academic work contributes facts and reveals ulterior motives in the public arena. These can be cooling antidotes to the poison of delusion administered to the public by the politically ambitious.

Civic Engagement, Success and the Gülen Movement

January 20, 2011

T he recent extraordinary interest in activities by and related to the Gülen Movement leads many to think about civic engagement and its efficacy and success.[202]

Civic engagement is vital for improving and enhancing conditions in any contemporary democracy. It means promoting the quality of life in a community through both political and non-political processes. It means working to make a difference in the civic life of our communities. It develops a combination of knowledge, skills, values and motivation to make that difference.

This kind of empowerment was developed mostly outside of and beyond partisan politics. It helps foster citizens' learning about democratic cultures, human rights and multiculturalism, especially in divided societies. Also, it brings socially responsible leadership into intercultural and democratic dialogue and engenders peaceful social change. However, judging by the high level of crime, conflict, corruption and violence in most countries, many organizations seem to offer little by the way of a roadmap or leadership. Key terminology and goals remain confined to the intellectual or academic field. They lack the resonance to galvanize a new generation of peaceful activists. So what can be done about this decline?

There are key factors or characteristics that deepen citizen engagement in public life: First, important issues need to be identified by the public. Then, non-contentious, peaceful and non-coercive means must be used for developmental models for citizens' civic learning, democracy building, respect for diversity and human rights, democratic dialogue, inclusiveness and social change. Also, citizens must know their cultural and political rights. Individual willingness or initiative should be accompanied by

---

[202] www.todayszaman.com/news-232784-author-of-book-on-gulen-movement-receives-muchinterest-in-ankara.html

organized mobilization for the common good. And lastly the civic engagement needs to be supported by altruistic giving.

Bearing these key factors in mind, let's turn to the Gülen Movement, now mostly described as "Hizmet," altruistic voluntary services to humanity or volunteer services. Many factors contribute to Hizmet's efficacy. Papers presented at international conferences maintain that Hizmet defines clearly the organization's goals. It mobilizes and puts to use effectively the available resources of people, material and ideas. It establishes legal and lawful institutions and so people and society at large take the movement's aims seriously.

Hizmet is a complex collective actor, composed of many decentralized civil society organizations and institutions pursuing similar goals but different strategies. It is argued that decisions on goals, that is, on what to do, are taken in a process of consultation, locally or in an individual project-network. The consultative process means that no one owns the services and authority in the name of Hizmet as a collective actor. The efficiency of decision taking in its service networks is seen to be the constancy and richness of the interaction of many individuals.

The most important factor in its success is that non-contentious, peaceful and non-coercive means must be used for developmental models. In this aspect the Gülen Movement really excels. It diffuses a discourse of dialogue, tolerance and a valuing of diversity. It has never shown any inclination whatsoever towards violence or extra-legal tactics of any kind. It has transformed the potential to use coercive means to induce changes in political systems into peaceful efforts to produce beneficial services. Hizmet is successful because of the interweaving of the service-project mentality with integrative peaceful strategies. It has convinced the public to use its constitutionally given rights to serve humanity positively, constructively and through self-motivated philanthropic contributions and charitable trusts.

For this reason, Hizmet has become, first, a vital component in providing an alternative and barrier to egoistic interests at the expense of others and a remedy for societal discord, conflict and violence. Second, it has become one of the most significant and leading actors in the renewal process towards a civil, pluralist, democratic and peaceful society.

I feel that an understanding of Hizmet can help to reverse the kind of decline in civic engagement that we see in many contemporary societies. It can show activists and other civic society movements how to expand their repertoire of action for societal peace and inter-civilizational cooperation. Very diverse people can come together to achieve very worthy goals. Hizmet has discovered this, reminds people of it and acts on this simple truth. For this reason, I believe that, in spite of opposition from groups that benefit from conflict between people, the Gülen Movement, or Hizmet, will continue peacefully and successfully in the way it always has.

Appendices

Appendix 1: What Is Deep State or Gang?

(by Mehmet Ali Birand / Turkish Daily News, Saturday, June 3, 2006
www.turkishdailynews.com.tr/editorial.php?ed=mehmet_ali_birand)

We are facing a confusion of concepts. What is 'deep state?' Who are its members? And there are these 'gangs' people are talking about. The two should not be confused. I have prepared a dictionary for those who are interested.

There are some often used concepts, the meanings of which the public knows very little about. We know what we are talking about, but these concepts create confusion among the public.

The questions are: 'What is the deep state?' and 'What is a gang?'

'Deep state' as a concept is understood by the public as representing elements of the military, police, National Intelligence Organization (MİT), the gendarmerie, the judiciary, some journalists and scientists and some youth wings of political parties. Deep state is a concept. It is not an organization or an association. However, it is believed that some people who think in the same way sympathize with some groups (gangs) that act in accordance with their beliefs.

A 'gang', on the other hand, can be divided into two categories.

According to public perception, one type of gang exploits the state's sympathies to commit public acts and flood the streets in the name of the state but in exchange is allowed to be involved in a range of crimes, including organized crime. These are just wannabe mafia groups. Among their members are well-known gangsters. They say they work for the state but are involved in drug trafficking and other illegal activities and are tolerated by the police. From time to time (especially in the 1990s) they were utilized by MİT, the police and the gendarmerie, some believe.

They are known to have been involved in many assassinations and unsolved murders.

The second type of gang is one that solely seeks financial benefit for its members. Among their members are retired military and police officials and some civilians who call themselves 'patriots'. Generally, members have links to some of the security institutions of the state. They are secretly supported and are provided with guidance. However, the state is a strange entity. It uses others to get things done. But when things change it targets the same groups it used and sends them to jail. Our history is full of such occurrences.

Deep state members, beware!

Appendix 2: Reasoned Decision Revealed: Gülen Does Not Aim at Changing Constitutional System

(Zaman, Saturday, 10 June 2006 at en.fgulen. com/content/view/2258/14/)

The Ankara 11th High Criminal Court has revealed the reasons promoting the acquittal of Fethullah Gülen.

The reasoned decision resolved that "There is no evidence proving that Gülen aimed at changing the Constitutional System or resorted to force and violence. On the contrary, he was threatened by fundamentalist terrorist organizations for his friendly attitudes towards the state."

The reasoned decision suggested the claims that Fethullah Gülen and associated institutions aimed at changing the constitutional system were not proven, and that Gülen never made a statement in relation to this issue, and that those claims were only comments and presumptions.

'No evidence was found to support the case; on the contrary, he was threatened by fundamentalist terrorist groups for his friendly attitudes towards the state. As it is stated in the law, at least two people are needed for the establishment of an organization, and as the file does not include another suspect; on the charges of organization and structure, the court was unable to prosecute. Fethullah Gülen and his associate can not be tried within law No. 3713 of the Counter Terrorism Act as charged in police reports, as the described crime and the elements of any crime do not exist in accordance with the 1st item of law No. 3713 of the Counter Terrorism Act.'

The court verdict noted that Gülen should be acquitted on the grounds of conscience and law, in accordance with the legislation and the evidence presented.

The court also awarded payment of expenses and court costs to the Turkish treasury.

Appendix 3: Special Usages

I have not used any terms that are either unusual generally, or unusual in sociological discourse about social movements—any specialist terms will be easily understood in the contexts where they occur. However, a handful of words or expressions are used which, because of the specific (Turkish) context of this case study, have particular shades of meaning or resonance that may not be intelligible from the context. I list these words/expressions below in alphabetical order for ease of reference.

- *Atatürkism* or *Kemalism:* the official political system and 'ideology' of Turkey, named after Mustafa Kemal Atatürk, who laid down the ideology of his Republican People's Party in six 'fundamental and unchanging principles'—'republican, nationalist, populist, etatist, laicist, and revolutionary'—later incorporated into the constitution to define the basic principles of the state.

- *Chief of General Staff:* the Commander of the Armed Forces. In wartime, he acts as the Commander in Chief on behalf of the President. Commanding the Armed Forces and establishing the policies and programs related with the preparation for combat of personnel, intelligence, operations, organization, training and logistic services are the responsibilities of the Turkish General Staff. Furthermore, the Turkish General Staff coordinates the military relations of the Turkish Armed Forces with NATO and other friendly nations.

- *counter-mobilization:* used in this study to refer to the systematic efforts by the *protectionist elitists* to oppose the activities of all civil society movements in Turkey, and in particular the Gülen Movement.

- *dominant interests:* i.e. the interests of the *elitist-statist-secularist* group who wield power in Turkey, not always from behind the political stage.

- *elitists:* those who believe in their inherent superiority over others with an unquestionable right to preeminence, privilege and power.

In Turkey, the *elitists* are the traditional Republican clique who define themselves as superior because of their 'Western' cultural preferences and practices, education, attitudes, etc. Their assumption is that these Western qualities give them a greater right to govern, if necessary by overturning the will of the people.

- *February 28 Process:* this refers to the sequence of measures and events that followed the *soft coup* of 1997: 'On the last day of February 1997, the regular monthly meeting of the military-dominated National Security Council [...] gave the Welfare-True Path coalition government a list of eighteen measures to be implemented without delay, including a clampdown on 'reactionary Islam'. [...] The military spent the next months waging a relentless public-relations campaign that turned society against the government and eventually forced the resignation on June 18 of Erbakan and his cabinet. The noose on civilian politics remained tight after that. Press freedom was severely curtailed, with many journalists and other public figures targeted by military-orchestrated smear campaigns. [...] What is called within Turkey 'the February 28 process' was not limited to the political wing of the Islamist movement. Islamic networks, sects, associations, and individuals were targeted for excoriation and sometimes prosecution or court-ordered bans on their activities.'[203]

- *hizmet:* word of Arabic origin (literally, 'service'), used in Turkish to mean disinterested voluntary beneficial service to others, especially provided by faith-inspired communities; the preferred term among participants in the Gülen Movement to describe their attitude and work.

- *Islamic:* adjectival form derived from Islam, referring to the traditional teachings of the religion, and expressly distinguished from *Islamist*.

- *Islamism, Islamist:* politically motivated understanding among Muslim activists, who believe in evolutionary or revolutionary transformation in society and political systems; Islam understood as ideology.

---

[203] Özel, 2003:87 in Çetin (2009).

- *laicism:* a militant (Jacobin) form of *secularism* that demands the exclusion of religious belief and practice from public life, and expects to use state power to achieve that exclusion. In Turkey until now there has been little real distinction between *laicism* and *secularism*.
- *mobilization:* used in this study to refer to the efforts of the participants in the Gülen Movement to direct resources to achieve their goals in the form of service-projects.
- *multiple belongings:* simultaneous, purposive and voluntary participation in or affiliation to various social networks, projects and SMOs.
- *National Security Council (NSC):* a council of state consisting of the President, Prime Minister, a number of other ministers (as necessary and relevant to the issues being discussed), five top-ranking generals from the Chief of Staff, plus other generals (the number of generals always exceeding the number of civilians on the council). The purpose of the *NSC* is to strongly advise the government on matters of national security, though its remit has gradually been extended to cover other aspects of Turkish public life, such as finance and culture.
- *protectionists:* those in the established leadership of Turkey with a strict nationalist, *secularist* and bureaucratic-authoritarian understanding who intend to perpetuate the status quo.
- *secularism:* legal and institutional separation of church and state, which, in the case of Turkey is understood to mean the separation/expulsion of religious authority from the state. In practice, *secularism* means regulation by the state, to a considerable extent, of the practice of religion through the Presidency of Religious Affairs (appointment of prayer-leaders to mosques, vetting content of sermons, religious education, etc.) The term *secularist* is widely used in Turkey to describe those who are actively opposed to religious practice in the public sphere—see *laicism*—and is so used in this study.
- *Social Movement Organization (SMO):* any formally established and institutionalized organization whose operations and goals coincide with the preferences of a social movement.
- *soft coup:* in February 1997, the newly elected government of Turkey was induced to resign by an open threat from a select group of generals at the Turkish Chief of Staff of a military coup. The gov-

ernment stood down and the military assumed control of the civil
authority of the state. The *soft coup* has sometimes been referred
to also as the 'postmodern coup'.

- *State-owned Economic Enterprises (SEEs):* Kamu Iktisadi Teskilat-
lari (KITs); monopolies, other state-sponsored and privileged businesses set up by the state.
- *statism, statists:* the doctrine that the state in Turkey should hold
control of the major part of political and economic activity in the
country and that this control should remain in the hands of the
Republican *elitists*.
- *symbolic challenge:* the production of new meanings, new social
relations and services, which point up failures in state policy or
inadequacies in the worldview of the *dominant interests*. (Different from physical or political challenge, which directly confronts
the legitimacy of the authority of the state or its agents.)
- *vested interests:* the privileged group who currently enjoy financial
and status benefits from the political and economic status quo in
Turkey, and who are determined to hold on to their privileges by
any means (including association with organized crime) and
whatever the cost to the people or the society.

Select Bibliography

Carroll, B. Jill. *A Dialogue of Civilizations: Gülen's Islamic Ideals and Humanistic Discourse*. Somerset, New Jersey: The Light & The Gülen Institute, 2007.

Çetin, Muhammed. *The Gülen Movement: Civic Service without Borders*. New York: Blue Dome Press, 2009.

Çinar, A. *Modernity, Islam, and Secularism in Turkey: Bodies, Places, and Time*. Public Worlds, Vol. 14. University of Minnesota Press, 2005.

Ebaugh, Helen Rose. *The Gülen Movement: A Sociological Analysis of a Civic Movement Rooted in Moderate Islam*. New York: Springer, 2010.

Esposito, John L. and Ihsan Yilmaz. *Islam and Peacebuilding: Gülen Movement Initiatives*. New York: Blue Dome Press, 2010.

Fuller Graham E. *The New Turkish Republic: Turkey as a Pivotal State in the Muslim World* United States Institute of Peace Press, 2007.

Fuller, Graham E. *A World Without Islam*. Little, Brown and Company; 1st ed., 2010.

Gülen, Fethullah. "A Comparative approach to Islam and Democracy." *SAIS Review* 21 (2001): 133–8.

Gray, John, *Heresies: Against Progress and Other Illusions*. UK, Granta, 2004.

Harrington, James C. *Wrestling with Free Speech, Religious Freedom, and Democracy in Turkey: The Political Trials and Times of Fethullah Gülen*. Lanham, Maryland: University Press of America, 2011.

Kalyoncu, Mehmet. *A Civilian Response to Ethno-Religious Conflict: The Gülen Movement in Southeast Turkey*. Clifton, New Jersey: Tughra Books, 2008.

Turam, Berna. *Between Islam and the State: The Politics of Engagement*. Stanford, California, Stanford University press, 2007.

Index

Economist, 203
EDL, 210, 212
EEC, 12, 17, 26
Egypt, 13, 209
elite, 4, 12, 24, 27, 39, 40, 43, 44, 49, 51,
  57, 67, 98, 111, 117, 125, 143,
  177, 203, 213, 233, 235, 239
elitists, 38, 40, 111, 140, 203, 218, 246,
  247, 249
Emeç, 103
Encümen-i Daniş, 116
Erbakan, 16, 17, 19, 20, 22, 26, 30, 31, 32,
  37, 41, 247
Erdoğan, 33, 136, 179
Ergenekon, 68, 69, 71, 72, 73, 85, 88, 89,
  90, 92, 105, 106, 107, 111, 112,
  113, 114, 117, 134, 138, 142, 149,
  153, 154, 155, 157, 158, 163, 164,
  180, 191, 192, 203, 213, 237
Ergil, 158, 238
Erzincan, 139
Europe, 12, 17, 36, 43, 44, 54, 73, 143,
  155, 159, 181, 183, 205, 206, 210,
  211, 219
European Union, 37, 38, 76, 90, 118, 130,
  137, 159, 183, 206
Evren, 23, 24, 25, 27

F

Faculty of Divinity, 2, 9
Far East, 51, 143
February 28 Process, 33, 41, 44, 247
FIFA, 217
Firat News Agency, 170
Foreign Policy, 175, 231
Fort Hood, 225, 227
France, 224
freedom, 7, 9, 15, 20, 26, 27, 46, 50, 63,
  69, 74, 75, 76, 77, 78, 85, 86, 88,
  89, 90, 102, 109, 112, 114, 118,

119, 120, 121, 122, 124, 135, 138,
150, 170, 176, 209, 211, 212, 217,
223, 229, 230, 238, 247
fundamentalism, 136, 154, 155, 185, 186,
  195

G

Gandhi, 71, 94, 126
Gaza, 199, 200, 201
Georgia, 182
Germany, 8, 205
Gladio, 68, 71, 153, 191
Glaswegian, 212
Goodhart, 175
Greece, 10, 20, 37, 70, 91
Greek Cypriots, 10
Guantanamo, 193
Gül, 80, 83, 87, 118, 137, 178, 179
Gülen, 69, 86, 108, 121, 122, 153, 154,
  155, 175, 176, 177, 195, 214, 225,
  226, 231, 232, 233, 234, 235, 236,
  237, 238, 239, 240, 241, 245, 246,
  247, 248, 251
Gülen-inspired schools, 232
Gülen movement, 108, 121, 122, 154,
  155, 176, 177, 195, 225, 232, 233,
  236, 237, 238, 240, 241, 242
Gulf War, 28, 151
Gürüz, 73, 74, 75

H

Hablemitoğlu, 104
Hacettepe University, 19
Hackney, 212
Hale, 42
Hamas, 200, 201, 209
headscarf, 27, 28, 74, 142, 179
hegemony, 58, 67, 73, 101
Hezbollah, 200
High Court of Appeals, 25